THE ISMAILI ASSASSINS

عمر خیام

Omar Khayyam

ماالعبتگانیم و فلک لعبت باز

از روی حقیقتی نه از روی مجاز

یک چند درین بساط بازی کردیم

رفتیم به صندوق عدم یک یک باز

خط سید حمیدرضا ابراهیمی

H. R. Ebrahimi
Dec. 2006

We are the puppets and the firmament is the puppet master,
In actual fact and not as a metaphor;
For a time we acted on this stage,
We went back one by one into the box of oblivion.

Early twelfth century, Persia.

THE ISMAILI ASSASSINS

A HISTORY OF MEDIEVAL MURDER

JAMES WATERSON

FOREWORD BY DAVID MORGAN

Frontline Books, London

For A&B&37

Frontline Books, London

The Ismaili Assassins

This edition published in 2008 by Frontline Books, an imprint of Pen and Sword Books Ltd, 47 Church Street, Barnsley, S. Yorkshire, S70 2AS
www.frontline-books.com

Copyright © James Waterson, 2008
Foreword © David Morgan, 2008

ISBN: 978-1-84832-505-0

CIP data records for this title are available from the British Library and the Library of Congress

For more information on our books, please visit
www.frontline-books.com, email info@frontline-books.com
or write to us at the above address.

Typeset and designed by JCS Publishing Services Ltd,
www.jcs-publishing.co.uk
Maps drawn by Red Lion Maps
Printed and bound in Great Britain by Biddles Ltd, King's Lynn

CONTENTS

Maps and Illustrations

Maps

Illustrations (Colour)

ILLUSTRATIONS (BLACK AND WHITE)

ACKNOWLEDGEMENTS

As a history writer I am totally indebted to the historians who have done so much to make the source materials available to we more linguistically challenged mortals. On a more personal level I would like to give thanks both to Dr David Morgan for introducing me, as an undergraduate, to the Assassins, Saljuqs and Mongols and to Dr Michael Brett for his lectures on the Fatimids and the Crusades period.

I would also like to thank Dr Abbas Khosravi and Mr Hamid Reza Ebrahimi for their superbly skilled calligraphy for the book's frontispiece that has brought Omar Khayyam's poem to life in the original Farsi.

One final thank you goes to Dr Brian Williams, formerly of the School of Oriental and African Studies, for his encouraging response after my first book *The Knights of Islam* was published. I remember his lectures, during my university years, being both erudite and enthusiastic and stirring a desire in me to bring Islamic history, and in particular the military history of the medieval Middle East, to a wider audience.

Once again I must thank my dear wife, Michele, for her forbearance at having Mongols, Mamluks, Crusaders and Assassins as permanent houseguests for these last two years and as visitors to our life together for far too long.

ACKNOWLEDGEMENTS

FOREWORD

O NE OF THE MORE regrettable consequences of the much greater
specialisation that characterised the historical profession in the
twentieth century was that historians seemed increasingly to
be writing only for other professional historians – and for a diminishing
number even of them. There came a time when the appearance of a book
on a best-seller list would be almost enough in itself to destroy its author's
scholarly reputation. In the years I have spent teaching the history of the
Middle East and Central Asia, both in London and, more recently, in the
United States, I have done my best to persuade my students – especially
graduate students, some of whom would be making careers as historians,
and therefore writing history – that historical writing does not have to be
boring and unreadable in order to qualify as worthwhile.

That time, fortunately, seems to have passed: no one has any doubts
about the scholarly credentials of, say, Simon Schama, despite his various
television series and the number of people who buy his books. There is,
at last, an increasing awareness of the fact that there is a large reading
public that is interested in being offered history that, on the one hand, is
well researched and has something significant to say; and on the other,
is written in jargon-free English that it is actually a pleasure to read. The
historiography of the medieval Islamic sect known (in the West) as the
Assassins (more properly the Nizari Ismailis) offers examples of both
tendencies.

For a number of years, the standard book in English was Marshall
Hodgson's *The Order of Assassins* (1955). That this was and is a work of
value, no one would deny – indeed, it was reprinted in paperback as
recently as 2005. And Hodgson, who died very prematurely in 1968, was
a strikingly original historian whose posthumously published three-
volume *The Venture of Islam* is, among surveys of Islamic history, quite
unparalleled as an intellectual tour de force. Even his greatest admirers,
however (of whom I am one), could not convincingly argue that he was
a master of the English language. He is more than worth the effort: but
it is indisputably an effort. A marked contrast came in 1967 with the
publication of Bernard Lewis's *The Assassins: A Radical Sect in Islam*. Lewis

has not only been, over a long career, a very prolific historian of the Middle East: he has also written about it more accessibly and readably than any other scholar writing in English in the twentieth century. *The Assassins* is a good example of Lewis at his best. When it appeared it was the ideal introduction to the subject. Even after forty years it remains well worth reading, whatever advances in research may have taken place since then. Today, a scholar would go first to books by such historians as Farhad Daftary of the Institute of Ismaili Studies. But Lewis is, deservedly, still in print (now with a new 2002 introduction, in which he very justly expresses serious reservations about the notion that there is any kind of terroristic continuity between the Assassins and al-Qa'ida).

James Waterson's book is nearer to the Lewis than the Hodgson tradition. He was a student of mine during my last years in London; and if this book and its excellent predecessor, *The Knights of Islam: The Wars of the Mamluks* (2007), are anything to go by, he seems to have taken to heart (if perhaps only subconsciously!) the advice mentioned in the first paragraph of this foreword. This is a book that is up to date, informative, and in no way difficult to read and understand. The subject is one of great fascination, and James Waterson's treatment of it is well calculated to pass on that fascination to the wide readership it richly deserves.

David Morgan
University of Wisconsin-Madison

TIMELINE OF KEY EVENTS

570	Birth of the Prophet Muhammad.
603–28	The war between Byzantium and Sassanian Persia leaves both of the main political powers in western Asia exhausted.
632	Death of Muhammad.
632–61	The *Rashidun*, or 'rightly guided', caliphs.
633	Muslim state most powerful political entity in Arabia. Risings crushed in Oman and Yemen in the Ridda Wars.
633–42	Arab conquest of Palestine, Syria, Iraq and Egypt.
643–707	Muslim conquest of North Africa.
644	Arab invasion of Iran.
651	Iran conquered, standard text of Quran completed.
656	Murder of the third caliph, Uthman, by Muslim mutineers.
656	The Battle of the Camel outside Basra. The Prophet's widow attempts rebellion against Caliph Ali but she is defeated.
657	Battle of Siffin between Caliph Ali and Muawiya, governor of Syria.
661	Murder of Ali by Kharijites, establishment of Umayyad caliphate under Muawiya.
661–750	Umayyad caliphate.
674–715	Conquest of Transoxania.
680	Massacre of Husain, Ali's son and the Prophet's grandson, and of his family and supporters at Karbala by Umayyad troops. The idea of the imam as the rightful ruler in Islam now applied to the descendants of Ali.
683–90	Civil wars in Syria between Arab tribes.
685	Shiite revolt in Kufa under Mukhtar. Claims that Ali's descendant, al-Hanafiyya, is the *Mahdi*.
711–16	Muslim conquest of the Iberian Peninsula.
732	Battle of Poitiers. Muslim advance into France halted.
740	Zaydite Revolt in Kufa in the name of Jafar al-Sadiq, the sixth imam.
744–8	Widespread Kharijite uprisings in Persia.
747–50	Abbasid revolution in Khurasan.

750	Overthrow of Umayyad dynasty, establishment of Abbasid caliphate.
751	Chinese defeated on the Jaxartes River, Muslim hegemony in central Asia established.
762	An Alid claimant to the caliphate, Muhammad, rebels in Medina but is killed with his supporters by the Abbasids.
765	Death of the imam Jafar al-Sadiq. The succession is disputed. Shiites divide into two branches. The Twelvers who follow the line of Musa and the Seveners or Ismailis who follow the line of Ismail.
788–809	Quasi-independent dynasties in Morocco and Tunisia. Sardinia conquered.
809–12	Independent dynasties in Oman and Yemen. Abbasid civil war, siege of Baghdad.
813–33	Reign of Caliph al-Mamun. Through the *mihna* he attempts to enforce orthodoxy across the Muslim world. The attempt fails and sets off more religious rebellion.
820	Independent Tahirid Dynasty in Khurasan. Abbasid dominion now shattered but Islam unites the empire.
836	Abbasid capital moved from Baghdad to Samarra.
861	Slave soldiers of Samarra riot and kill the caliph. Caliphs are the puppets of their own bodyguards.
867–72	Independent Saffarid Dynasty defeats Tahirids and occupies all of Persia.
869–83	Black slaves revolt in Iraq.
877	Quasi-independent Tulunid governors of Egypt take Syria from direct Abbasid control.
899	Ismaili Shiite republics set up by the Qarmatians in eastern Arabia and in Yemen.
907	The Khitai conquer Northern China and start to push steppe Turks from Central Asia into the eastern Islamic lands.
909	The Fatimids establish a rival Ismaili Shiite caliphate in Tunisia and occupy Sicily and Sardinia. Large-scale Ismaili missionary work spreads the creed across Islam.
927	Qarmatians nearly seize Baghdad.
930	Qarmatians seize the holy black stone from the Kaaba and massacre pilgrims.
944	Kharijite rebellion against the Fatimids suppressed in North Africa.

945	The Shiite Buyids from Iran occupy Iraq but retain the Abbasid caliphs for political reasons. The tenth century is the 'Shiite Century'.
960	The Fatimids conquer Egypt from the Ikhshidids. The Saljuq Turks enter eastern Islam from Central Asia and convert to Sunni Islam.
962–1024	Former Islamic slave soldiers, the Ghaznavids, forge an empire in Afghanistan and northern India and occupy eastern Iran.
969	Foundation of Cairo by the Fatimids. Ismaili House of Propaganda founded.
1040	Battle of Dandanqan, the Saljuqs defeat the Ghaznavids and take control of Iran.
1055	The Saljuqs take Baghdad and 'liberate' the Abbasid caliphate from the Shiite Buyids, their sultanate begins.
1065–97	Fatimid–Saljuq war in Syria.
1070–92	The Ismailis, soon to become the Assassins, take castles in northern Persia as strongholds. Hasan-i-Sabbah, the founder of the Assassins starts his career as a Fatimid missionary.
1071	Saljuqs defeat Byzantines at Manzikert.
1092	Murder of the Saljuq great *wazir* Nizam al-Mulk by the Assassins. The Saljuq Empire is shattered.
1094	The Fatimid succession is contested. Nizar is murdered in favour of his brother by the *wazir* and the Nizari Ismailis, the Assassins, formally split away from the Fatimids.
1099	First Crusade takes Jerusalem.
1099–1105	Fatimids engaged repeatedly by the Crusaders.
1100	First Assassin missionaries sent to Syria.
1100–10	Assassins' murder campaign against the sons of Nizam al-Mulk in Persia.
1101	Sultan Berkyaruq regains some control over Persia and begins a campaign against the Assassins.
1106	First castle seized by Assassins in Syria.
1108–9	Sunni religious leaders in Nishapur and Isfahan killed by Assassins.
1111	Aleppo's lord, under pressure from the Assassins, closes the city's gates to the sultan's army as it is on its way to fight the Crusaders.
1113	The Sunnis of Aleppo massacre the Assassins in their city.

1113   The emir Mawdud leads an expedition against the Crusaders but he is killed in Damascus's great mosque by the Assassins.

1118   Almost constant Saljuq raids on Assassin territories in Persia ending only with the sultan's death.

1119   Battle of *Ager Sainguinis*. Before the battle a Sunni judge preaches to the troops. Hatred of the Assassins by both groups is a catalyst for the union between Sunnism and the Turkish military men and *jihad*.

1120–40s The rise of Zangi, lord of Mosul.

1121   The King of Georgia invades Islam and the Assassins begin a campaign of murder to stop the Georgians. Al-Afdal, the Fatimid *wazir*, is assassinated in Cairo. Fatimid resistance to the Crusaders in Syria collapses as the state undergoes sustained political crises.

1122   Balak, the new lord of Aleppo, takes on the *jihad* against the Crusaders and persecutes the Assassins' sect.

1124   Death of Balak at siege of Manbj. Death of Hasan-i-Sabbah, the first Assassin grand master.

1125   Sunni judge of Aleppo murdered by the Assassins.

1126   Sultan Sanjar resumes war with the Assassins.

1129   In Damascus a Sunni mob massacres Assassins and sympathisers.

1130   The Fatimid caliph, al-Amir, is murdered by the Assassins.

1130–40 Rise of the Khwarazm shahs in Transoxania. Syrian Assassins consolidate their position by obtaining castles.

1131   Buri, the lord of Damascus, is assassinated.

1135   The Assassins kill the Abbasid caliph with the collusion of the sultan.

1138   The Assassins kill their second caliph.

1141   Battle of Qatwan Steppe, Saljuqs defeated by the Khitai.

1143   The Saljuq governor of Rayy builds towers out of the skulls of suspected Assassins as he goes to war with them. The Saljuq sultan of Baghdad is assassinated with the collusion of Zangi, the new lord of Mosul.

1144   The Zangi's counter-crusade takes Edessa.

1146   Death of Zangi.

1148   The Second Crusade reaches the Holy Land.

1149   Assassin irregulars fight in the army of Raymond of Antioch against Nur al-Din.

1152	Count Raymond II of Tripoli is the first Crusader murdered by the Assassins.
1153	Sultan Sanjar is defeated by the Ghuzz Turks; they hold him captive for three years.
1154	Nur al-Din takes Damascus. Sunni *jihad* against the Assassins and Crusaders.
1157	Death of Sanjar, break up of eastern Saljuq Empire.
1162	Rashid al-Din becomes chief missionary for the Assassins in Syria.
1164	The Assassin grand master announces the end of the *sharia* and the Resurrection. He is portrayed as a direct agent of God.
1171	Saladin brings the Fatimid Empire to an end and holds Egypt.
1174–92	Career of Saladin. The Assassins try to kill him three times but eventually make an accord with the sultan. Saladin defeats the Crusaders and takes Jerusalem.
1192	The Third Crusade arrives in Syria. King Richard of England saves the Crusader state. Assassination of the Marquis Conrad of Montferrat as he awaits coronation as the new king of the Crusader kingdom. Third Crusade leaves Syria after agreement with Saladin over Jerusalem and the Syrian coast.
1193	Death of Saladin and of Rashid al-Din.
1194–6	The Khwarazm shahs make war on the last Saljuqs and on the caliph.
1199	First clash between the Assassins and the Khwarazm shahs.
1210	Assassins accept authority of the Abbasid caliph and become 'neo-Muslims'.
1213	Raymond, son of Bohemond of Antioch, is assassinated.
1215	Chinggis Khan takes Beijing.
1218	The Khwarazm shah provokes war with the Mongols.
1219	First Mongol invasion of Islamic lands.
1220	Mongols conquer eastern territories of Islam, Bukhara is sacked.
1223	Mongol reign of terror in eastern Persia. Khwarazmians in disarray.
1227	Death of Chinggis Khan.
1228	Crusade of Frederick II. The emperor pays protection money to the Assassins.

1230   Mongol offensive into western Islam. In Syria the Assassins fight with the Hospitallers against Bohemond of Antioch.

1231   Death of last Khwarazm shah.

1238   Failure of Assassin and caliphal embassies seeking alliance against the Mongols in France and England.

1242–3   Mongols invade Anatolia, Battle of Kose Dagh.

1244   Khwarazmians desecrate the Holy Sepulchre in Jerusalem, Battle of Harbiyya.

1249–50   Louis IX crusades to Egypt, birth of Mamluk sultanate. King Louis receives an embassy from the Assassins.

1253   Four hundred Assassins are sent to Mongolia to assassinate the Khan but the mission fails.

1253–4   Hulegu Khan is sent to Persia by the Great Khan to punish the Assassins and to end the Abbasid caliphate.

1256   Hulegu Khan invades Persia with specific mission to eliminate Assassins. The grand master's castle, Alamut, surrenders.

1258   Mongols murder the last Caliph of Baghdad and sack the city.

1259   Mongke Khan dies, the Mongol Civil War begins.

1260   The Mongols invade Syria but are defeated by the Mamluks of Egypt at Ain Jalut.

1261–91   Mamluk–Sunni *jihad* against Crusaders ending with fall of last Crusader city, Acre. The Assassins' castles in Syria are also taken by the Mamluks in their Holy War.

1270   The great Assassin castle, Girdkuh, finally falls to the Mongols. Philip of Montfort is assassinated in Acre on the orders of Baybars, the Mamluk sultan.

1271   Bohemond of Tripoli employs Assassins to kill the Mamluk sultan, but the attempt fails.

1272   Baybars sends Assassins to kill Edward of England while he is on Crusade. The Assassins are now controlled entirely by the Mamluk sultans.

1275   Assassins recapture Alamut castle from the Mongols.

1336   The Mongol state of Persia collapses. Assassin refugees spread over Asia and become the peaceful community of Ismaili Muslims that exists today.

GENEALOGICAL AND SUCCESSION TABLES

ASSASSIN GRAND MASTERS

Hasan-i-Sabbah	1090–1124	Muhammad II	1166–1210
Buzurg Umid	1124–38	Jalal al-Din Hasan	1210–20
Muhammad I	1138–62	Ala al-Din Muhammad	1220–55
Hasan II	1162–6	Rukn al-Din	1255–6

THE RASHIDUN CALIPHS

Abu Bakr	632–4	Uthman Ibn Affan	644–56
Umar Ibn al-Khattab	634–44	Ali Ibn Abi Talib	656–61

THE UMAYYAD CALIPHS

Muawiya Ibn Abi Sufyan I	661–80	Umar Ibn Abd al-Aziz	717–20
Yazid I	680–3	Yazid II	720–4
Muawiya II	683–4	Hisham	724–43
Marwan I	684–5	Al-Walid II	743–4
Abd al-Malik	685–705	Yazid III	744
Al-Walid I	705–15	Ibrahim	744
Sulayman	715–17	Marwan II	744–50

THE ABBASID CALIPHS

Abu'l-Abbas al-Saffah	750–4	Al-Mutawakkil	847–61
Al-Mansur	754–75	Al-Muntasir	861–2
Al-Mahdi	775–85	Al-Mustain	862–6
Al-Hadi	785–6	Al-Mutazz	866–9
Harun al-Rashid	786–809	Al-Muhtadi	869–70
Al-Amin	809–13	Al-Mutamid	870–92
Al-Mamun	813–33	Al-Mutadid	892–902
Al-Mutasim	833–42	Al-Muktafi	902–8
Al-Wathiq	842–7	Al-Muqtadir	908–32

Al-Qahir	932–4	Al-Mustarshid	1118–35
Al-Radi	934–40	Al-Rashid	1135–6
Al-Muttaqi	940–4	Al-Muqtafi	1136–60
Al-Mustakfi	944–6	Al-Mustanjid	1160–70
Al-Muti	946–74	Al-Mustadi	1170–80
Al-Tai	974–91	Al-Nasir	1180–1225
Al-Qadir	991–1031	Al-Zahir	1225–6
Al-Qaim	1031–75	Al-Mustansir	1226–42
Al-Muqtadi	1075–94	Al-Mustasim	1242–58
Al-Mustazhir	1094–1118		

THE GREAT SALJUQ SULTANS

Toghril Beg	1055–63	Berkyaruq	1094–1104
Alp Arslan	1063–72	Malikshah II	1104–5
Malikshah	1073–92	Muhammad Tapar	1105–18
Mahmud	1092–4	Sanjar	1118–57

Thereafter the empire split into petty states controlled by numerous claimants to the title of Great Sultan.

THE FATIMID IMAMS AND CALIPHS

Al-Mahdi	909–34	Al-Mustansir	1035–94
Al-Qaim	935–46	Al-Mustali	1094–1101
Al-Mansur	946–53	Al-Amir	1101–31
Al-Muizz	953–75	Al-Hafiz	1131–49
Al-Aziz	975–95	Al-Zafir	1149–54
Al-Hakim	996–1021	Al-Faiz	1154–60
Al-Zahir	1021–35	Al-Adid	1160–71

THE KHWARAZM SHAHS

Atsiz	d.1156	Tekish	1172–1200
Il-Arslan	1156–72	Ala al-Din Muhammad	1200–23
Sultan-Shah	1172 (Reign disrupted by civil war)	Jalal al-Din Muhammad	1224–31

THE HOUSE OF THE PROPHET

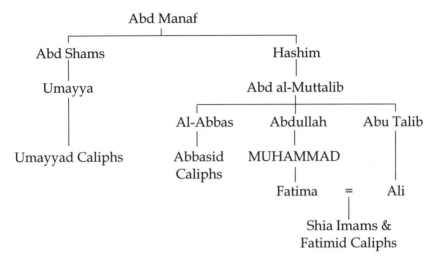

THE GREAT KHANS

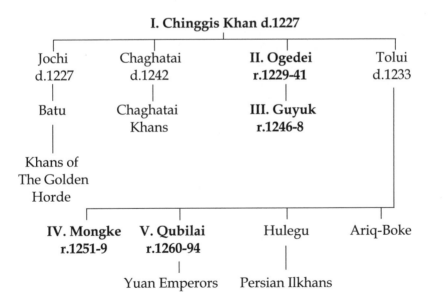

A NOTE ON TRANSLITERATION, TITLES AND DATES

THERE ARE MANY WAYS of rendering Persian, Arabic, Turkish and Mongolian into English. I have generally opted for the most commonly used 'short' forms of names rather then the more scholarly forms simply because the vast swathe of names that the reader encounters whilst reading any history of the medieval Middle East means that any familiar faces are welcome.

For city and country names I have used the nomenclature of the period. The Crusader cities are given their Frankish names rather than the Arabic, as this is how they are most commonly denoted in other texts that the reader might be led to review. Persia has been preferred over Iran simply because the medieval entity of Persia covered a larger geographical area than modern Iran does and denotes the area of the pre-Islamic Persian-Sassanian Empire more closely than do the borders of the present-day state. Similarly, medieval Syria was far larger than the modern state of the same name and embraced all of Lebanon and modern Israel.

Of course, the events of the medieval Middle East were recorded by contemporary Islamic writers in the Arabic calendar, which is based on a lunar cycle and dated from the *hijra* – the Prophet's flight from Mecca to Medina. I have, however, used the Christian calendar and all dates are Anno Domini as I want the reader to be able to parallel the events described with what was happening in Europe at the same time.

MAPS

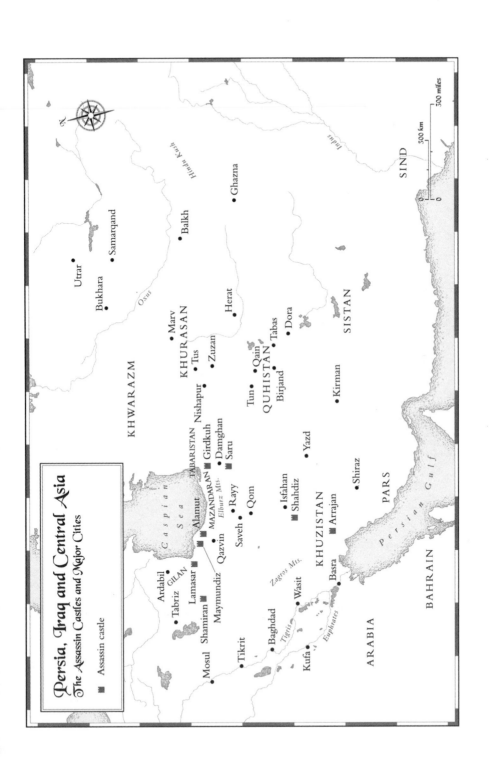

Persia, Iraq and Central Asia
The Assassin Castles and Major Cities

■ Assassin castle

Utrar
Bukhara
Samarqand
Balkh
Ghazna
Oxus
Marv
Herat
Hindu Kush
Indus
KHWARAZM
KHURASAN
Tus
Zuzan
Nishapur
Tun
Qain
Tabas
Dora
SISTAN
QUHISTAN
Birjand
Kirman
SIND
TABARISTAN
Girdkuh
Damghan
Saru
Yazd
Alamut
MAZANDARAN
Elburz Mts.
Rayy
Qom
Isfahan
Shahdiz
Shiraz
PARS
Caspian Sea
Qazvin
Saveh
Arrajan
KHUZISTAN
Ardabil
Tabriz
GILAN
Lamasar
Shamiran
Maymundiz
Zagros Mts.
Wasit
Basra
Persian Gulf
Mosul
Baghdad
Tigris
Euphrates
Kufa
BAHRAIN
Tikrit
ARABIA

300 km
300 miles

Manbj •

Azoz •

al–Bab • • Buzaa

• Aleppo

Antioch •

St. Symeon •

Ma'arrat Masrin •

■ Sarmin

Inab •   • Kafarlatha

■ Balis

Afamiya •

■ Shaizar

Maniqa •

Ulayqa • • Khariba   Hama •

Qadmus •

al–Kahf • ■ Masyaf

Tortosa • ■ Khawabi   • Salamiyya

• Homs

Tripoli •

Beirut •

S Y R I A

Sidon •

Hasbayya • • Damascus

Tyre •   Banyas •

Hattin

Acre • ✕

Ain Jalut ✕

Caesarea •

Arsuf •

Jaffa •   Ramla •

Ascalon • • Jerusalem

Gaza •

Harbiyya ✕

Mediterranean Sea

Orontes

Jabal al Summaq Mts.

Euphrates

Leontes

River Jordan

Lake Tiberius

Dead Sea

P A L E S T I N E

N

0   50 km
0   50 miles

Syria and Palestine
The Major Centres, Battlefields
and Assassin Castles

■   Assassin castle

✕   Battlefield

INTRODUCTION

History is a discipline widely cultivated among nations and races and eagerly sought after. The men in the street, the ordinary people, aspire to know it. Kings and leaders vie for it. Both the learned and the ignorant are able to understand it. For on the surface, history is no more than information about political events, dynasties, and occurrences of the remote past, elegantly presented and spiced with proverbs. It serves to entertain large, crowded gatherings and brings to us an understanding of human affairs. It shows how changing conditions affected human affairs, how certain dynasties came to occupy an ever wider space in the world, and how they settled the earth until they heard the call and their time was up. The inner meaning of history, on the other hand, involves speculation and an attempt to get at the truth, subtle explanation of the causes and origins of existing things, and deep knowledge of the how and why of events.

*Ibn Khaldun (d.1406)**

THE DIFFICULTIES ENCOUNTERED IN writing about the Assassins fall into two main areas. First, most of the history of the medieval Middle East is, to all intents and purposes, a military history. The 'men of the sword' were the body politic or at least its *sine qua non* throughout this entire period and if we look at the great events of the period from the Arab conquests of the seventh century, through the Crusades period and into the Mongol invasions of the thirteenth century, this seems startlingly clear. The Assassins are, at first glance, the very antithesis of such a military history. They generally avoided battle, substituting political killing in its stead, and there are almost no great campaigns or bloody battles to recount about them directly.

The second problem relates to the old truism that history is written by the winners. The Assassins disappeared from importance in the affairs of Persia and the Levant in the thirteenth century, crushed out of existence by the Mongols and by the Turkish Mamluks of Egypt. Both these enemies, and the many foes the Nizari Ismaili Assassins had faced before, were either Sunni Muslims or later converts to that division of

---

* From the foreword to Ibn Khaldun, *The Muqaddimah: An Introduction to History*, translated from the Arabic by Franz Rosenthal, English translation by N. Dawood. London, 1958, Vol. I, pp. 5–9.

Islam. Sunni writers, right from the birth of the Ismaili sect, stigmatised the movement as the greatest heretics ever to have arisen from within Islam. Indeed their vitriol extended so far as to call the followers of Ismailism, the parent movement of the Assassins, adherents of *Dajjal*, the Antichrist whose appearance will herald the advent of the Last Days. The eleventh-century writer Al-Baghdadi neatly encapsulated the feelings of mainstream Islam:

> The damage caused by the *Batiniyya* to the Muslim sects is greater than the damage caused them by the Jews, Christians and Magians; nay, graver than the injury inflicted on them by the Materialists and other non-believing sects; nay, graver than the injury resulting to them from the Antichrist who will appear at the end of time.*

Finding the truth amid chronicles that condemn one side whilst panegyrising the other's leaders is, of course, vital if we are to follow Ranke's dictum for historians, 'wie es eigentlich gewesen' – to show simply how it really was. But the period covered when one chases the Ismailis and Assassins through history is a long one, and, as Jean Cocteau once said, 'over time myth becomes history and history becomes myth.' How the writings and ideals of 750, however erroneous, affected the culture of ideas and sentiments in the thirteenth and fourteenth centuries is also of vital importance to us if we are to grasp a fuller idea of how it really was. So myth is recorded here too, but all due warning is given to the reader whenever it is encountered.

Returning to the first problem, this is a military history simply because the Assassins, through both their successful and failed political killings, fractured and divided the Islamic world before the arrival of the army of the First Crusade in Islam's western lands and were very much centre stage during the Mongol devastation of Persia and Iraq. In both of these episodes there are enough bloody battles and inspired stratagems, acts of extreme heroism and of depraved cruelty, skilled statecraft and deplorable blundering to satisfy any reader.

What is most difficult about writing this military history is that during the writing of any kind of history of the Middle Ages complex theology frequently rears its ugly head. This is particularly the case with medieval

---

* *Batiniyya* was a term commonly applied to the Nizari Ismaili Assassins. Abu-Mansur Abd-al-Kahir ibn Tahir al-Baghdadi, *Moslem Schisms and Sects Being the History of the Various Philosophic Systems Developed in Islam*, trans. A. Halkin, Tel-Aviv, 1935, Part II, p. 107.

Islam as it lacked the apparent unity and 'uniformity' that Catholicism still retained at this juncture. It is not my intention to discuss in depth, as others have done, the highly complex and often confusing arguments and divisions within Islam, Shiism and Ismailism that led to the birth of the Assassins. However, as James M. McPherson demonstrated in his superb study of the American Civil War, *Battle Cry of Freedom*, leaving battles and campaigns divorced from the politics they grew from and shaped leaves the reader uninformed about why men fought and how states waged war. Furthermore the fact is that in the medieval world, just as today, politics is religion and religion is politics.

Not many people in the West have heard of the Nizari Ismaili Assassins although the word 'assassin' itself, derived from the Latin *assasinus* and born, most likely, of the Arabic *hashisiyyi* (plural *hashishiyyun*) or hashish, is ubiquitous in its usage to describe cold-blooded political murder. But these men and the dread they engendered are worthy of study if for no other reason than that we are still living with the consequences of the successful establishment of a Latin kingdom in Syria in the eleventh century and of the Mongol irruption into the Middle East in the thirteenth century. Since they were catalysts for both events, a 'rediscovery' of the Assassins is therefore vital for understanding both what happened then and what is occurring now in the world's central lands.

1

A HOUSE DIVIDED

THE ORIGINS OF THE ISMAILI ASSASSINS

The Prophet said: A man will come out of the East who will preach in the name of the family of Muhammad, though he is the furthest of all men from them. He will hoist black flags which begin with victory and end with unbelief. He will be followed by the discards of the Arabs, the lowest of the *mawali*, slaves, runaways, and outcasts in remote places, whose emblem is black and whose religion is polytheism, and most of them are mutilated.*

I N 1253, AT THE command of an adored imam, four hundred men left remote castle strongholds in the high mountains of northern Persia and set off to travel across Asia to the Mongol capital of Qaraqorum. They were an army of murderers, disguised as merchants, mendicant preachers and messengers; their intention was to assassinate Mongke, the Great Khan and grandson of Chinggis Khan. Each man's plan would have been simple. They would get close to the Khan and then strike him down with a consecrated dagger before the Mongol bodyguard hacked them to pieces. The assassin would certainly be killed – tortured and killed more likely – after striking down Mongke, but that was part of the divine plan too. For the man who struck down the Khan of the Mongols would be assured a place in the highest Garden of Paradise, there to be attended by virgins for eternity.

Ultimately, this army of killers failed, but such was the fear that their poniards, of terrible length and sharpness, placed in the hearts of Mongol chiefs that body armour was worn both day and night by every man of importance in the Khan's dominions. The response of the Mongols, the superpower of the Middle Ages, to these men began with enslavement and massacre of their women and children and ended with a brutal invasion

* Al-Muttaqi in B. Lewis, *Islam from the Prophet Muhammad to the Capture of Constantinople*, New York, 1974, Vol. II, p. 53.

of Persia and an ensuing genocide that even today, eight hundred years later, still resonates in the consciousness of Iranians.

In 1092 a man from the same sect, armed only with a sanctified blade, had effectively destroyed a great Islamic empire with one political killing. This single murder divided and weakened the Muslim states of Iraq and Syria to such a degree that it gave the knights of the First Crusade the chance they needed to be able to take Jerusalem and create the Latin Kingdom of Heaven on Earth. Later, in a violent and ironic twist of fate they acted as a catalyst for the Islamic *jihad* that would eventually eradicate the Frankish Kingdom of Jerusalem.

These were the Assassins of the Nizari Ismailis, Muslims whose emergence into the religious and political landscapes of Persia and Syria was viewed by the rest of Islam as a trumpet blast heralding the Last Days. Their devotees eradicated whole political dynasties in Persia through campaigns of assassination and numbered caliphs among their victims. Even Saladin, the most famous leader of the Holy War against the infidel Crusaders, lived in fear of their ability to penetrate a sultan's close bodyguard and to infiltrate royal households. The Ismaili grand masters never left the safety of near-impenetrable castles in Persia and Syria and yet no man of importance, from Cairo in the west to Samarqand in the east, could consider himself beyond the reach of their disciples' knives.

Their infamy did not end, however, at the borders of the *Dar al-Islam*. Beyond the lands of the Muslims the Assassins' assaults on the Crusaders of Syria led to warnings travelling as far as the royal court of France. It was believed that there were agents planted in every king's household ready to undertake political murder at the word of the grand master. The life of Edward I of England was very nearly ended by the Assassins' blades and Richard the Lionheart's reputation as the avatar of chivalry was sullied by association with them after they murdered Conrad of Montferrat, the hero of the Crusader resistance to Saladin, in the streets of Acre.

The Assassins operated as a military power, not through direct confrontation but through their skilled and selective political killings and by fifth-column infiltration. Their selection of these tactics was due to the requirements of the asymmetrical wars they were forced to fight against numerically superior, militarily advantaged and logistically dominant enemies who could not be met on the battlefield with any real hope of success. In these uneven wars the Nizari Ismaili Assassins maintained an impressive record of frustrating the ambitions of great princes and their mission to slay the Khan drew on chameleonic skills of concealment learned over the course of a century and a half of eliminations and intimidation and was driven by an unswerving devotion to their grand master.

Had they been able to kill the Khan, the Assassins might just have been able to save Islam from the Mongol rage that was soon to engulf it. As it was, their failure only hastened the galloping horses of the coming Apocalypse.

Such was the action during the waning of the golden age of Islam. To uncover why the Ismaili Assassins came about, and how their methods evolved we have to go back to the seventh century, when Islam was just beginning its incredible journey of conquest, and to the death of the Prophet Muhammad.

Muhammad's death left the Muslim Arabs with a succession dilemma as the Prophet had always insisted that he was not divine but just a man. Therefore succession to his leadership could not logically be based on being God's anointed as the enthronements of Byzantine emperors and western kings were. This meant that although Ali was both the cousin and son-in-law of the Prophet he was only equal to other lifetime companions and comrades of Muhammad in the right to succession. The succession crisis was solved in the short term by the creation of the position of *khalifah* or caliph. The word simply means deputy, in this case to the Prophet, and was neutral enough to avoid any idea of divine right of succession by any man or of continued descent of the title through one family. This decision also has to be viewed against the pre-Islamic traditions of the Arab tribes, where leadership was by election and based on success or ability rather than by consanguinity.*

The problem was that there was a faction within the new nation that felt that Ali, despite the denial of personal divinity by the Prophet, had a better claim than other candidates of the Quayrash, the leading tribe of the Arab Muslims. The admittedly apocryphal statement of a deputy of Mecca as quoted by Gibbon,† 'I have seen the Chosroes of Persia and the Caesar of Rome, but never did I behold a king among his subjects like Muhammad among his companions,' at the very least gives credence to the fact that any relative of the man who had brought the Arabs a unifying faith of their own and a sense of nationhood was going to attract

---

* B. Lewis, *The Arabs in History*, Oxford, 1992, pp. 49–60.

† E. Gibbon, *The Decline and Fall of the Roman Empire*, first published 1776, Everyman edn, London, 1910, Vol. V, p. 255.

at least some supporters who believed in a God-given right to rule for Muhammad's direct descendants through his daughter Fatima.

Furthermore, at this time politics and the religion of Muhammad were indivisible. The Prophet's religious revelation was what had unified the early Arab converts and what had set them on their road to conquest. The series of documents that have been called the Medina Agreement* very definitely show how Muhammad's social and political message was bound up in the new faith. The actions of a Muslim towards fellow believers and towards unbelievers are expressed very clearly in the Medina papers: 'Believers are patrons and clients one to the other to the exclusion of outsiders.' The *hadith* or customs and sayings of the Prophet, which found expression in the Medina Agreement, were what regulated Muslim society after Muhammad's death and the same religio-social message can be found in the Quran. The emphasis was on social justice and the redistribution of riches throughout the Muslim community and the nature of Islam was such that it required a change of consciousness in the individual, from viewing himself in the singular or in terms of family or tribal ties to viewing himself rather as part of the *umma*, a community of the faithful.† Therefore, whilst Muhammad's message was ostensibly religious, it could not be implemented without large-scale social and political change; in this way religion, society and politics were indivisible. This synthesis of faith and government was an immediate cause of strength for the nascent Arab-Muslim state, as it would later be for the Assassin Missions, but it would soon enough ensure immense difficulties in securing a stable and progressive Islamic polity.

In only a short period of time, the faction backing Ali had become definable enough to be recognised as the *Shia-tu Ali*, or the party of Ali, later known as the Shia. At this point, however, there was no true religious schism in Islam as there would be later. The Shia were simply the political supporters of Ali for the top job. In this, they were immediately disappointed as, in what was perhaps not an altogether open or fair election, the close companions of the Prophet put up Abu Bakr, Muhammad's father-in-law, as the new leader without consulting the tribes – according to one tradition, whilst Ali was preparing the Prophet's body for burial. Later Shiite radicals would claim that it was at this point

---

* F. Peters, *Muhammad and the Origins of Islam*, New York, 1994, pp. 198–202.

† M. Hodgson, *The Venture of Islam: Conscience and History in a World Civilisation*, London, 1958, Vol. I: The Classical Age of Islam, pp. 172–93.

that, whilst Ali and his supporters followed the commandments of the Quran, the rest of the people, 'went astray like a blind camel'.*

Ali finally succeeded to the caliphate only after two other caliphs had occupied the throne. This period of the four *Rashidun* or 'rightly guided' caliphs was, on the surface, a hugely successful one for the Arab-Muslim community. By 651 Egypt, Syria, Iraq, the central lands of Persia and parts of North Africa had all come under Arab control either by conquest or by treaty, and in 654 there was even a naval victory over the Byzantines at the Battle of the Masts. There were, however, also portents of what was to come for so many caliphs and sultans in the future as three of the four *Rashidun* caliphs died bloodily. The second caliph, Umar, was killed by a Persian Christian slave; his successor, Uthman, was murdered by Muslim mutineers; and Ali was slain by a religious fanatic who was supposed to be on his side in Ali's civil war against the Umayyad clan – a distant branch of the Prophet's family tree. It was with Ali's death and the victory this gave to the Umayyads in Islam's first civil war that the Shia began the transformation from being simply a political faction to being a discernable religious division within Islam. Some of its adherents were of course Arabs, but it was among the *mawali*, non-Arabs who would soon begin converting to Islam in newly conquered Persia, that it made its greatest appeal.

Islam's conquests were so rapid, in part at least, because the long war between Sassanian Persia and the Byzantines (603–28) had totally exhausted both of western Asia's main powers. It had only drawn to an end with the Emperor Heraclius's forces driving the Persians from the very gates of Constantinople and forcing their retreat from Egypt and the Holy Land. The later Byzantine sack of Ctesiphon, deep in Persian territory, had effectively ended the conflict but at enormous cost to the Byzantine Empire and to its reputation in the Levant. Sassanian Persia collapsed into near anarchy after the higher lords of the state had slowly shot their monarch King Chosroes to death with arrows as a punishment for his folly in attacking the Greeks and in order to appease Heraclius. All this left a power vacuum that the now unified and well-organised Arab forces were able to fill. This said, there was still hard fighting to be done for the Muslims in the Sassanian heartland around Fars, where loyalties to the old order died the hardest.

---

* E. Kohlberg, 'Some Zaydi Views on the Companions of the Prophet', *Bulletin of the School of Oriental and African Studies*, Vol. 39, No 1, 1976, pp. 91–8.

Antipathy towards Greek Orthodox Byzantium came from its hard-taxed and religiously persecuted Syrian and Egyptian subjects, who were chiefly Aramaic and Coptic Christians, and from the Jews of Palestine who were being punished by Byzantium for their support of the Persians in the long war. This undoubtedly also assisted the Arabs in their rapid conquest of the Byzantine dominions in the Middle East.

The only hiatus in this seemingly unending catalogue of success was the civil war that began with the murder of the third caliph, Uthman, in 656. The murder of one man essentially threw the entire empire into chaos and this peculiar feature of medieval polity is worth noting at this juncture, as we start to determine both the use and effectiveness of assassination as a policy. In a period where an individual was not just the leader of a state but also essentially embodied the state, then his removal would almost certainly cause the state to stumble and even in certain cases to disintegrate entirely. What is also worth noting, politically, is that Uthman's murder was almost a direct result of his favouring of his own clan – the Umayyads, a leading family of the Quayrash. The Quayrash were the old elite of pre-Islamic Mecca and Uthman gave them preference over other groups with longer histories of conversion to Islam and loyalty to the Prophet. Muhammad had in fact been of the Quayrash himself but from one of its less aristocratic branches and he had never therefore been part of the more exclusive pre-Islamic aristocracy. This nepotism went against the equality professed in early Islam and set off a series of small revolts in the armies against what was seen as a hijacking of the Islamic Arab nation by the Umayyad family.

Uthman's murderers came from the Arab army stationed in Egypt and they killed him in Medina where they had travelled ostensibly to discuss dissatisfaction within the Egyptian forces. A desire for social justice, and the perceived lack of it in the Islamic polity was a major cause of the later formation of radical Shiite sects that ultimately led to the birth of the Assassins. It was also a primary factor in the later ability of the Ismaili Assassin sect to recruit abundant numbers of lay supporters and devotees with their 'New Preaching' or *dawa jadida*, which appealed strongly to townsfolk, low-ranking military men and peasants.

The murder of Uthman brought the much-delayed ascension of Ali to the caliphate, but his apparent lack of either remorse for Uthman's bloody death or desire for revenge on the perpetrators prevented a smooth succession. It was even suggested in higher political circles that the new caliph had a vested interest in the death of his predecessor and soon enough rebellion was brewing again. Furthermore, by taking into his government men of Kufa, a garrison city of Iraq, who were clearly implicated in the murder, Ali only worsened matters.

The role of women is not large in recorded Islamic history, but at this juncture the opposition of the Prophet's widow Aisha to Ali was decisive as she called for war against the fourth caliph. The Umayyads of Syria took the opportunity of the political chaos this war cry caused in Medina and Mecca to bring Syria fully under their dominion and break away from the empire. Ali defeated Aisha's forces at the Battle of the Camel, so named because the majority of the action took place around the dowager's camel, in 656 near Basra. The lady was soon enough sent back to Mecca and Ali was in control of Arabia and Iraq, at least for a little while.

The Battle of the Camel, by its very nomenclature, sounds like a small-scale battle and it might indeed have been, as 'pure' Arabian warfare was based on a principle of avoiding unnecessary loss of life. The limited manpower available in the peninsula precluded large-scale engagements and there was an accepted code of conduct in warfare that the sort of 'absolute war' described and decried by von Clausewitz so many centuries later should not take place. *Razzia* or raiding was the most common tactic employed by the Arabs in this early period and it was used against both the Byzantines and Persians with great effectiveness, to make the holding of territory by the two empires untenable. The Assassins also found themselves disadvantaged in terms of simple numbers against all their foes, their selection of methods of both attack and defence reflecting this disparity, as did those of the early Arab conquerors.

There was also a degree of 'chivalry' present in warfare in Arabia, even before the advent of Islam. Single combat was not uncommon between champions of either side and Abu Bakr had laid out the rules of war in 632:

> O people! I charge you with ten rules; learn them well!
> Do not betray or misappropriate any part of the booty; do not practice treachery or mutilation. Do not kill a young child, an old man or a woman. Do not uproot or burn palms or cut down fruitful trees. Do not slaughter a sheep or a cow or a camel, except for food. You will meet people who have set themselves apart in hermitages; leave them to accomplish the purpose for which they have done this. You will come upon people who will bring you dishes with various kinds of foods. If you partake of them, pronounce God's name over what you eat. You will meet people who have shaved the crown of their heads, leaving a band of hair around it. Strike them with the sword.

> Go, in God's name, and may God protect you from sword and
> pestilence.*

In many ways assassination, which eliminated the commanders at the
top and thereby denied those at the bottom of belligerent orders, could
theoretically avoid much of the wanton destruction of war and there may
have been a sprinkling of Abu Bakr's philosophy of righteous war in the
approach of the Assassin sect in later centuries. There is certainly no record
of the Assassins ever harming children or women in their murders, and
civilians generally were never caught up in what we today, somewhat
euphemistically, label 'collateral damage', in any of the Assassins'
missions. This said, it is certain that both their and Abu Bakr's clemency
was also highly pragmatic. The desertion of the populations of Syria and
Iraq from the Byzantine and Persian causes to the Arabs in the seventh
century has been described briefly above; part of the appeal of the Arabs
as new masters were the easy conditions of surrender and occupation
that they imposed on their new subjects. Much later, the Assassins
would need to preserve their base of support from both townspeople
and the peasantry, and the avoidance of total war and the horrors this
always brought to civilians was central to this, especially as their Persian
powerbases were in regions that had a fragile agricultural structure†
built almost entirely on the laborious management and maintenance of
complex underground irrigation canals or *qanats*. The disruption of war
could soon enough lead to failure of this water system, with subsequent
crop loss and famine. This was something the Mongol invaders of the
thirteenth century would quickly discover to their cost.

The chivalry of Arabia made an appearance in the Battle of Siffin on
the Euphrates between Ali and the Umayyad forces of Syria in 657; it
was Ali's undoing. Ali was advancing into Syria from Iraq at the head
of a tribal army, to remove Muawiya, the Umayyad governor of Syria,
from his position. Muawiya had not directly challenged Ali's position
as caliph at this juncture, but he had demanded the punishment of
Uthman's murderers, to which Ali had replied that no crime had been
committed as Uthman had acted as an oppressor of the Muslims. There
was also evidently an unspoken political divide appearing within Islam
as Uthman and then Muawiya spoke for the aristocratic rights of the old

---

* Al Tabari in Lewis, *Islam from the Prophet Muhammad to the Capture of Constantinople*,
Vol. I, p. 213.
† A. Lambton, *Continuity and Change in Medieval Persia, Aspects of Administrative,
Economic and Social History: 11th to 14th Century*, Albany, NY, 1988, p. 161.

Arab families, whilst Ali's support base cut right across the new society as he had tried to reinvent the role of the caliph. Ali seems to have felt that the leader of the Muslim world should not be an administrator and tax collector but rather a spiritual leader or imam. This idea particularly appealed to those at the bottom of the social order: the *mawali*, the new Muslim converts.

Muawiya knew he could rely on the fighting men of Syria, who had become deeply attached to him and his family. It was almost certainly this that made him confident enough to refuse to give the *baya*, the oath of loyalty, to the new caliph, and now Ali was marching with his army to force him to do so. Ali's army met Muawiya's Syrian forces in April, but there was little stomach for a fight on either side and the action was limited to skirmishes. Both sides would have been concerned over the opportunities their dispute gave to the enemies of Islam. The Byzantine border, a Syrian concern, was far from pacified and the north-eastern marches of Persia were also unstable, with Turkish incursions increasing in frequency. Muawiya's intransigence over the *baya* was enough, however, eventually to force a confrontation, and battle was joined on 26 July. Ali's forces, despite facing some of the toughest troops in Islam, were soon close to victory and only desisted from their attacks when Muawiya's men hoisted Qurans aloft on their spears with a cry of 'Let Allah decide!'

Ali, despite personal misgivings, and under pressure from factions within his own forces who viewed the Syrians' demands for financial autonomy as being valid, agreed to further negotiations and even arbitration from neutrals in the conflict. The armies withdrew from the field, but Ali was doomed by his gallant act. In the negotiations Muawiya refused the title of *amir al-muminin* or Commander of the Faithful to Ali. This fatally weakened Ali's position with many elements of his rainbow coalition and, together with the interminable slowness of the negotiations, it was enough to cause the desertion of a group of his most ardent followers. The name they were given, *Khawarij* or Kharijites, reflects this abrupt abandonment. It literally means 'those who leave' and they were only an extreme illustration of the wide-ranging discontent that was present in Ali's forces. Ali failed to push the real issue – who should lead the Muslim world – and he allowed the negotiations to continue to drag on, even though he could see that they were draining his army's morale.

Many others, like the Kharijites, were now voting with their feet; Muawiya had also used the time that the talks consumed to detach Egypt diplomatically from Ali's dominion. The loss of Islam's richest province eroded Ali's powerbase even further. It is likely that he was even considering a formal truce and partition of the empire with Muawiya when he was murdered by a Kharijite in January 661. Certainly his son, Hasan, immediately gave up all hope of challenging Muawiya, who had become, almost by proxy, the new caliph of all Islam. Hasan took a large payment from Muawiya and retired to Medina, where he was poisoned by one of his wives eight years later. The lessons of Ali's failure as a result of his reliance on coalitions and his expectation of honourable actions by his opponents were not immediately learnt by the Alids* and Shiites that would follow him. The Nizari Ismaili Assassins' later challenge to the Islamic world was, however, built on an exclusive, not inclusive, faith base that stressed dogma and single-minded devotion to the cause above all else and which gave absolutely no quarter to opponents.

Under the Umayyads, the successes on the borders kept coming and compared to the factional anarchy of Ali's caliphate the state was in much better shape. By the end of Muawiya's reign the north-east of Persia, the huge province of Khurasan, was being occupied and colonised with *mawali*, slaves and former prisoners from Iraq. Up to fifty thousand families were, to all intents and purposes, forcibly relocated to the region. By 716 Spain had been conquered with the help of armies of newly converted Berbers from a now consolidated North Africa. Charles Martel's hammer and the Franks' new belief that they were the People of God defeated the Muslims at the week-long Battle of Poitiers in 732 and kept the Muslims from taking France, but in the east the area corresponding to modern-day Pakistan became part of the empire.

So the Umayyads were successful kings, indeed the chroniclers recorded their dynasty by using the Arabic for kingdom, *mulk*. The writers declined to call the Umayyad state a caliphate,† and despite all the glory of conquest the chronicles of this period show an absolute disillusionment with the empire so acquired. The reasons for this are easy to find. First, there was division and jealousy. Syria, at this time one of the jewels of the empire, was reserved for settlement by the Quayrash clan. Others looked on green-eyed, which only deepened divisions that had never fully healed since the Ridda Wars of the early 630s in which Arab tribes who had attempted to break away from the nascent Arab-Islamic state were savagely brought to heel. Later Islamic writers describe the Ridda Wars as being against desertion of the faith by these clans – *ridda* literally

---

* This title has long been applied by historians to the extended family or clan of Ali.
† P. Crone and M. Hinds, *God's Caliph*, Cambridge, 1986, pp. 80–93.

means apostasy – but it is just as likely that the war was about reasserting the authority and pre-eminence of the men of Mecca and Medina over the other tribes of Arabia as much as any question of a loss of faith. Indeed, war aimed at conversion of any populace was an anathema to the ideals of Islam in the medieval age and large-scale voluntary conversion, when it took place in Islam's new lands, was essentially the cause of the destruction of the Umayyad caliphate and the end of the Arab Empire.

Conversion took place without any semblance of active encouragement from the Arab overlords in the occupied lands, but there were immediate advantages to accepting the faith that meant no urging was needed. For example, a community made up of the descendants of sixth-century Sassanian-Persian occupation forces in Yemen converted to Islam simply to gain support against local hostility. In Iraq Sassanian nobles and military men converted to try to maintain their old positions in the new society and government order; fighting for the Arabs was relatively lucrative – up to eight dinars per month could be expected.* The Arabs needed manpower as the Arabian Peninsula could not possibly produce enough men to garrison the empire, huge as it now was, and whilst military slavery was already prevalent in this period† the shortfall could not be made up just by human bondage. The initial response from the Muslim Arabs was that these new converts could be classified as *mawali* or clients of Arab families, but a two-tier Islam was oxymoronic given the precepts of the Quran on the equality of the *umma*. The class divisions that this conversion introduced into the empire and its armies were made all the more obvious by the new converts' exclusion from the *diwan*: the 'share' that Arab Muslims were entitled to from the booty of new conquests. These were conquests that *mawali* soldiers were now helping to secure.

The sense of injustice that the above engendered in the *mawali* and the fact that they had often only perfunctorily converted to Islam and retained much of their prior religious beliefs made them ready to accept new traditions within Islam that seemed to promise social justice and that were centred on ideas of divinity. It is beyond the scope of this book to look too deeply into complex theology, but it is notable that the central tenet of Zoroastrianism, the official belief system of Sassanian Persia, and of many of the minority folk religions of Iran today, is that a saviour named Saoshyant will arrive at the end of time to renew all life. These

---

* D. Nicolle. *Armies of the Muslim Conquest*, London, 1993, p. 26.

† For the evolution of the institution of military slavery in early Islam see J. Waterson, *The Knights of Islam: The Wars of the Mamluks*, London, 2007, pp. 35–40.

new adherents also perhaps wanted to embrace an Islam that could be identified as being distinctly different to, and standing in opposition to, the more orthodox ideas of the Islam of the Arabs. In 680 an event occurred that would sow the seeds of just such a religious movement, based on 'saints', and which would give the new Muslims an alternative to 'conventional' Islam.

Husain, the youngest son of Ali and the grandson of the Prophet, upon hearing of the death of Muawiya, left his refuge in Medina and started on his way to Kufa. Kufa was now a key centre on the Euphrates; a city whose Arab population held a strong attachment to Ali and whose *mawali* were already showing a reverence for the family of the Prophet that went well beyond what could be found in accepted Islamic practice. Whether the slaying of Husain and his family in the desert near Karbala was as tragic and dramatic as it has since been portrayed we shall never know, but the tales of the small party of Husain's seventy men and his family being surrounded by Umayyad troops, allowed to thirst almost to death and then being slaughtered by cavalrymen did not take long to reach Kufa. It was then embellished with further gory details including how Husain, having seen all of his compatriots killed and having carried their bodies back to his tent, charged at the Umayyad lines and was butchered. His head was inspected with the tip of a stick by the Umayyad governor, despite the pleadings of his own troops not to despoil the face that the Prophet's lips had touched in life.

At this point the truth of Ali and Husain's lives, their deeds and deaths, and those of all the other Alids who followed them, became somewhat academic. Revolts were raised in the names of both Ali and Husain and of their descendants, whether these individuals were politically active or not, simply because the revolutionaries needed a rallying point for the numerous discontented factions within the empire by this time. Ali and Husain became, to all intents and purposes, divine imams within a short period of time.

In 685 a rebellion among Persian Muslims failed in Kufa. It had been called in the name of Ibn al-Hanafiyya, who was of the line of Ali, but was the child of another of Ali's wives and not of Fatima's bloodline. It seems likely that the young man was not entirely supportive of the revolution instigated in his name and he may have simply decided to lie low for a time while the whole thing blew over. This did not, however, prevent Mukhtar, an old associate of Ali, from declaring Ibn al-Hanafiyya to be both an imam and the *Mahdi*, the divine one, who after going into concealment for an undisclosed time would once again rise up and usher in a new era of justice. With this and the rapid evolution of the idea that Ali and his descendants were the true imams, Shiism moved from being simply a political movement based around support of the right of Ali's line to head Islam, to being a distinct sect within Islam with a definable and different belief system to that held by the majority of Muslims. The idea of the *Mahdi*, the man of *ilm* – full knowledge of the Quran and of all its hidden meanings – would became one of the most powerful tools of religious propaganda that the Ismaili Assassins would later use to attract new adherents to their faith. That the *Mahdi*'s reappearance would also usher in a realm of justice on earth was of particular importance in the recruitment of the *fidai'in*, the devotees who were willing to murder and to lay down their lives for the creed.

Mukhtar demanded absolute binding loyalty from his followers just as the Ismailis would from each *fidai*:

> Then he [Mukhtar] alighted and entered, and we came to him together with the nobles among the people, and he stretched out his hand, and the people hurried to him and swore allegiance to him, and he said. 'Swear allegiance to me, on the Book of God and the Sunna of His Prophet, to seek vengeance for the blood of the Prophet's kin and to wage Holy War against those who treat that blood as licit, to defend the weak, to fight against those who fight us and be at peace with those who are at peace with us, to be faithful to our pact of allegiance, from which we shall neither give nor seek release.'*

The Umayyads would spend the remaining seventy years of their rule putting down revolts like Mukhtar's all over Islam. Many of these were raised in the name of Alid imams but there were also revolts in Syria among their most trusted troops and a continued fallout from the bloody Battle of Marj Rahit, which had been fought successfully by Caliph Marwan in 684 but had essentially divided the province into two camps. The defeated Qays Arabs in the north remained antagonistic to the caliphate of Marwan, whilst his supporters, the Yamani tribes, held the south and a continuing hot–cold war rumbled between the two. Syria's decline into the distracted and exhausted state it had become by the eleventh century, when the Assassins were able to infiltrate it with relative ease and the Crusaders able to conquer it quickly and almost completely, began in the Umayyad period.

---

* Al-Tabari (citing Abu Mikhnaf) in Lewis, *Islam from the Prophet Muhammad to the Capture of Constantinople*, Vol. II, p. 53.

The Umayyads had a particular problem with Iraq, which was reflected by their choice of governor for the rebellious province:

Al-Hajjaj set out for Iraq as governor [in 694–695] with twelve hundred men mounted on thoroughbred camels. He arrived in Kufa unannounced, early in the day. Al-Hajjaj went straight to the mosque, and with his red silk turban, he mounted the pulpit and said. 'Here, people!'
They thought that he and his companions were Kharijites and were concerned about them. When the people were assembled in the mosque he rose, bared his face, and said. 'I am the son of splendour, the scaler of high places. When I take off my turban you will know who I am. By God, I shall make evil bear its own burden; I shall shoe it with its own sandal and recompense it with its own like. I see heads before me that are ripe and ready for plucking, and I am the one to pluck them, and I see blood glistening between the turbans and the beards.
By God, O people of Iraq, people of discord and dissembling and evil character! I cannot be squeezed like a fig or scared like a camel with old water skins. My powers have been tested and my experience proved, and I pursue my aim to the end. The Commander of the Faithful emptied his quiver and bit his arrows and found me the bitterest and hardest of them all. Therefore he aimed me at you. For a long time now you have been swift to sedition; you have lain in the lairs of error and have made a rule of transgression. By God, I shall strip you like bark, I shall truss you like a bundle of twigs . . . I shall beat you like stray camels. Enough of these gatherings and this gossip . . .'*

Despite such threats and the slaying of some one hundred and twenty thousand people during the governor's reign of twenty-two years there *were* more gatherings and gossiping and revolts and sedition in Iraq. In 740 Zayd ibn Ali, the uncle of the sixth imam after Ali, Jafar al-Sadiq, raised the standard of rebellion and it was almost predictable that he should do so in Kufa. He was let down by the men of the city soon after, however, which perhaps only validates al-Hajjaj's above characterisation of them. A more loyal faction of his followers did, though, keep faith with him and managed to set up two small militant communities in Tabaristan and to the south of the Caspian Sea. His failed revolt also set a precedent: it made it clear that legitimacy for an imam should be based more on a willingness to take up armed struggle than on having a 'pure' Alid bloodline. This idea would be driven to its logical conclusion first by the Fatimids and then by the Assassins.

---

* Al-Jahiz in Lewis, *Islam from the Prophet Muhammad to the Capture of Constantinople*, Vol. I, pp. 23–4.

The last Umayyad caliph, Marwan II, tried to reform the state as it
became more and more obvious that the dynasty's time was up and that
its nemesis would come from within Islam. The work of military advice
that Marwan wrote for his son in 747 concentrated on the threat of the
continued rebellions of the Arab Kharijites in south-east Persia and not
on the dangers beyond the borders. The tensions within the empire as
a whole came to a head in 750 with the Abbasid Revolution, but it has
been suggested that the Umayyad caliphate, with its Arab hegemony
and investment of a few favoured individuals with all the power of the
empire was simply so unstable that it could not survive the pressure
from so many disaffected groups and would have fallen even without
the Abbasids' rebellion.* Of course, one could equally argue that a family
firm cannot really be expected to have enough individuals within its
household to run an empire that stretched from Spain to Transoxania.†

The Abbasid revolution was given a religious character by the raising
of black banners by its forces under the Persian *mawali* Abu Muslim in
distant Khurasan. Black flags, as alluded to in the Prophet's portent at
the head of this chapter, are an allusion to Armageddon and the Last
Days and the revolutionaries made a 'vague messianic promise of a just
and equitable society' to come.‡ Abu Muslim was acting for the family
of the Abbasids, who called for a return of the caliphate to the house
of the Prophet and who were descended from an uncle of Muhammad,
whereas the Umayyad claim on the blood line of the Prophet was much
more tenuous. They had also managed to gain the support of a Shiite sect
formed around Hasim, the son of al-Hanafiyya, upon whom the hopes
of the Kufa rebellion of 685 had been based. Hasim was childless and
allegedly transferred his rights to the imamate of Ali over to the family of
Abbas. The Abbasids therefore commanded a wide coalition in which the
hopes of *mawali* Persians, Shiites and mainstream Muslims, disgusted by
the secular and nepotistic nature of the Umayyad state, were merged.

The Abbasids relied for military force on the army of Khurasan and
mawali forces of Iraq. The Khurasani army was used to fighting with the
Turks on its northern border and were the best troops within Islam at this

---

* P. Crone, *Slaves on Horses: The Evolution of the Islamic Polity*, London, 1980, pp.
30–50.
† Transoxania roughly corresponds to what is today Uzbekistan and South
Kazakhstan. They lie, of course, east of the Oxus River.
‡ E. Daniel. 'Arabs, Persians and the Advent of the Abbasids Reconsidered', *Journal
of the American Oriental Society*, Vol. 117, No 3, July–September 1997, pp. 542–8.

time. It is difficult to be sure of these troops ethnicity, but it is likely that up to 80 per cent of the Khurasani army was non-Arab.* The Khurasanis won a series of victories over the Umayyad troops of Syria, who were certainly no slouches: they had fought the Byzantines in the Taurus Mountains over a protracted period and had been involved in several seaborne attempts on Constantinople. It was the Khurasanis' victories that brought the Abbasids to power.

The Abbasid revolution was a success, but only inasmuch as it was a straightforward Arab coup d'état. Abu Muslim should perhaps have raised red herrings rather than black banners; his murder by his ungrateful patrons and the large number of Umayyads left in position as judges and governors by the Abbasids† are strong evidence that an ongoing Arab Empire was planned – not a new Islamic society. Unfortunately for the new Abbasid caliph a Muslim polity of fairness and equality was exactly what the peoples of the Islamic lands wanted and they were voting for it by converting to Islam.

The Arab hegemony of numbers was essentially over by the end of the eighth century; there was a 'bandwagon' period of conversion in this period that led directly to the later establishment of independent Islamic-Persian dynasties and the almost immediate breakdown of the caliphal authority throughout the empire.‡ Conversion appears to have been a springboard for a re-emergence of regional identities and revolts against the Arab centre. The Abbasid caliphate was unrecognised in Spain as an Umayyad refugee had established a caliphate there that lasted until the Christian Reconquista of the eleventh century. In 788, what is today Morocco became the domain of the Idrisids and also the first obviously Shiite state. Syria was simply lost to civil war and banditry.

Persia especially showed a resurgence of national feelings. The Saffarid Dynasty that emerged in eastern Persia in the ninth century used this rebirth of national identity to separate itself and its subjects from the Arab Abbasids. The notion of a superiority in terms of culture, heritage and 'breeding' to the 'new' Arabs certainly contributed to the later formation of the Assassin sect as a breakaway Persian movement from its parent, the Arab Fatimid Empire, in the eleventh century. This sense of the Assassins being a distinctly Persian enterprise even survived

---

* Daniel, 'Arabs, Persians and the Advent of the Abbasids', pp. 542–8.

† A. Elad, 'Aspects of the Transition from the Umayyad to the Abbasid Caliphate', *Jerusalem Studies in Arabic and Islam*, Vol. 19, 1995, pp. 89–115.

‡ R. Bulliett, *The View from the Edge*, Cambridge, MA, 1994, pp. 37–47.

the order's spread to Syria and helped maintain it during its wars with the alien Turks and Mongols. Persian nationalism was also a defining characteristic of the Shiite Persian Buyid Dynasty of the tenth century – there was an attempt made by the Buyids to link themselves with the pre-Islamic past of Persia, through fictional genealogies that gave them illustrious ancestors with Sassanian bloodlines. Buyid coinage even showed its kings wearing the winged crowns of old Persia and carried the legend 'may the glory of the shahanshah increase'.* Significantly, there was heavy recruitment by the Assassins among the Daylamites of the Elburz Mountains, who had formed the body of the Buyids' army before its dissolution, and that they remained its most steadfast pool of *fidai'in* recruitment even late into the Assassins' history.

The Abbasids were then effectively the inheritors of a dying Arab kingdom. Even the great Caliph Harun al-Rashid of Charlemagnic legend, who ruled between 786 and 809, was willing to appease the people of Khurasan with virtual autonomy and exemptions from taxes† in order to prevent their secession. And it is notable how much time the early Abbasid caliphate spent using the military to suppress Islamic grass roots revolutions. Their response to the military men breaking away to form dynastic states was to separate fiscal control of provinces from military governance and to create an immense espionage network. These policies on the whole failed, although the spy network was later a useful weapon against the Ismaili missionaries, who were the bricks and mortar of the Assassin movement. The immediate results were both fiscal and administrative oppression that led to more revolts, first among the Copts of Egypt in 798 and then among the peasants of both Transoxania and Khurasan. These smallholder revolts were often instigated by 'prophets' and this is an indication of the growing abundance of self-legitimising Islamic leadership amongst the grass roots in this period. It was this disaffection and desire for politico-religious leadership among the peasantry that the Ismaili Assassins would later tap into to build their organisation, and from which they progress to recruitment in the cities of Islam.

It is notable too that this fiscal oppression and these revolts were taking place during a period of relative affluence and success for the Abbasids. In this period their armies reached the Asian shore of the Bosporus opposite

---

* D. Morgan, *Medieval Persia*, Oxford, 1988, pp. 19–24.
† T. El-Hibri, 'Harun al-Rashid and the Mecca Protocol of 802: A Plan for Division or Succession?', *International Journal of Middle Eastern Studies*, Vol. 24, 1992, pp. 461–80.

Constantinople and the Byzantines were forced to make peace and pay tribute to the tune of 'sixty-four thousand Byzantine dinars, two thousand five hundred Arab dinars, and thirty thousand ratls of fine wool'.* During the financial crises that would come in the future, radicalisation of the sort propagated by the Assassins during their missionaries' attempts to indoctrinate the peasantry, would find even more fertile soil in which to take root.

The Ismaili Assassins' direct attack on the orthodox caliphate was, however, still in the future and, broadly speaking, during the eighth and ninth century the Shiite response to the betrayal of the house of Ali by the Abbasids following the revolution seemed essentially muted. Many of Ali's descendants acquiesced to the new rule and some of the Alid family even lived at the Abbasid court. The Abbasids were, however, evidently peeved at the ongoing reverence that many Muslims still expressed for the family of Ali. The Abbasid caliph al-Mansur is given this speech by the ninth-century historian al-Tabari, delivered from the pulpit of a mosque in Khurasan:

> Al-Hasan his [Ali's] son succeeded him, and God knows, he was no man for the job: money was offered to him and he accepted it: Muawiya intrigued with him, and said 'I'll appoint you my successor after me', and that deceived him, and he divested himself of the office he held and delivered it over to Muawiya. Then he turned to women, marrying a new one every day, and divorcing her tomorrow, and he kept that up until he died in his bed. After him, Husain ibn Ali made an uprising, and the people of Iraq, the people of Kufa, the people of schism and hypocrisy and of submersion in discords, the people of these boroughs of misfortune – here he pointed towards Kufa – who by God are neither so hostile to me that I should make war on them or so submissive that I should make peace with them; may God keep me and Kufa separated – forsook him and delivered him to his enemies, so that he was killed.†

Given the Abbasid caliph's real sentiments towards them, his under-standable feelings about their main centre of support Kufa, and since every one of them was under surveillance from the Abbasid secret police, the Alid family's generalised submission can hardly be surprising. Indeed if any credence can be given to a court functionary's tale this submission would have been a simple matter of survival. Al-Mansur's perfumer

---

*   Al-Tabari, *The Early Abbasi Empire*, trans. J. Williams, Cambridge, 1989, Vol. II, p. 102.

†   Al-Tabari, *The Early Abbasi Empire*, Vol. II, pp. 34–5.

claimed to have discovered how the caliph kept a vast cavern under his palace in which were stored all the bodies of the family of Ali that he had had secretly executed. The bodies were all perfectly preserved and each corpse could be identified by a tag in its ear. The bodies ranged from young children to old men and women and each tag identified the place in the genealogy of the house of Ali of each one.

That the caliph could not give public burial to his victims was obvious: a shrine would quickly spring up around each Alid saint, which could quickly become a focus for opposition. But even more significant was the 'tagging'. It meant that the total extirpation of the Alids was a deliberate policy of Caliph al-Mansur and that he was cataloguing his progress.*

Despite the Alids' apparently calm acceptance of their fate, what did occur at this point within the section of society holding allegiance to the family was the definite conjoining of the idea of the imams with that of the *Mahdi*. It was now believed that the imams would sustain the Shiite community whilst it awaited the coming of the *Mahdi*. The death of the Alid Muhammad, who fought with a small handful of supporters against a powerful force of Abbasid cavalry outside Medina, effectively sealed the deal. From the time of his death in battle while holding the Prophet's sword and being struck down by arrows, before being beheaded and having his head displayed by the Abbasid caliph on a silver dish, the idea of the imam, the *Mahdi* and the house of Ali were inseparable. The fact that Muhammad tried to repeat the exact defence plan that his ancestor the Prophet had used – digging a trench to fight from – only added to the romance and legend. The Prophet's Battle of the Trench in 627 had been a success. In 762 however the Abbasid cavalry merely tore the doors from houses and bridged the ditch before surrounding its defenders.†

The Abbasid caliph al-Mahdi who ruled from 775 to 785‡ seems to have realised how all these failures were making the Alids into successful imams and he abandoned his own family's traditional claim to the imamate and instead based their right to rule totally on consanguinity with the Prophet. 'Mahdism' had by now, however, developed even further as an idea. It was now believed that the *Mahdi* would also spread

---

* For the perfumer's tale see H. Kennedy, *The Court of the Caliphs*, London, 2004, pp. 15–16.

† Kennedy, *Court of the Caliphs*, pp. 25–6.

‡ The Abbasids commonly took throne names that had a propaganda value. The appeal of al-Mahdi is obvious given the influence of the idea of the *Mahdi* in the medieval Muslim world.

the faith to the limits of the world and conquer Constantinople before ushering in the perfect Islamic state. In fact the Abbasids had even encouraged such ideas in the early eighth century, during the build-up to their revolt against the Umayyads, through their sponsorship of radical Shiite groups that professed this idea, and used the hidden messages that they claimed were built into the Quran as evidence for their millenarian ideas. Of course, there were also enough overt messages in the Quran to bring hope to those at the bottom of the empire too: 'And verily We have written in the scripture, after the Reminder: My righteous slaves will inherit the earth.'*

In this period too, we see the beginnings of extensive preaching of the Shiite cause, including both the idea of the imam and of the coming of the *Mahdi* throughout the empire, by wandering missionaries or *dais*. Passages of the Quran such as the above were selected and the Quran's approval of rebellion against, and regicide of, sinful rulers was stressed. The sufferings of the *Ahl al-Bayt*, or house of Ali, were also emphasised and the reversal of the injustices carried out against both the imams and the downtrodden in what must have felt, to a large group of Muslims, to have become the 'wrong empire', was promised. There was also a further evolution of the idea of secret messages or *batin* in the Quran and the exegesis of these by mystical processes known only to initiates of the sects. The formation of secret societies and the chasing down of them by the Abbasids' intelligence agencies are a constant feature of this period.

At this point there was also a division within the Shiites that has remained constant to this day. The majority of the Shiite camp recognised the line of the family that ended with the death of the eleventh imam, Hasan al-Askari in 874 and the going into occultation or *satr* of his son in 878. In simple terms this means that Hasan al-Askari's son mysteriously and miraculously disappeared and it was believed that he was being kept in some immortal condition until some unspecified date in the future. His return from *satr* as the twelfth imam Muhammad al-Muntazar is still awaited by the Twelver Shiites of Iran and southern Iraq, indeed by the majority of Shiites in the world today. For them, his return as the *Mahdi* will herald the end of time. The Twelver Shiites, however, in the early medieval period, whilst remaining distant from the ruling Abbasids and disenfranchised, were on the whole quiescent.

A smaller division, however, broke away much earlier in 765 with the death of Jafar al-Sadiq, the sixth imam and the 'succession' to the imamate

---

* Quran, Sura 21, v. 105.

of his son Musa al-Kazim whose line led to the Twelver Shiites discussed above. This succession was disputed by a group that declared Ismail to be the sixth imam.* Ismail was another son of Jafar, who had been disinherited by his father either because he was a radical, and therefore a danger to the tactic of survival by submission to the Abbasids, or because he was an inebriate. Needless to say, the sources differ dependent on the particular chronicler's religious and political colours and the later Sunni writer Juvaini goes so far as to state that Jafar said of his son, 'Ismail is not my son; he is a devil that has appeared in his shape.'† Ismail died before his father, and his son Muhammad disappeared mysteriously – he may well have been secretly murdered by Abbasid agents. Muhammad was recognised as the seventh imam by this new division within Islam which took the name of the Ismailis.

It was this group, and more specifically their wandering propagandists, who caused the Abbasids real problems. They would usher in what has become known as the Shiite Century and would, in time, give birth to the terror tactics of the Assassins. Indeed, such was the success of the New Preaching that the Abbasids went to great pains to make sure the story of Ismail's body being inspected by well-respected notables and elders of Medina before being buried in Baqi, the cemetery of Medina where the Prophet's only son and daughters were also buried, was disseminated all over the Islamic lands. There was also a propaganda campaign to spread the word that the new creed was not of Ismail's making, but was that of an individual who was variously branded a Jew, a Christian and a Zoroastrian. In short, there was an attempt to pull Ismail posthumously back into the world of orthodoxy, but in fact he was already long lost to radical Sevener Shiism and there were other tales – that he was not even dead – that proved impossible to counter.

The death of Musa al-Kazim after he had been imprisoned by the Abbasids certainly gave a boost to the Ismaili cause, as followers of the House of Ali could see that compromise with the caliphs was evidently not an option. The idea that Musa had laid down his life for Ismail to escape into hiding became popular and within a very short period of

---

* The Ismailis do not count Ali's son Hasan as an imam, probably because of his collaboration with the Umayyads. The Twelver Shiites do recognise Hasan as an imam, hence Jafar ends up as number five for the Seveners and number six for the Twelvers.

† Ala-ad-Din Ata-Malik Juvaini, *Chinggis Khan: The History of the World Conqueror*, trans. J. Boyle from the text of Mizra Muhammad Qazvini, Manchester, 1997, p. 643.

time many Shiite intellectuals had gone 'underground' to propagate the Sevener Ismaili cause.

One of the most important factors in the spreading of the new Ismaili creed was the *Pax Islamica* itself – never before had such a vast swath of Asia and Africa enjoyed almost unfettered communication. Whilst the provinces of Africa and eastern Persia had certainly slipped from Abbasid control, in that they could not exact taxation from the powerful families and governments controlling these areas, there was still an underlying sense of the wholeness of Islam, and travel within the lands that professed the faith was, at this point, relatively easy. Furthermore, Islam had allowed for the formation of a network of trade within the region far beyond anything that had ever preceded it, and this both facilitated transport for the missionaries and made financing them from distant centres relatively simple too. The invention of the *saqh* or cheque, cashable in almost any centre against distant funds was an Islamic invention as was the *diwan*, which the French Crusaders later took back to Europe as *douane*, but it was only concerned with revenue collection and not the movement through trade ports of dangerous agitators.

To whom were these agitators preaching? It seems that whilst in earlier centuries the peasantry had been the main locus of the more successful rebellions, and the Ismaili *dais* continued to appealto this group, they also preached to the growing and increasingly discontented urban populace. The populations of the formerly Byzantine cities of Syria had exploded under the Umayyads and early Abbasids as a response to the new trade routes that now stretched from China to the Mediterranean, and the new garrison towns and cities of Persia and Iraq had attracted more and more of the previously rural population to the growing conurbations. The populations of these cities were a mix of rich and poor, Arab and non-Arab, and every shade of persuasion within the Islamic faith. Later, the Assassins' missionaries would bring their New Preaching through the same 'journey'. Their appeals first to the peasantry before moving onto the people of the cities and, in particular, to the members of the 'brotherhood' of craft guilds may not have been entirely opportunistic. Certainly, early Shiite rebellions had failed because of their reliance on the allegiance of one city which, when lost, meant the end of the revolt. Consolidation of the revolution in the countryside before moving on to the more politically valuable but equally more difficult-to-indoctrinate cities made more sense if the Assassin movement was to survive. Their strategy has a modern parallel in Mao Ze Dong's campaign in China, which reversed the 'normal' practice of communist revolution by initiating class war among the peasantry rather than among the workers.

The cities were important potential hotbeds of dissent simply because obvious and outrageous wealth was displayed openly within the gaze of the lower orders:

> Al-Zubayr ibn al-Awwam built his house in Basra, where it is well known at the present time, the year 332 of the Hijra [943–944], and provides lodgings for merchants, sea-going traders and the like. He also built houses in Kufa, Fustat and Alexandria. These houses and estates are well known to the present day. The value of al-Zubayr's property at his death was fifty thousand dinars. He also left a thousand horses, a thousand slaves, male and female, and lands in the cities we have mentioned.*

Ethnicity, as discussed above, was also important. It is notable that many of the early *dais* about whom we have any knowledge were Persians and in preaching to the descendants of old Sassanian government families, who had now either lost their aristocratic position or were reduced to managing only 'local' affairs of the empire, they would have found willing listeners for their ideas, which might just have been laced with a sprinkling of xenophobia against the Arab dominion.

In fact, such ideas of an exclusively Arab Empire were fading fast as early as the eighth and ninth centuries. Many of the caliphs, including the famed contemporary and alleged correspondent of Charlemagne, Harun al-Rashid, were sons born of one of their father's non-Arab concubines, rather than of Arab princesses. Similarly the administration, especially of the eastern empire, was falling more and more to Persians and other *mawali*. A better way of describing the divisions in the caliphate might be simply to say there were the ruling and the ruled and there were certainly plenty who identified themselves as not having anything to do with the rulers of the Abbasid state.

During this time the *mihna*, an attempt by Caliph al-Mamun (813–33) to impose orthodoxy on the whole of Islam and thereby to create a central 'church', where the caliphate would be similar to the papacy – able to make *ex cathedra* rulings and use both the definition and accusation of heresy as a political weapon – ultimately failed. The caliph showed a readiness to spill blood to see his project through but he was opposed wholeheartedly by the religious intelligentsia, the *ulama*, and by the

---

* Al-Masudi in B. Lewis, *Islam in History: Ideas, Men and Events in the Middle East*, London, 1973, p. 243.

Muslim community as a whole. His violence against religious leaders simply isolated the *umma* from the caliphate.* Indeed Sunnism, or the following of the practice of the Prophet as delineated by the teachers of the Hanbali religious school and later by the Hanafi, Maliki and Shafi schools, developed quickly during this period. Sunnism was then, in many ways, a distinct alternative to caliphal doctrine. The Shiites already had a distinct feeling of identity through their following of the imams but now mainstream Islam had it too. The distinct division into Sunni and Shia camps would come later, early in the tenth century, as a reaction to the growing strength of Shiism. The origins of the 'schism' were created by al-Mamun: by losing the theological battle with the *ulama* over the *mihna* he also lost practically all the Abbasids' political capital with orthodox Muslims. His next political blunder, naming the eighth imam of the family of Ali as his successor, made the split in Islam impossible to repair. The rapidly crystallising orthodox faction that would later become known as Sunnism could now directly identify the Shiites as their adversaries in the fight to claim the title of 'true believers'. Being able to claim that their form of Islam was the only true version of the religion was vital to both factions as it was tied directly to political power in the state.

For those unconcerned with the minutiae of religious matters, there was simple justice to trouble them. The *qadis* or religious judges appointed by the Abbasids had no credibility with the people who believed that an honest judge would never serve the caliphs. Such was the people's opinion of these individuals that a contemporary writer recorded, 'we have seen an adulterous judge, a judge used for sodomy, and a judge committing sodomy, but now behold us observing a judge who is hired as a pimp!'†

People without a care for either religious or judicial argument could be angry about taxation. Unwillingness to pay tax to a distant and unrepresentative government was enough to set off a revolution in 1775 in a British colonial outpost, and this was among a people who at least had had some experience of tolls and taxes, and who even continued them after independence. The introduction of taxation in the name of the Abbasids of Iraq would have been an anathema to Syrian nomads, and by the end of the ninth century the position of the nomadic Arabs had slipped so far down the social scale that they had in fact dropped off it. They had been replaced, as described above, by Persians and other *mawali*. Over the course of the ninth century even the Persians began to

---

*   Bulliett, *The View from the Edge*, pp. 37–47.
†   Bulliett, *The View from the Edge*, p. 59.

lose the most important positions of power at court due to an explosion in military slavery. The caliphs had decided that *mamluks,* slave soldiers, would provide more loyal supporters for their increasingly shaky rule than either Persians or Arabs did. From this point onwards mamluks would to a very large degree dictate Islam's military and political fortunes and this would remain the case right up until the dissolution of the Ottoman Empire.

The mamluks selected by the caliphs were Turks and in this period we also see the beginning of Turkish domination over the old empire of the Arabs that would be completed in 1055 by the Turkish Saljuq conquest of Persia and Syria. Turks had been harvested as young boys for the slave trade from the steppe lands beyond the north-eastern Persian border since the advent of Islam into the region. The victory in 751 of the Abbasid caliphate's Persian-Khurasani army over a Tang Dynasty Chinese field army just east of the Jaxartes [Syrdarya] River, in what is today Kyrgyzstan, brought the entire western steppe into the orbit of the Islamic Empire. China's subsequent inability to assist the princes of the Turks was because the Tang Dynasty was simultaneously fighting an internal rebellion, fomented by one of its own Turkish officers.

The area was, in fact, never conquered or colonised by the Muslims but it became the main source both for the caliph's new army and for the men who would come to rule Islam. Perhaps the Muslims should have looked at how the Chinese lost the battle in 751: their Korean general was deserted by his Turkish levies and crushed between them and the Arab army.* The Muslims would also soon be reliant on forces just as foreign as these men were to the Chinese. By pushing the Islamic Empire so far to the east the Abbasids also gained more and more new Turkish neighbours, who were now unrestrained by a strong China. Gibbon's *Decline and Fall of the Roman Empire* gives one of the key reasons for the barbarian invasions of the third century into Roman territory as being the over-extension of the empire into Dacia under the Emperor Trajan at the end of the first century AD. Dacia was too tempting for the Goths to resist, and Khurasan was too rich a prize for the now unrestricted Turks to ignore, once the Arab Empire had begun its decline.†

Al-Mutasim was the caliph who really started the Turkish Mamluk revolution in the early ninth century. He formed a new aristocracy from his slave soldiers, which was able to take over the highest positions in the

---

* H. Gibb, *The Arab Conquests in Central Asia,* London, 1923, pp. 96–9.
† Gibbon, *Decline and Fall of the Roman Empire,* Vol. V, chs 1 and 10.

state. He personally supervised their training and seems to have become somewhat 'Turkified' himself from the amount of time he spent with his 'slaves'. He also arranged for the Samanids, one of the many independent dynasties of Islamic Persia in this period, who controlled the area around Samarqand, to send him boys directly without them passing through the regular slave market.

The caliph also cut all the Arabs from the military salary roll and used the funds this released to build up his new slave army and to house the army and himself at Samarra beside the river Tigris about eighty miles north of Baghdad. The new city was over thirty miles long. It required its own canal system to meet its needs for water and was chiefly composed of huge walled compounds, with endless successions of living quarters, courtyards, racing tracks and game enclosures, halls, harems and a grid-like web of boulevards and side streets to link each zone. The Jawsaq al-Khaqani, the heart of Samarra, has been described as a palace the size of a city, the monumentality of which was designed to impress and awe visitors. The city of Samarra itself was designed to be self-sufficient and to seclude the ruler from the ruled.*

It was a tacit admission by the caliph that the empire had become ungovernable and the oppressive Turkish military regime he let loose on it only made it easier for Ismaili missionaries to stir up national feeling among Persians. The missionaries were also aided by the worsening, outside of Samarra's walls of course, of oppression and extortion by petty government officials. A contemporary poet's lines make the level of misery clear: 'Would that the tyranny of the sons of Marwan would return to us, would that the justice of the sons of Abbas were in Hell!'†

The realm as a whole also continued to splinter and yet oddly the very thing that had caused its disintegration – mass conversion to Islam – now held it together as a civilisation if not as an empire per se. The Abbasid caliphate was, however, now little more than a cipher to the dynastic ambitions of powerful families such as the Samanids in the east and the Tulunids of Egypt who ruled in its name but offered little in the way of revenue. Indeed, a dynasty in the far east of Persia, the Saffarids, could be seen as a truly independent Persian state, in that they evolved completely without reference to Baghdad as a result of the coming together of

---

* R. Ettinghausen and O. Grabar, *The Art and Architecture of Islam 650–1250*, New Haven, CT, 1987, pp. 82–8.

† Lewis, *Islam in History*, p. 252. Marwan was the progenitor of the Umayyad family.

militias formed locally to protect villages from the raids of the Kharijites of Sistan. The Persian states of the east therefore paid little more than lip service to the caliph but oddly enough continued to send Turkish slaves to the caliphs as a form of tribute payment. The ability of such states to exist within what should have been, in theory, a united Islamic Empire with the caliph as its undisputed head, would have given succour to the later Assassin statelets that often had to survive while being virtually cut off from each other and being assaulted by armies intent on achieving just such a universal state.

The Abbasid caliphate's nadir as a viable political entity was pretty much completed by their eventual inability to pay their Mamluk army. Their slave soldiers subsequently rioted and murdered Caliph al-Mutawakkil in 861. This ushered in a period that has been described as the 'Anarchy at Samarra'.* Four caliphs followed in quick succession and three of them were killed either by straightforward murder or during rebellions – this only mirrored the chaos outside the palace walls.

In 869 a claimant to the line of Ali sacked the town of Asna in Upper Egypt and massacred all its inhabitants. He then defeated and crucified the commander of the army sent to capture him, and as a denouement, cut off his hands and feet, mimicking the way that Shiites were being executed by the Abbasid state. Shiism was becoming more militant and the risings were no longer confined to Arabia and Iraq. As a response the Abbasids cranked up their anti-Shiite legislation. Shiites were forbidden to acquire estates, to buy horses or to own more than one slave. Perhaps this last edict was wise – between 869 and 883 the Zanj, black East African slaves employed in the salt marshes around Basra, were in revolt and beyond government control, attracting many Arabs and Shiites to their cause. The bloody and difficult repression of the uprising required the alleged leader to be skewered from mouth to anus and then slowly turned as a spit-roast over an open fire whilst being forced to reveal the names and whereabouts of his associates.

Although it seems likely that some of the resistance to the Abbasids was spontaneous there was certainly also a large-scale, centrally directed, missionary movement active in this period. The locus of this movement remained hidden from the Abbasids' secret police and remains so for historians today, though it seems likely that Syria may have held a number of training centres, particularly on its coast. One of the reasons

---

* H. Kennedy, *The Prophet and the Age of the Caliphates: The Islamic Near East from the Sixth to the Eleventh Century*, London, 1986, p. 171.

for the difficulty in tracking down Ismaili missionaries and subsequently for detecting Assassins who had infiltrated the palaces and bodyguards of sultans and emirs was that their faith expressly directed them to dissimulate their true religious belief in order to carry out their work. This concept, the *taqiyya*, evolved in an age where religion was a key identifier of an individual's allegiances, social position and politics and as a rule was very much worn on one's sleeve. It allowed Ismaili *dais* such as the celebrated Ghiyath, a composer of many books and treatises, Abu Hatim, who was apparently an expert on pre-Islamic Bedouin warfare and a fine poet, and emirs such as al-Marwazi to propagate the Ismaili doctrine throughout Persia and as far as Tabaristan.

Things improved marginally for the Abbasid caliphate at the beginning of the tenth century. This was mainly because the internecine fighting between rival Turkish leaders, each wanting to place a puppet caliph on the throne, had burnt itself out. Through the actions of two exceptional merchants and financial wizards working within the government the almost-bankrupt state's finances had also stabilised enough to satisfy the army's demands. The fact still remained, however, that the Abbasid caliphate was in terminal decline as a political entity and that the Turks were de facto rulers of the empire. Caliph al-Radi who 'ruled' from 934 to 940 said:

> By God, I suppose people ask, 'is this caliph content that a Turkish slave should run his affairs and even control finance and exercise sole control?' They do not know that this [caliphal] authority was wrecked long before my time . . . I was handed over to the life-guards and palace guards . . . [if] one of these dogs asked me for something, I had no power to refuse.*

Then, in the late tenth century a slave soldier, Sebuktigin, who had been captured during tribal fighting among Turks across the border from Islam and sold into bondage as a young man, formed a confederation around him that under his son Mahmud of Ghazna would deprive the Abbasids of much of eastern Persia and Transoxania. The Ghaznavid state developed to become something that the people of Persia would experience first under the Turks and then under the Mongols for the next four centuries: not a state that maintained an army, but rather an army that had simply become a state. The only purpose of civilians in this realm

---

* Al-Suli in Lewis, *Islam from the Prophet Muhammad to the Capture of Constantinople*, Vol. I, pp. 39–42.

was to pay taxes to the men of the sword.* The Assassin Revolution of the eleventh century was, in effect, a reaction to this and would even reverse it to a degree, at least in the lands held by the Ismailis. The daggers of the *fidai'in*, who essentially constituted the military wing or army of the Ismaili state, were entirely at the service of the head of the state, the grand master. The grand master's chief function was to preserve the religion of the sect and to protect the state *and* its populace.

Much of Persia had therefore fallen to the Abbasids' former Turkish slaves but at least the Ghaznavids remained orthodox in their religion. Before the Ghaznavids' secession an even greater insult was made to the Sunni caliphs by a confederacy of men – the Daylamites who came from the mountains to the south-west of the Caspian Sea. The Daylamites were famed for their military prowess as infantry and they came under the leadership of the Buyid family, a clan that retained a heritage of fighting for the Iranian kings long before the arrival of Islam and who now embraced Shiism. Their espousal of all things Persian has been discussed earlier and now these Persians came to conquer the Arab city of Baghdad. Backed by Ghuzz-Turkish and Kurdish cavalry, they had effectively conquered Iran and Iraq by 970.

It would be hard to classify the ramshackle arrangement of power-holding warlords that this drive to Baghdad left in its wake as an empire per se, but the Buyids' achievement in bringing Shiism to the political centre of the Islamic world and effectively holding the Abbasid caliphs as hostages was certainly an impressive feat. It was mirrored by the almost simultaneous creation of an Ismaili Empire in North Africa and of other Ismaili states in Yemen and Bahrain and for a brief period of only eighty years it seemed that the house of Ali had finally triumphed in the lands of Islam.

---

* Lambton, *Continuity and Change*, p. 3.

2

STATEHOOD AND SEPARATION

THE ASSASSINS ARE BORN

As he sat upon his horse in readiness for the attack, splendid in red and gold arms and armour, girt with the sword of his ancestor Ali and wielding two lances, the animal pranced and one spear fell. The evil omen turned to good when the prince recited the tale of Moses's staff, thrown down to confute the wizards of Pharaoh; and the narrator to whom the verse was addressed saluted the light of prophecy which laid the meaning of the Holy Book open to his lord and master, the Son of the Messenger of God, the Imam of the Community.

> *Qadi al-Askar al-Marwarrudhi, describing the Crown Prince Ismail of the*
> *Fatimid Dynasty before an assault on Kharijite rebels in 947**

THE GAINS FOR THE followers of the house of Ali were built on the backs of missionaries who were willing to undertake the dangerous task of propagating their faith and political message throughout the *Dar al-Islam* whilst under constant threat of discovery by or betrayal to the secret police of the Abbasids. Of these missionaries, the Ismailis were the most radical and far reaching in their preaching, and it is far away from Persia, among the Berbers and Arabs of *Ifriqiya* and of Bahrain, that their preaching crystallised as a force ready to challenge the Sunni world, both on the battlefield and in the souls of its citizens.

The *mihna* of Caliph al-Mamun was a turning point in the fortunes of the mission in North Africa and the particular incident for this was the flogging to death of a religious jurist who refused to accept the caliph's doctrines. As always happens when governments attempt suppression of

---

* M. Brett, 'The Realm of the Imam: The Fatimids in the Tenth Century', *Bulletin of the School of Oriental and African Studies*, Vol. 59, No 3, 1996, pp. 431–49, quoting from Al-Maqrizi Itti az al-Hunafa. After the rebellion was crushed its leader's body was sent around the whole of North Africa as a dire warning to any other potential rebels.

religions by brutal acts,* the caliphate of Baghdad subsequently lost all control of the religious and political allegiances of its subjects in Tunisia and Morocco, and left a religious vacuum in which the Shiite *dais* could recruit all the more easily.

In 909 an Ismaili imam emerged from *satr* in Tunisia and claimed direct descent from Fatima, the daughter of the Prophet and wife of Ali. Fatima was a revered personage throughout Islam – the tale of her kind treatment of the wounded during the Battle of Uhud in 625, at which the Muslims had been led to victory by the Prophet himself and in which Ali had killed the champion of the polytheistic Arabs of Mecca in single combat, was by the tenth century the stuff of legend, as was Fatima's suffering after Ali's death. These poignant lines are traditionally attributed to her and added to the affection of the populace for her memory:

> There have befallen me calamities such that did they
> Befall the days they would become nights

Unfortunately, in writing of the imams who claimed descent from Fatima and would create the Fatimid caliphate, historians have had to contend with fighting their way through a great deal more legend in the form of the dynasty's own propaganda and the vitriol of later Sunni chroniclers. The famous libraries of the Fatimids were destroyed during Saladin's capture of Cairo in 1171, and whilst many texts made their way through Yemen to India with refugee Ismailis, these were primarily theological texts and not chronicles of the deeds of the caliphs and their armies. This has made a clear reconstruction of the Fatimids' rise to power and conquest of North Africa a difficult task, but it can also be said that the events of the years between 910 and 969 can only be recomposed fully if the Fatimid Ismaili vision of the 'Kingdom of Heaven on Earth' and of the evolution of 'God's purpose in God's good time'† is entered into. Without at least allowing for the fact that the Fatimids really believed in their own divinity, and that their followers were convinced that they were being led by an imam initially, and then the *Mahdi*, we cannot begin to understand how they achieved their conquests. To attempt such an

---

* Latimer's words of comfort to his companion at the stake before their being burnt as heretics, 'We shall this day light such a candle. By God's grace, in England, as I trust shall never be put out,' meaning that their sacrifice and indeed any persecution would make their faith stronger still, seems to be one of the world's great universal truths.
† Brett, 'The Realm of the Imam', pp. 431–49.

undertaking would be similar to trying to comprehend the success of the First Crusade or the creation of the Mongol world empire from a purely secular angle.

The ground had been prepared for this imam's coming out of *satr* by a particularly energetic *dai* named Abu Abdullah from Yemen, who had preached among the Bedouin, Berbers and Arabs of North Africa for some considerable time before the imam revealed himself as the *Mahdi* – it is certain that the miraculous coming out of *satr* by the 'Mahdi-Imam' was carefully choreographed. This required the murder of Abu Abdullah in 910 – *Mahdis* by their very nature can have no past and can hold no debts to anyone. It was vital that there should be absolutely no doubt over the divinity of the *Mahdi* as the forces that brought the Fatimids to power did not share any particular ethnic uniformity or indeed any real political identity before the advent of the Fatimids. And yet they carried the dynasty all the way from the fringes of the Islamic world right to the walls of Baghdad – it could be argued that success breeds loyalty, but the Fatimids rode a hard road of failures and setbacks up to their conquest of Egypt in 969. It could only have been their own unshakeable belief that they themselves were divine, and their ability to project this messianic belief to their troops, that maintained both themselves and their army through this period. This deep personal belief is reflected in their throne names, the first imam being named al-Mahdi, which is of course the 'awaited one' of the Shiites; North Africa was a hotchpotch of faiths, the Fatimids also used its identification with the Messiah of Jewish and Christian traditions to good effect – al-Mahdi's successor took the throne name of al-Qaim, another Islamic term for Messiah.

The Fatimid army was initially made up of the Berbers of Kutama, but after the first imam al-Mahdi conquered the Aghlabids of North Africa it absorbed both Anatolian Greeks, who were known as the *Rum*, a corruption of Rome, and black slave soldiers from the Aghlabids' now disbanded forces. The Fatimids also carried off slaves from the coast of Italy to add to their contingents of European slave soldiers; their taking over of the Aghlabid colony of Sicily in 914–15 added to this influx of 'recruits'. The question of the ethnic make-up of the Fatimid army is particularly problematic when discussing one of its key components: the Zuwayla. They may have been Arabs, Berbers or black Africans; the region from where they were drawn, just north of Lake Chad, is a mixed area. Certainly, they were trusted early followers of the Fatimids as they took part in a failed amphibious assault on Egypt in 920, and such was their degree of association with al-Mahdi that after the Fatimid fleet was destroyed off Rosetta by the Abbasid-Egyptian navy and its crews and mariners taken prisoner, only the Kutama, Berbers and Zuwayla were executed, whilst the Sicilian sailors were freed.*

A suburb of al-Mahdiyya, the Fatimids' first capital in Tunisia, was called Zuwayla, and these troops were instrumental in turning back a rebellion of the Kharijites at the walls of the palace-city in 944. The rebellion came very close to crushing the Fatimids' nascent state even though the Kharijites had earlier been strong supporters of the Fatimids. We last met the Kharijites murdering Ali in disgust at his truce-making with the Umayyads, and raiding Iraq from their mini-state in eastern Persia. So it says a great deal about the wide-ranging activities of the wandering *dais* that such an extreme and isolated group of religious anarchists, whose rallying cry was 'Man owes no obedience to rulers who disobey God!' had ever been brought into the Fatimid fold, even if they later rebelled against the new Shiite champions.

Meanwhile, the most important *dai* in Iraq, Hamdan Qarmati, started an independent movement in the 870s that would culminate in yet another revolt in Kufa. The revolt gave birth to the Qarmatians who, 'began to murder Muslims, pillage their goods and carry off their children'.† They then carried their banner to the east coast of the Arabian Peninsula to establish what can conveniently be called a religious republic, just prior to the Fatimid revolution in 899. From this wide geographical range of activity, it is obvious that the Ismaili *dais* were both numerous and effective. Certainly, the Sunni writers of the period went out of their way to warn solid orthodox citizens of their wiles:

> The first thing to which I bear witness, as I shall explain and make clear to the Muslims, is that he has deputies whom he calls the authorised missionaries, and others whom he nicknames the trained dogs likening them to the dogs of the hunt, because they set snares for people and deceive them with cunning tricks. They shrink from every intelligent person and cling to every ignoramus. By stating a truth with false intent they urge him to practise the laws of Islam concerning the ritual prayer, the alms-due and the fast, like someone who scatters seeds for birds so they will fall into his net. They devote more than a year to watching over him observing his patience and scrutinising his condition. They deceive him with misquoted reports from the Prophet [Allah bless him and give him peace] and falsified

* Y. Lev, 'Army, Regime, and Society in Fatimid Egypt, 358–487/968–1094', *International Journal of Middle East Studies*, Vol. 19, No 3, August 1987, pp. 337–65
† Juvaini, *Chinggis Khan*, p. 648.

sayings. They recite the Quran to him incorrectly, and the words out of their contexts.*

The writers suggested that once their target was selected the *dais* would move to indoctrinate him with their perverse ideas of the *batin*, or hidden meaning, in the Quran and give him the idea of joining a privileged and select group:

> As you have surely noticed, the egg has an outer aspect and an inner aspect. The outer aspect is that which human beings have in common, and it is familiar to both the elite and the ordinary folk. As for the inner aspect the ordinary folk have no knowledge of it, and only a few are acquainted with it. That is alluded to in His sayings [Glory be to Him]:
> And only a few believed with him.
> And they are few
> And few of My servants are very thankful.†

Such was the success of the missionaries' work in Bahrain‡ and Yemen that both states were completely lost to the Abbasids in short order. The Qarmatian sect was soon, however, also to reject the claims of al-Mahdi's Fatimid successors after initially supporting them and they generally remained antagonistic to the Fatimid caliphate. They even fought against the Fatimid armies during their invasions of Egypt and Syria between 953 and 975, but that did not prevent them being even more of a threat to the economy of Abbasid Iraq, since their state effectively dominated the trade routes of the Persian Gulf and they raided shipping with impunity. Their attempt to extend their empire to Syria failed, but they remained a thorn in the side of whoever controlled Persia until their extinction in the eleventh century – for orthodox Muslims they were the epitome of the excesses of radical Ismailism.

They came close to seizing Baghdad itself in 927, and continually raided *hajj* caravans and pilgrims. They outraged the entire Muslim world in 930 when they seized the holy black stone from the Kaaba; they then massacred perhaps as many as thirteen thousand *hajj* pilgrims and subsequently desecrated the holy well of Zamzam with the bodies during a sack of Mecca. Their *Mahdi*'s abolition of *sharia* law also helped

---

* The jurist al-Hammadi al-Yamani, *Disclosure of the Secrets of the Batiniyya and the Annals of the Qaramita*, trans. M. Holland, Cairo, 2003, pp. 36–7.
† Al-Yamani, *Disclosure of the Secrets of the Batiniyya*, p. 39. The verses are from the Quran: Sura 11, v. 40; Sura 38, v. 24 and Sura 34, v. 13.
‡ Medieval Bahrain encompassed much of the eastern coast of Arabia.

them become the greatest bête noire of Sunni writers until the advent of the Assassins. In fact, the Qarmatians did show a few of the social and religious traits that the Ismaili Assassins would later develop. They were accused of sharing their women amongst themselves by Sunni writers and, whilst this has not been proven, it does seem that there was some degree of community of property, sharing of labour to create for the whole community and an attempt to create a state with equality for all. Later, one of the appeals of the Ismaili Assassins to local populations would be a message of egalitarianism, with very real evidence of social order and of a community working together to maintain their common agricultural and economic base.

In the increasingly insecure society of the Abbasid caliphate, banding together was the only form of security the lower orders of the populace could utilise, and such groups would have found the opportunity of joining a larger, stronger band such as the Ismaili Assassins very appealing. The Assassins would also, at one point in their history, abandon *sharia* law as the Qarmatians had.

Ironically enough, one of the Qarmatians' key leaders was eliminated by a Sunni Assassin in 915. This individual, a skilled physician, worked hard, just as the later Shiite Ismaili Assassins would, to gain access to the inner sanctum of the leader al-Qarmati. He started by treating the lower-ranking leaders of the ruling clique. His particular forte was that medieval staple of medicine – bleeding. He was so skilled at opening veins painlessly that soon enough he was able to tend al-Qarmati. We are told he then hid poison in his hair so that he might smuggle it past the ruler's ever-vigilant guards:

> He took out the scalpel and sucked it . . . Then he rubbed his head with it, so the necessary amount of poison stuck to it from his hair. He performed the venesection on him, and then departed immediately, mounting his riding animal and fleeing away. When the enemy of Allah felt the presence of death, he commanded the killing of the physician but he was absent, so they caught him below Naqil Said in front of Qinan. They killed him there [may Allah the Exalted bestow His mercy upon him], and al-Qarmati died [may Allah not bestow His mercy upon him].*

Despite all the above blood and anger, Qarmatian Bahrain was in many ways just a side-show whilst Egypt was the main attraction – only its conquest could prove that the Fatimid dynasty and Ismailism

---

* Al-Yamani, *Disclosure of the Secrets of the Batiniyya*, pp. 109–10.

were viable alternatives to the Sunni-Abbasid caliphate. However, even Egypt's reduction could only be a staging post to the taking over of the entire Islamic world – the millenarian nature of the Fatimid movement required nothing less. Both al-Mahdi and his heir al-Qaim made attempts on Egypt, which had experienced the collapse of the Tulunid dynasty back in 905, followed by a reversion to direct Abbasid control. Since 935, however, it had been practically autonomous again under the Ikhshidids who only recognised the Abbasids as their overlords in theory.

In 968 Kafur al-Ikhshidi, a former Ethiopian slave of the ruling dynasty who had usurped their power in the 940s, died, and the political and economic strife this brought to a state that had long endured both the attacks of the Fatimids and internecine fighting in its own army, made the Fatimids' final conquest fairly easy:

> In Kafur's time the flood of the Nile was deficient. In that it only reached twelve cubits and some fingers. Foodstuffs became dear, and death was rampant so that they could not shroud and bury the dead. It was rumoured that the Qarmatians were advancing on Syria and Kafur's slaves, consisting of 1070 Turks, apart from Greeks and local blacks turned against him. He died when ten days remained of Jumada I, 357 [13 April 968], at the age of 60. He ruled Egypt and Syria and the two Holy Cities [Mecca and Medina] for twenty-one years, two months and twenty days, of which two years, four months and nine days he ruled alone, after the deaths of his master's children. After him Egypt was on the verge of destruction until the coming of the armies of al-Muizz, under the commander Jawhar, when Egypt became the seat of the [Fatimid] Caliphate.*

Al-Muizz had used the sword for the bringing down of Egypt but he reached for his pen to subvert the eastern lands of Islam.† His correspondence documents a campaign aimed at persuading the Shiites of Iran and Iraq that the time for the return of the caliphate to the line of Ali was at hand and that action was required to ensure that it

---

* Al-Maqrizi in Lewis. *Islam from the Prophet Muhammad to the Capture of Constantinople*, Vol. I, pp. 45–6.
† Al-Muizz spoke the language of complex genealogy and theocracy in his letters to the East to claim the universal caliphate for his family, but with the nobles of Egypt, after his conquest of that country, he was decidedly blunt. When asked what his claim to be of the family of Fatima was, he drew his sword half way from its scabbard and said, 'this is my genealogy.' Then he showered his audience with gold coin and this was enough, it would seem, for his claim to be accepted by his pragmatic new subjects.

took place.* The fact that Kafur had been the guardian of Mecca and Medina and that Kafur's possessions had now all fallen to al-Muizz was, of course, a huge propaganda boost. Al-Muizz's evangelism was a careful balance of claiming full rights to the imamate for his house by descent through Fatima, whilst allowing Jafar al-Sadiq, the sixth imam, and Ismail, the seventh imam, places in his genealogy. It was this manipulation and misrepresentation of the blood line that finally set the Qarmatians against the Fatimid mission, but it brought many Iranian Ismailis completely into the Fatimid camp and these were the bravest, most numerous, articulate and influential Ismailis to be found anywhere in the *Dar al-Islam*.

So Ismailism was spreading throughout the House of Islam through the travelling preachers, but what were they preaching now? The Quran itself was the most powerful weapon the revolutionaries had: the esoteric meanings or *batin* they claimed it held, which they claimed were more important than the *zahir* or the 'plain' meaning evident to all, were used to entice new adherents as the *batin* could only be seen by the initiated. Indeed, such was the importance of this aspect of their indoctrination that the followers they accrued were often termed *Batini* by Sunni writers because of this heresy.

Another aspect of their propaganda was that time was cyclical. This was a central tenet of the preaching because it gave hope of change and that those at the bottom might soon be at the top. According to Ismaili theory, dynastic changes were 'due' every 240 years. It might be a little cynical to point out that one of the major works on this important element of Ismaili theocracy, *The Epistles of the Sincere Brethren*, was composed almost exactly 240 years after the establishment of the Abbasid caliphate.† Another central belief that grew out of the idea of the *batin* of the Quran was that one's teacher was owed total loyalty and that there were grades of knowledge through which a convert passed. The need to accrue knowledge, but only under 'correct' tutelage, is made clear by the following Ismaili text:

> Both reason and a true teacher are required. Through reason we realize the
> need for the authoritative imam to lead us to knowledge of God.

---

* For the best and clearest explanation of the complexities of these negotiations, particularly as relating to the potential minefield of entitlement to the title of *Mahdi* by the Fatimids, see M. Brett, *The Rise of the Fatimids: The World of the Mediterranean and the Middle East in the Fourth Century of the Hijra, Tenth century CE*, Leiden, 2001, pp. 20–60.
† Lewis, *Islam in History*, p. 254.

> Unity is an indication of the true religion; diversity of the false. And unity stems from the acceptance of the authority of the imam, while multiplicity of sects derives from the use of individual judgement.*

The hierarchical structure and total dependence on a tutor or guide that this simple tenet implies sounds dangerously close to brainwashing and was certainly responsible later for the Assassins' blind devotion, which made them prepared to give up their lives for the cause. They were equally devoted to their grand master who was, of course, also their teacher and later their imam. The incredible resilience of the sect when faced by attack from powerful enemies was built on this allegiance to both teacher and creed.

With the conquest of Egypt in 969 by the Fatimids, and their construction of Cairo, 'The Victorious', with its new universities and the great college mosque of al-Azhar to produce even more religious agents and missionaries, the Ismaili world was given its first real headquarters. But the new Shiite caliphate did not stop there – the Fatimids moved on to take full control of Arabia and, by that act, of the Red Sea. Their armies' progress was slowed, but not stopped, in Syria by Qarmatian opposition more than by the armies of the Hamdanids, the autonomous dynastic Sunni power of the region. The bringing under control of all the Islamic lands seemed almost inevitable and the Fatimids had proven that a *Mahdi* could be a real entity and not just a dim vision of future hope. Their *Mahdis* were flesh and blood and had countless banners and vast armies, but then that became the central problem with the Fatimid state – with the establishment of Cairo, the religious revolution they headed lost much of its dynamism. There was now the state or *dawla*, which so often lay at odds with the *dawa* or divine mission of the dynasty. The caliphate and imamate were essentially unable to survive this secular–spiritual dichotomy. The secular requirements of a leader were to collect taxes, maintain a police force and army and to normalise relations with neighbours so that trade, the lifeblood of the state, could continue uninterrupted. The *dawa*, however, called for an ongoing religious revolution. Indeed, in its purest sense such a movement would have to be similar to the 'perpetual revolution' called for by Mao Ze Dong in 1966 in China – and was likely to be just as catastrophic for the Fatimid state as the Cultural Revolution would later be for the People's Republic.

---

* M. Hodgson, *The Order of the Assassins*, The Hague, 1955, pp. 54–6.

In 996 a caliph, al-Hakim, came to the Fatimid throne; his behaviour has been seen as madness by many historians, but his actions can also be viewed as an attempt to bridge this divide between the worldly and divine natures of Fatimid rule.* Certainly under al-Hakim, the Fatimid dream of conquering the entire Islamic world gathered pace again and both Kufa and Mosul fell briefly under Fatimid influence, if not their complete control. But whilst those far away from Cairo were perhaps willing to come into Caliph al-Hakim's embrace, those closer to home were finding him increasingly dangerous to know. Juvaini tells us how the caliph would write notes:

> some saying, 'Give the bearer of this note 1,000 dinars, or such or such-and-such a costly robe of honour' and some saying, 'Kill the bearer of this note, or take such-and-such a sum from him, or cut off this or that limb of his, and torture him'. And he would seal the notes with wax, ambergris or sealed earth, and on audience days he would scatter them about and everybody according to his luck would avidly snatch up one of these notes and bear it off to the local administrators and whatever the contents of the note might be they were put into effect immediately.†

Dogs, secretaries and women also did pretty badly under Caliph al-Hakim:

> He had both hands of Abu-l Qasim al-Jarjarai, who had been the secretary of Ghayn, cut off. He had Ghayn's remaining hand cut off, so that he lost both hands. Then after cutting off his hands al-Hakim sent him a thousand pieces of gold and garments but then later he also had his tongue cut out. He abolished a number of taxes, had all the dogs killed and rode by night. He forbade women to walk in the streets . . . The shoemakers were forbidden to make women's shoes and their shops fell into disuse.‡

But it was al-Hakim's indiscriminate killings of judges, 'stirrup holders' and beer makers that provoked an uprising in the name of the Umayyads in 1006. However improbable such a rebellion in the name of the Sunni caliphs of Spain might seem, it proved to be very difficult to put down.

Al-Hakim ordered the Church of the Holy Sepulchre in Jerusalem to be knocked down in 1009 and there were intermittent persecutions of Jews and Christians. The caliph's favourite intimidations seem to have been

---

* Kennedy, *The Prophet and the Age of the Caliphates*, pp. 330–7.
† Juvaini, *Chinggis Khan*, p. 656.
‡ Al-Maqrizi in Lewis, *Islam from the Prophet Muhammad to the Capture of Constantinople*, Vol. I, pp. 51–9.

forcing Jews to wear bells, and Christians to 'wear' large crucifixes of one cubit's length.* At this time the pilgrimage to Jerusalem from Europe had been flourishing. Although al-Hakim's destruction of the Sepulchre Church's fabric (along with the Fatimids' reputation for tolerance) was quickly repaired by his successor, this desecration of the holiest place in Christianity by a Muslim monarch was a major theme of the call for the First Crusade by Pope Urban II at Clermont in 1095.

Al-Hakim himself disappeared whilst on a hunting trip with some nobles in 1021 – it seems highly likely that he was murdered by a group led by his own sister, who felt, given his past form, that it was wiser to strike first. However, the story of his being taken up into heaven caused a small schism within Ismailism and remains the central creed of his followers, the *duruz* or Druze of Lebanon and Syria. To this day they await his return.†

After his death, the Fatimid state seemed to lose all of its energy. Indeed, al-Hakim's generous sponsorship of a *Dar al-Ilm*, or House of Wisdom, for extending the Ismaili revolution, and a Palace of Initiates for the *dais* that carried this revolution abroad, was neglected by his successors. It is notable too, that he created a new post of 'Trustee of the Sword and Pen' – this was uncommon in Islamic medieval government where civil and military administrations were most definitely separated. Al-Hakim was the last Fatimid caliph to conjoin these offices – in the same way that they would be unified in the person of the grand master of the Assassins.

The Fatimid caliphate retained its economic threat to Baghdad through its control of the Red Sea, the ports of Yemen and its extensive European commercial connections. The state continued to grow in prosperity as well as territorially – indeed in the middle of the eleventh century, just as Iraq collapsed into complete anarchy, a Fatimid army even entered Baghdad itself and for a brief period of time the Friday prayer, the *khutba*, was called in the Fatimid caliph's name. However, the Fatimid caliphate's religious dynamism had disappeared and it was falling more and more under the control of the military – the men of the sword. Just as the Abbasid caliphs of Samarra and Baghdad had become the helpless puppets of their own praetorians, so now the Fatimids became mere figureheads for a series of military dictators.

---

* One cubit is equal to about forty-five centimetres.
† A description of the formation of the sect is given by M. Hodgson, 'Al-Darazi and Hamza in the Origin of the Druze Religion', *Journal of the American Oriental Society*, Vol. 82, No 1, 1962, pp. 5–20.

After Egypt had been taken, the imams had begun to rely more and more on imported slave soldiers and Turkish mercenaries. This was inevitable given that the Fatimid push into Palestine and Syria pitted them against armies of a far greater quality than they had faced in North Africa. Army reform had therefore begun in the reign of the imam al-Aziz in the late 970s and he relied on his *wazir* Ibn Killis to institute many of the changes needed. The first Turkish troops to arrive in Cairo were in fact the remnants of the defeated cavalry forces of a rebellious emir of Damsacus who had tried to secede from the Fatimid Empire. In the 1040s, the Ismaili *dai* and writer Nasir-i-Khusrau described how he saw ten thousand Turks and Persians parading in Cairo alone.

The Turks provided the army with much needed cavalry archers, an arm of the army that could not be formed from within the Berbers.* Whilst a more balanced army in terms of specialised roles was a positive result of the reforms, the other more deleterious effect was the loss of direct identification with the dynasty that the early Fatimid army had held. Furthermore, the army now had the problem of racial tension. This was chiefly between the black African troops and the Turks; on occasion these simple confrontations grew into free-for-all melees in which the major casualties were the civilian population of Cairo. Nuwayri, a chronicler of the regime, wrote that during the reign of al-Hakim the Turks often attacked foreign *dais* when they visited Cairo, and that the caliph revenged himself on the Turks by putting black officers in command of them. This resulted in a vast fight between the two divisions of the army in 1020 but such disturbances were often simply orchestrated between 'opponents' to allow for looting of the city's markets. The situation worsened in the late 1020s, as an economic crisis caused pay riots among the black troops and recriminations between all the racial groups in the army. In fact the army nearly disintegrated in 1025: after being reduced to eating dogs just to survive, the black Africans mutinied. They attacked the city of Fustat and Caliph al-Zahir had to send Turkish slave troops to defend it. He also authorised the populace to arm itself against the mutineers. Involvement of civilians in military affairs had been unheard of in Islam since the civil war between al-Amin and al-Mamun and the siege of Baghdad in 816.

Given this situation, the caliphs, in order to survive in this divided state that they had created, had to choose a side, and they settled on the Turks. Their favouritism for this faction is evident from al-Hakim's address to his Turkish troopers in 1000, 'You are those whom al-Aziz fostered and

---

* Lev, 'Army, Regime, and Society in Fatimid Egypt', pp. 337–65.

you have the status of offspring.' This position of privilege in the state made the Turks into potential kingmakers. They could not, at this point, use their political muscle to decide who would be caliph, but the office of *wazir* was most commonly filled by their favoured candidate and the *wazir*, not the caliph, controlled the state by the late eleventh century. The *wazirs* were military men and many of the members of the ruling junta that backed the *wazir* were not even Ismailis; the Fatimid caliphate and its messianic mission had lost its *raison d'être*.

In 1094, the *wazir* al-Afdal even went so far as to divert the caliphal succession. The caliph al-Muntasir was dying and the succession should almost certainly have fallen to his son, Nizar. Al-Afdal, however, saw that Mustali, a younger son, could be made into a more pliable puppet than the older Nizar would ever be. Furthermore, Nizar was already married with an adult son, whilst Mustali was about sixteen and therefore just coming up to marriageable age, as was the *wazir*'s daughter. Al-Afdal's ambitious plan succeeded – Mustali ascended the throne and married al-Afdal's daughter. Nizar fled with his son to Alexandria, where he hoped to raise an army from the local garrisons, but he was easily captured and imprisoned in Cairo. He was probably killed there, although another account says that he and his son were murdered in an Alexandrian jail.

Initially, the response across the Ismaili world to this judicial murder seems to have been muted, and it could be that the schism in the Ismaili movement, which gave birth to the Assassins, was only retrospectively proclaimed in Nizar's name as a later justification – for a decidedly earlier and well-planned desertion of the Fatimid cause by the Persian Ismailis. Indeed the Persian-Ismaili sources seem to indicate that the need for a new *dawa* to replace the outdated religious mission of the Fatimids was the prime reason for the division. In 1092, a full two years before Nizar's death, but in the same year as the first identifiable political murder of the Assassins, chroniclers recorded that there were 'two sects' within Ismailism: the pro-Fatimid followers of Nasir-i-Khusrau, and the newly sworn enemies of the caliphs of Egypt – the followers of Hasan-i-Sabbah.

It seems likely then, that the Persian Ismailis responded to the failing *dawa* of the Fatimids and to new threats to their own existence in Persia with a new radicalisation of their doctrine and a radical overhaul of their methods of resistance. These methods would be assassination, infiltration and fortification. These three facets made up the Ismaili Assassin defence plan. The strategy was the brainchild of a truly remarkable individual – Hasan-i-Sabbah.

Hasan had been born to a Twelver Shiite family in Qom in north-west Iran, around 1040. He studied as a cleric in the city of Rayy, a university town and long a stronghold of Shiism, and it seems that his education was wide enough to embrace study of mathematics, astronomy and astrology, as well as the natural sciences. In Rayy, he claims he came into contact with the doctrine of the caliphs of Egypt and with Nasir-i-Khusrau, who was the most important Ismaili propagandist of the time, known by his fellow *dais* as 'the Proof of the Faith'. If Hasan actually met Nasir, then it would be hard not to be dazzled by the great man's fame as a traveller, poet and writer. Such a meeting does in fact seem possible, as in this period Nasir had just returned to Persia from Egypt, where he had devoted himself once more to the caliph, and to the expansion of Ismailism throughout the east. Hasan, in his autobiography, suggests that Ismaili teaching had affected several of the more powerful magnates of the region and, because of his intellectual ability, Hasan would naturally have been a prime candidate for recruitment. Hasan says he was swayed from his Twelver beliefs by the Ismaili preachers being able to disprove his doctrine through argument and debate. He was also impressed, he says, by their abhorrence of alcohol and because they were God-fearing, pious and charitable.

It seems that Hasan was converted by Attash, a physician who was a *hujja*, a high-ranking *dai*. Hasan nearly died during this time from a serious illness but subsequently recovered and this experience encouraged him to complete his conversion. He took his final oath of allegiance in 1072 and was active as a *dai* from then on. In 1078, he set off from Isfahan for Egypt, the epicentre of any *dai*'s world, and, like Martin Luther in Rome in the early sixteenth century, Hasan was shocked by the decay of the imamate, by the petty social climbing of Cairo's politics, and how Caliph al-Muntasir had fallen under the power of his *wazir*, Badr al-Jamali.

Hasan's relationship with Badr al-Jamali, the Fatimid *wazir* and father of al-Afdal whose kingmaking would cause the Nizari schism, was a highly strained one. This was certainly because al-Jamali was setting a course for the caliphate that had more need of 'real' soldiers like himself than of radical missionaries. His son, al-Afdal, who continued his father's policy, may have fully realised what he was doing when he put Nizar aside. Perhaps he had even wished to divide the two halves of the Ismaili world simply because he viewed the empire as a soldier would – territorially, and not ideologically, as a revolutionary would.

Al-Jamali, and al-Afdal after him, also set themselves the task of maintaining what had been directly conquered. Al-Jamali may have realised that the Fatimid dream of total domination in the lands of Islam was over, even before it became obvious to the caliphs themselves.

Despite the internal problems of the army discussed above, it would be wrong to dismiss the Fatimid state as a rapidly collapsing one at this juncture. In the late eleventh century, it was still probably the richest and most cultured state in the entire western world and Nasir-i-Khusrau recorded that during a visit to Cairo in the middle of the eleventh century he found that,

> Everyone has perfect confidence in the sultan, and no one stands in fear of spies or evil officials. There I saw wealth belonging to private individuals such that if I would speak of it or describe it the people of Persia would refuse to credit my statements. Nowhere have I seen such prosperity as I saw there. One year the waters of the Nile fell short and corn became dear. The sultan's *wazir* summoned a Christian trader and said, 'the year is not good, and the sultan's heart is weighed down with anxiety for his people. How much corn could you supply, either for a price or as a loan?' The Christian answered, 'thanks to the fortunate auspices of the sultan and the *wazir* I have in store so much corn that I could supply all Egypt with bread for six years.'*

The army was also impressively large, despite its problems. The most powerful European monarch of the medieval period, Frederick II Hohenstaufen, ruler of Germany, Italy and Sicily, fielded an army of between ten to fifteen thousand men in his Italian campaigns, much of which would have been made up from the temporary addition of the troops of his vassal lords and mercenaries. Nasir-i-Khusrau records the *standing* Fatimid army as retaining sixty thousand North African cavalry, twenty thousand North African black infantry troops, thirty thousand Nubians and Sudanese, ten thousand Turks, thirty thousand Central African troops and ten thousand caliphal guards.

The problems of the state were deep seated, but not likely to drag it under just yet. The simple presence, however, of Badr al-Jamali at the helm of the state was very much a symptom of what was wrong with the proclaimed Fatimid *dawa* (mission), if not the *dawla* (state). He was an Armenian slave soldier, who had fought for the Fatimids in Syria and had shown immense ability as an administrator and military strongman in the province. He had been brought to Cairo primarily because of the deterioration in the relations between the various branches of the army in Egypt, and after stabilising the situation, largely through favouring

---

* E. Browne, *A Literary History of Persia*, Cambridge, 1902, Vol. II, pp. 400–1.

the Turkish slave soldiers and gaining the full confidence of the sultan, he also had the bureaus of justice and the *dawa* placed in his care. So, just as al-Jamali was gaining control of the *dawa* and could begin using it to aid his vision of a conventional state, the revolutionary firebrand Hasan arrived in Egypt. Al-Jamali, now *wazir*, would have been concerned about maintaining his hegemony over the *dawa* if the Persian missionary began to draw support from the other *dais* resident in Cairo.

No doubt there was also resentment on Hasan's side against the Armenian *wazir*, whom he viewed as a foreign impostor backed by other outsiders – Turkish troops. Hasan's homeland, Persia, was already under the domination of the Turks and in later, highly xenophobic, writings he referred to the men from the steppes as *jinn*, or devils, rather than as humans. Despite his disgust at the *wazir*'s nationality and the condition of the imamate, Hasan spent a year and a half in Egypt and left to serve in the international *dawa* for the Fatimids. Whilst some sources claim that al-Jamali tried to have him deported to the *maghrib*,* it seems that he was merely very strongly encouraged to leave. There were other tales of his imprisonment in a Cairo prison, which promptly collapsed, allowing his escape; and Hasan also complained in a letter that the Abbasids 'sent three mules heavily loaded with gold silver, and other goods to Badr al-Jamali so that he may arrest me and send me alive to Baghdad or he may kill me and send my head there'.†

Hasan boarded a ship at Alexandria in 1075 and there is a tale of a huge storm hitting the vessel, and of weeping and crying among the other passengers, whilst Hasan sat calmly through the tempest. When questioned by the other passengers about his serenity, he replied that God had assured him a safe passage in order that he should complete his life's mission. When the ship arrived safely in Syria, all of the crew and passengers immediately swore to become his adherents. The story is doubtless apocryphal but reflects the powerful attraction of Hasan's preaching as he undertook a series of travels throughout Persia and Iraq in the 1080s and 1090s.

While he was obstensibly working for Cairo headquarters, it also seems likely that he was already looking for a command centre for himself and planning secession from the Fatimids. He also had a great number of men already under his command, scouting for him, and attracting adherents

---

* The Arabic word *maghrib* denotes North Africa but is also the word for sunset. The implication here might be that al-Jamali wanted to send Hasan very, very far away.

† J. Al-Muscati, *Hasan Bin Sabbah*, trans. A. Hamadani, 2nd edn, Pakistan, 1953, p. 30.

in his name, not in the name of the Fatimids. The great college mosque of al-Azhar may actually have been the training ground of many of these men and if this is so, it was a severe backlash against the old regime, as the training given to *dais* was extensive – designed to make them able to bring converts to Ismailism from every part of the Islamic world. For example, al-Kirmam, an eminent Ismaili philosopher and the most learned *dai* of the Fatimid period, was well acquainted with the Hebrew and Syriac languages; every *dai* familiarised themselves with the religions and languages of all the peoples of western Asia. Hasan also appears to have fully comprehended the religious and cultural patchwork that was Islam in this period, and he also used the fact that he was born in north-west Persia to good effect in creating enthusiasm for his new *dawa* among his countrymen.

There is a whiff of a conspiracy, in the chronicles, between Hasan and Nizar, who may have already realised he was being pushed aside by the *wazir*, al-Afdal. Ibn al-Athir has Caliph Mustansir himself tell Hasan that the imam was to be Nizar, but that Nizar already knew he would be thwarted. Given the long-standing compliance of the caliph to his *wazir's* orders, this seems unlikely, but not as unbelievable as the tale that Hasan had smuggled the grandson of Nizar out of Egypt to Persia, to be brought up in the Nizaris' new stronghold of Alamut Castle. The tale of the infant's escape was, however, a useful propaganda tool and it seems to have been believed at the time; among the later Assassins, the tale would take an even more elaborate form and would directly affect the policy of the order's leaders.

Hasan's Ismaili revolution was taking place in Persia, despite the presence of the new Sunni sultans' troops, the Saljuq Turks, in both his homeland and in Iraq. The Saljuqs' dismembering of the Twelver Shiite Buyid sultanate in the 1050s may actually have assisted him, as the Daylamites, on who the Buyid state had largely been built, started to convert to Ismailism as a form of resistance to the Turks. Their mountainous homeland in the north of Persia had never been conquered – in the seventh century there is a tale of their leaders being so confident of both their men and the redoubtable peaks which they would be defending, that they sent a map of their lands to the Arab invaders with a note inviting them to try an attack. Their mountains were therefore the ideal area in which to make a stand against the Saljuqs.

In the 1070s, Saljuq invasions of Syria made for a renewed Sunni challenge to Fatimid power. There was extensive Saljuq settlement in

Syria and also in Anatolia; the full implications of the Anatolian invasion became apparent later. For now it is enough to say that the advent of Badr al-Jamali's regime, the decline of the Fatimids into mere figureheads and the militarisation of the Fatimid state were inevitable as the Sunni world now had new champions who were already in full control of Persia and had begun to push the Fatimids back into Egypt in the late 1070s.

The Shiite Buyids had been swept away and the Ismailis of Persia, whilst beginning to organise their resistance under the formidable Hasan, were faring little better than the other Shiites at this point. Earlier in the eleventh century, it had seemed that the entire Islamic world might become Shiite, but just as this seemed attainable the Alid cause was smashed by the the new Sunni champions, the Saljuqs. Violent disorders call for violent remedies and the Assassins and their killings were born of a desperate response to the seemingly unstoppable progress of the Turks.

3

WHETTING THE BLADE

ASSASSINATION AS WAR

Brothers when the time comes, with good fortune from both worlds as our companion, then by one single warrior on foot a king may be with terror, though he own more than a hundred thousand horsemen.

*From an Ismaili poem in praise of the Assassins**

A	T THE BEGINNING OF the tenth century the Khitai, a Turco-Mongolian people from the steppes to the north of China, swiftly subjugated a large area of what is today Mongolia and Northern China. The Chinese had been dealing with the nomads of the steppes for hundreds of years from the Xiongnu, or Huns, through to the Tanguts, by a combination of military action, treaty, buying off, marriage alliances and ensuring that the 'cooked' barbarians buffered the empire from the 'raw' savages – but this time it was different. The Khitai were strong enough and China was sufficiently weak, due to civil wars that had wracked the empire since 860, for them to take a dynastic name, the Liao, and rule as emperors in northern China from 907 to 1125.

The presence of an empire in China that also spread into the 'free' steppes made the Turks of the region to the north-east of China uneasy and when the Liao started to place garrisons in the steppes it seemed clear that submission and regulated taxation were the likely consequence. The Turks therefore did what nomadic people have a tendency to do when faced with interference in their affairs by centralised governments – they began to migrate. They headed west and into the *Dar al-Islam*. Such was the volume of steppe nomads that entered Islam at this time that Arab writers started to differentiate them from the Turks who had been a part of the military forces of Islam for some time – they called these new arrivals the Turcomen.

---

* W. Ivanow, 'An Ismaili Poem in Praise of Fidawis', *Journal of the Bombay Branch of the Royal Asiatic Society*, New Series, No 14, 1938, p. 71.

The movement became extensive at the beginning of the eleventh century, but even before this there had been a movement of tribes into Transoxania. At first, the Islamic states of northern Persia tried to hold back this influx; Maqdisi wrote of strongholds and frontier posts against the Turcomen, but it was useless, and dynasties such as the Samanids simply disappeared amid the chaos that ensued.

The most significant group among the Turks were the Ghuzz tribes, and within these tribes the most important clan to enter Islam at this time were the Saljuqs. Duqaq was the progenitor of the family, but his son Saljuq was the eponymous state-builder. The family converted to Sunni Islam late in the tenth century and involved themselves, probably quite lucratively, in the wars, essentially caused by the migration of the Turks, in Transoxania and Khwarazm, south of the Aral Sea. It is likely that the Saljuqs chose the Sunni branch of Islam over the Shiite simply because the wandering *Sufis*, or holy men, with whom they would have come in contact on the fringes of the *Dar al-Islam*, practised a form of Islam that carried a large component of mysticism and folk religion – much akin to the shamanistic beliefs of the steppes. These *Sufis* were part of a much looser and much more catholic Sunnism.

In 1026, Saljuq's successor, Arslan Israil settled with the tribe in Ghaznavid territory, but they were troublesome tenants and the Ghaznavid sultan, Mahmud, pushed them out and seized Arslan. Arslan's brothers, Toghril Beg and Chaghri Beg, fled and sought refuge with another of the new Ghuzz arrivals, the Qarakhanids, who also involved themselves with mercenary warfare against the Byzantine and Armenian frontiers to Islam's north-west. Meanwhile, more and more Ghuzz kept flowing into the Ghaznavid lands and the Saljuqs profited from this new military muscle to deprive Masud, who had succeeded his father, Mahmud, as the Ghaznavid sultan of the cities of Marv, Herat and Nishapur in 1038. Toghril Beg proclaimed himself sultan, and in 1040 a Saljuq-Ghuzz army made up almost entirely of horse archers – a concept previously unheard of in the Islamic world – defeated a huge Ghaznavid army at the Battle of Dandanqan, just north of Marv. By this one battle the Saljuqs took the whole of Khurasan, and the Ghaznavids withdrew to their lands in India, where they commenced the process of Islamisation of the north of the sub-continent.

After consolidation of the province they had taken from the Ghaznavids, the Saljuqs moved west and, no doubt due to their continued successes, they attracted a great many more bands of Ghuzz Turks to their banner.

They were able to campaign in all seasons – they were inured to hardship and their supply train was made up of two-humped camels, which were able to withstand brutal winters and also travel great distances every day. They moved rapidly across the eastern Islamic lands, moving through Azerbaijan and into the Jazira, until they were halted and defeated by Kurds near Mosul. This was, however, only a temporary setback, and they moved on to the removal of the Buyids and the 'liberation' of the Sunni caliph in 1055. The caliph accepted the Saljuqs readily, although really he had no choice. Officially, he was the head of the Islamic world, but everyone knew where the real power lay – with the men of the sword.

The Saljuq achievement was impressive – with their defeat of the Ghaznavids and Buyids, they had shown the total superiority of cavalry warfare over armies that deployed infantry as their main force and only used cavalry as an auxiliary arm. They had also managed to maintain an army in the field over repeated campaigns – this was highly unusual anywhere in the medieval world. This had been achieved by their creation of the *askari* – technically, a bodyguard of Mamluks for the sultan, but actually more like a small standing army, around which the more ephemeral and temporary tribal troops or auxiliaries were arranged. They had also moved from simple booty share-outs at the end of campaigns to pay their army, to adopting the Islamic *iqta* system – at least to provide payment for their *askari*.

A Saljuq trooper's *iqta* bears some parallels to the fief of a western knight, to the extent that it provided his salary. However, in many ways, the *iqta* was more complex, in that it could be a 'share' of an industry, such as the spice trade, a textile production centre or simply a piece of land, but unlike the western knight, the *iqta* holder was not resident on the land from which the *iqta* was drawn. Local government officers, often civilians, managed it for him and collected the taxes or rents for him. Furthermore the *iqta*, in theory, was not hereditary like a fief, so in some ways it paid for service and not family loyalty. The distribution of *iqta* was therefore a powerful means of ensuring loyalty to the sultan and of rewarding emirs.

The Saljuqs also showed themselves to be much more than mere tribal warriors, with the speed in which they brought relatively orderly and effective, if oppressive, government to Persia and Iraq. Afdal al-Din relates an apocryphal story of Sultan Qavurt's firmness, which illustrates nicely the arbitrary but effective justice of these military men. Qavurt, he states, had visited one of his provinces one winter. When he left the province, bread was selling at one dinar for one hundred *manns*, but when he returned later, it was reported to him that the price of bread had risen to one dinar for ninety *manns*. Immediately, he went with ten horsemen and summoned all the bakers. He asked them, 'Have locusts attacked the town since I left?' They answered, 'No'. He then asked, 'Has there been some other natural catastrophe?' Again they answered, 'No'. He said, 'Praise be to God. When I left with my entourage, the expenses laid upon the province were halved and the price of bread should have fallen to one dinar per one hundred and twenty *manns*.' He then cast several of the well-known bakers into their ovens to be burnt and left the province.* Such rough and ready efficiency, and the project of consolidation that the Saljuqs were embarked on, immediately began to affect the embryonic Ismaili communities in the north-west of Persia. Taxation of these areas first required them to be brought under control, and the Saljuqs started consolidating their rule with aplomb.

The Ismailis always flourished during times of government chaos, but now they faced a determined and organised foe – whilst the Sunni world had the military power of the new Turks to deploy against Shiites of all colours, it was also rearming itself intellectually, to try to win the doctrinal battle that fed into the loyalties of the *ulama* and *umma*. The key agent in this Sunni scholarly renaissance was the great *wazir* of the Saljuq state, Nizam al-Mulk. A long section of his *Siyasatnama*, or Book of Government, is dedicated to denigrating both the independent Persian branch of the creed and their 'parents', the Fatimid Ismailis. He wrote that the object of the Ismailis was to abolish Islam, to mislead mankind and to lead them into perdition, and that they were the companions of the Antichrist; he also accused them of being Mazdakdites.†

The Saljuq 'party line' was built on these thoughts and the theocratic message was subtly linked to a more nationalistic one when it was claimed by the authorities that the Ismailis, a sinister perverted and deviant group, were plotting harm to Persia and seeking to destroy its religion. The new Nizari Ismailis of Hasan-i-Sabbah were also singled out and accused of general vices and murders. The writing of controversial

---

* In Lambton, *Continuity and Change*, p. 57.
† Mazdak, who died between 524 and 528, was a Persian religious reformer who was hanged by the Sassanian king Chosroes I, who also massacred Mazdak's followers. There was a large component of socialist or even communist ideals in his religious message. To call someone a Mazdakdite became a standard slur in medieval Islam that clerics enjoyed hurling at each other.

works against the Ismailis had, in fact, started in 1011 with a polemic written by leading Sunni and Twelver Shiite jurists at the behest of the caliph, which stated that the Fatimids had no Alid family link. This was obviously an attempt to ensure any unity between the Seveners and Twelvers, both Shiite groups, would be disrupted. The proclamation was read in mosques throughout the Abbasids' realm. Such writings became the stock in trade of some of the great Sunni theologians and jurists of the Saljuq period. Al-Ghazali was the creator of the political doctrine that reasserted the importance of the office of the caliph as leader of the faithful, whilst allowing all political power to flow through the sultan.* He worked at the Nizamiyya, the great *madrasa* or Islamic university that Nizam al-Mulk founded in Baghdad to challenge al-Azhar in Cairo, as well as the later secret training schools of the Nizar Ismailis. After Nizam al-Mulk's death in 1092, al-Ghazali continued to write anti-Ismaili treatises under the patronage of the reinvigorated Abbasid caliphs, in particular al-Mustazhir, who held the caliphate from 1094 to 1118. These texts were disseminated around the Saljuq Empire through Nizamiyya *madrasas*, which the great *wazir*, Nizam al-Mulk, had sponsored in the cities of Nishapur, Herat, Marv, Damascus, Basra and Mosul. Al-Ghazali constructed arguments to show that the Ismailis were specifically excluded from the *umma*. Making war on them and enslaving them was therefore entirely acceptable – indeed it was a virtuous act for all true believers.

The espionage services that had failed so spectacularly in the past were also reinvigorated, and within a short period of time Hasan-i-Sabbah's disciples found it much more difficult to disseminate their teaching in the larger cities. He himself had had to avoid the city of Rayy, probably Persia's largest city at this time, because one of Nizam al-Mulk's chief agents – the city's governor, Abu Muslim – had been informed of his intended visit to the city in 1090. It was not surprising that the Saljuqs were watching Rayy carefully – an Ismaili *dai* had once advised a younger colleague of the support to be found in the city: 'Go to Rayy, because

---

* Al-Ghazali defined a new relationship between the caliph and the sultan. Constituent authority belonged to the sultan, who designated the caliph, but the validity of the sultan's government was made dependent upon his oath of allegiance to the caliph, and the latter's appointment of him. The institutional authority of the caliph rested primarily on the Sunni community, and his functional authority was built on the *sharia*. This was vital if the Saljuqs were to be the 'anointed' kings of Islam and if their swords were to the consecrated tools of the Sunni revival.

there in Rayy, and in the provinces of Tabaristan and Mazandaran there are many Shiites, who will listen to your call.'*

As discussed earlier, the Ismailis had gained a strong position in Daylam among the now-converted Twelver Shiites of the region, but now Nizam al-Mulk and Sultan Malikshah commenced a campaign to drive them from the region. The campaign started as a police action with a wave of arrests. It seems that Nizam and Malikshah knew that they were up against an enemy who was well integrated into the local communities, as they attempted first to weed them out rather than to commit the whole region to the hammer blows of a full army occupation. The Ismailis of Saveh, a city between the metropolises of Rayy and Qom, were the first to be targeted. Eighteen of them were arrested on charges of having joined together in prayers separately from the Sunni inhabitants of the city, and for praying according to the Shiite rites. They were interrogated and then released, but subsequently one of the city's muezzins was found murdered. It is possible that he was the first victim of the new form of resistance by the Ismailis, that of assassination, but he may equally have been the victim of a Sunni fanatic, as it was rumoured in the town's markets that he was a secret convert to Ismailism. Whatever the case, Nizam al-Mulk used the opportunity to bring a known Ismaili, Tahir the Carpenter, to trial, claiming that the murder had been committed to stop the muezzin – a wavering convert to Ismailism – from revealing a far larger conspiracy, of *Batini* in the city, to the authorities. The great *wazir* also insisted on the death penalty once Tahir was found guilty.

At first glance, it seems a little strange that Nizam al-Mulk should take such a keen interest in what appears to be a decidedly local issue, but, as was seen in the evolution of the Qarmatian state of Bahrain, Ismailism had a element of radical social and political change inherent in its religious teachings. Since Nizam al-Mulk's great project was the consolidation and control of all of the loose association of territories that made up the Saljuq Empire, the growth of any alternate sources of political doctrine was alarming to him. What was more, the Ismailis, as will be seen below, had begun to literally carve out distinct mini-states inside the Saljuq lands. By 1085, Hasan was already being discussed in court circles as a successful preacher of heresy in both Khurasan and Iraq. The heresiarch Hasan

---

* S. Stern, 'The Early Ismaili Missionaries in North-West Persia and in Khurasan and Transoxania', *Bulletin of the School of Oriental and African Studies*, Vol. 23, No 1, 1960, pp. 56–90.

would have been viewed as a political threat by Nizam al-Mulk simply because that is how the great *wazir* viewed heterodoxy:

> What a king needs most is right religion, because kingship and religion are two brothers. Whenever any disturbance appears in the kingdom, disorder also occurs in religion; and people of bad religion and malefactors appear. Whenever there is disorder in the affairs of religion and the kingdom is disturbed the power of malefactors increases. And they cause the kings to lose their dignity and make them troubled at heart; innovations appear and rebels become powerful.*

The minister went on to single out the Ismailis for special attention:

> Never has there been a more sinister, more perverted or more iniquitous crowd than these people, who behind walls are plotting harm to this country and seeking to destroy the religion . . . and as far as they can they will leave nothing undone in the pursuit of vice, mischief, murder and heresy.†

Nizam al-Mulk's character was also likely to be unforgiving. His own life had been hard and he was unlikely to give quarter to anyone. Ibn al-Athir, speaking of his early years, said:

> His father lost all his property and belongings and his mother died while he was still a nursling. So his father used to take him round to various nurses for milk and they nourished him. As a young man God gave him great aptitude for hard work and for acquiring knowledge. He then entered the service of the sultans and as time passed by he rose from rank to rank very rapidly. Nizam al-Mulk, in spite of his excellence, high position, love of learning and the learned, was an intriguer, prone to haughtiness and influence.‡

In truth, Nizam was no worse that any other Persian minister in terms of his scheming. During the rise to power of a Persian bureaucrat, it was de rigueur to bring down at least one of your rivals through a whispering campaign and to cause the death and impoverishment of his family too, if possible. Nepotism was also standard practice and Nizam installed several of his sons in positions of power.

The Nizari Ismailis must then have realised that they were up against a resolute and single-minded foe and the Saveh incident made it clear to Hasan that he and his followers were standing directly in the path of a

---

* From the *Siyasatnama*. In Lambton, *Continuity and Change*, p. 211.
† H. Darke, *The Book of Government or Rules for Kings: The Siyar al-Muluk or Siyasatnama of Nizam al-Mulk*, London, 1960, p. 231.
‡ Al-Muscati, *Hasan Bin Sabbah*, p. 46.

Saljuq juggernaut. The sheer numbers of men available to Nizam al-Mulk and the Saljuqs meant that direct confrontation could not be considered. Throughout the entire Saljuq period, vast armies took the field under the sultans. The sultan's nephew, according to Ibn al-Qalanasi, took four hundred thousand men with him into Anatolia to meet the Byzantine emperor in battle at Manzikert in 1071, and whilst al-Qalanasi may have fallen victim to the hyperbole that has affected so many recorders of armies over the years, it certainly took a month to transport Sultan Alp Arslan's army across the Oxus in 1072. Even as late as the 1130s, during the state's waning as a great power, Sultan Sanjar fielded an army of one hundred thousand cavalrymen, made up of his own men and the armies of the emirs of Sistan, Ghur, Ghazna, Mazandaran and Khurasan.

The army had also evolved from the largely tribal-based forces of the early Saljuq state. By the reign of Malikshah, there was a growing reliance on Mamluks, although there was still, judging by the sultans' attitude to the free Turcomen, a large degree of reliance on the men of the tribes for campaigns. Nizam al-Mulk wrote in his *Siyasatnama*, that the Saljuq dynasty was under an obligation to the Turcomen due to blood ties with them, and because of the part they had played in the foundation and maintenance of the empire and its armies.*

Malikshah wrote confidently to Hasan of the consequences of challenging the Saljuq state:

O Hasan-i-Sabbah. It is surprising that you have invented a new faith and religion and have enticed people into it by various devious means. You have been traitorous to the ruling authority. You have beguiled many brave and simple mountain-folk by exploiting their simple nature and have formed an army of them who, wherever they go, kill innocent people and make them targets of their daggers. Moreover you revile against the Abbasid Caliphs who are responsible for the maintenance of Islam, of the empire, of the nation and who are the upholders of religion and the State. It is they who are the foundation of the organisation and administration. You should desist from following this wrong path and become a good Muslim, or else we might be forced to send troops against you. The commencement of this action depends on your behaviour or upon the receipt of your reply. Keep away from the dangerous policy you are following. Have mercy on your own self and on your followers and do not unnecessarily hurl them into disaster, do not let your strong defences and fortresses deceive you and make you conceited. With this sincere advice, I may add this also very clearly that even if Alamut were

* Darke, *The Book of Government*, pp. 90–100.

one of the fortresses of the heavens, I could level it to the ground by the grace of God.*

The Saljuqs' army did, however, have some exploitable military weaknesses and its simple size and composition were chief among these. As discussed above, the core of the sultan's army was his *askari*, and in order to create a true field army for campaigns, he was reliant on his emirs and provincial governors joining him with their military forces, as well as the short-term employment of the tribal Turcoman auxiliaries. The main weakness of this composite force was that it lacked cohesion and was liable to disperse of its own accord – this was particularly true of the Turcomen who, being free nomads, had other concerns like moving their flocks to new pastures and less mundane tasks like simple raiding and being a nuisance to the peasantry. The allegiance of the emirs could reasonably be expected by virtue of the simple fact that the sultan, in this early period, led the army in person and therefore by example – he also gave and took away *iqtas*.

Another concern was that the army was composed almost entirely of cavalry and there was always the problem of providing fodder, especially as each trooper almost certainly took at least two horses – a charger and a pack horse – on campaign with him. Whilst the logistics in terms of 'pasture or fodder per animal' are difficult to compute exactly, the average consumption of a small pony of the sort used by the Turks and Mongols has been suggested as being about five kilograms per day.† In the early fourteenth century, when the Mongols were attempting to avoid living off the land in their preparations for an invasion of Syria, a daily ration of about six kilograms per horse per day has been suggested as the rations allowed by the Ilkhan Ghazan for his cavalry.‡ Nishapuri wrote that, at the apogee of the dynasty in the reign of Malikshah, the Saljuq standing army was about fifty thousand strong, though of course this would be swollen by Turcomen auxiliaries during campaigns.§ As discussed earlier, the agriculture of Persia was fragile and therefore easily strained, and only about 10 per cent of it was true pastureland, with another 10 per cent being farmed cropland.¶ Keeping a cavalry army

---

* Al-Muscati, *Hasan Bin Sabbah*, pp. 29–30.

† D. Engels, *Alexander the Great and the Logistics of the Macedonian Army*, Berkeley, 1978, p. 73.

‡ Lambton, *Continuity and Change*, p. 22.

§ Zahir al-Din Nishapuri in Lambton, *Continuity and Change*, p. 8.

¶ Morgan, *Medieval Persia*, p. 4.

in the field would have strained the resources of any area in which it was decamped, as well as those of the state granaries.

Then there was straightforward monetary expense. Certainly the *askari*, and probably the standing army, were equipped by the sultan. Whilst armour and arms were usually family heirlooms, due to the sheer expense of buying mail,* the Saljuq system of warfare had other expenses. It required the production, transport and replacement of vast numbers of arrows; the Turks, and the Mongols, both avoided close combat until the enemy was sufficiently weakened by their archery. A Turkish archery manual from the fifteenth-century Mamluk Dynasty of Egypt describes the Pillars of Archery as being, 'the infliction of injury, the ability to strike from a distance, the ability to strike swiftly and the ability to protect oneself'.† The tactic used for achieving this was a long-range assault by high-volume, rapid-fire 'shower shooting' into the ranks of the enemy as the army was advancing. As the Saljuqs closed on their enemies they would begin to choose individual targets for their arrow strikes and then finally move to sword and spear only when the enemy was in a state of near disintegration.

Writers from the time of Saladin and of the Mamluk sultanate describe the huge camel-loads of arrows taken on campaign.‡ Added to this logistical expense there was the problem of simply paying the army. The Saljuq army was paid mainly in cash and partly in treasury drafts. There was therefore a requirement for the transport of vast amounts of coin for each campaign and long campaigns would, of course, drain the state's revenues. Booty taken in battle was a bonus and a further inducement to loyalty among the sultan's troops, but, obviously for this to occur there had to be booty to be taken. This was almost guaranteed during campaigns of straightforward conquest, but when the army was being used internally to suppress sedition, there was little hope of accruing treasure. The problem of fodder and provisions for the men was alleviated, to some degree, by the *iqta* system, which, being spread over the entire state, ensured that there was, at least in theory, well-managed

---

* For a description of the expenses of equipping oneself for the *Dar al-Harb* see H. Robinson, *Oriental Armour*, London, 1967, pp. 33–51.

† For a more complete exposition of the philosophy by the archery master al-Yunini, see J. Latham and W. Paterson, *Saracen Archery*, London, 1970, ch. 1.

‡ For a fuller explanation of Turkish archery and its use, logistics, effectiveness and the training required for troops to be able to carry it out effectively, see Waterson, *Knights of Islam*, chs 5 and 6.

government land in every area, from which supplies could be drawn by a campaign force.

The final point about the Saljuq army was that whilst it was predominantly made up of Turkish cavalry, it relied for its infantry and camp guards on the Daylamites. This would be significant for the later infiltration of sultans' and *wazirs'* bodyguards by the Assassins, since Hasan's *dais* had, as discussed earlier, been proselytising in the Daylamite regions for many years now. There was already a history of Shiism in this group – the opportunities this gave for a 'ready-made' fifth column in the Saljuq army cannot have been overlooked by Hasan.

Malikshah's letter to Hasan spoke of a fortress named Alamut and the initial Ismaili response to the Saljuq threat was to seek fortified places in which to base their headquarters. The difficulties of keeping an army in the field for the Saljuqs have been alluded to above. Added to this was the fact that, before the late thirteenth century, the Mongols' arrival in Persia with Chinese siege engineers and the tenacious destruction of the Crusader strongholds of Syria by the Egyptian Mamluk sultanate, meant that siege warfare in the Middle East had not been well developed, and relied to a great extent on the ability to starve out the occupiers of a castle. A well-prepared and fortified foe was, needless to say, a difficult proposition – especially for a large army consuming provisions at a faster rate than the besieged were.

In classic castle warfare, as practised with exemplary skill by the Crusaders of Syria – up until King Guy's disastrous decision to engage Saladin at the Battle of Hattin – the defenders of a fortified place aimed simply to hold out until the arrival of the state's field army or a relief force from an ally.* Hasan's Ismailis had no such hope of relief as their forces were comprised of what amounted to little more than a local militia, even though the Daylamites, as discussed earlier, were infantry warriors with a long and proud heritage. Therefore, despite the fact that the Saljuqs would find reducing castles extremely difficult, having no hope of relief certainly meant that the surrender of even 'fortresses of the heavens' could not be put off forever. In 1747, Frederick the Great instructed his generals that, 'the art of defending fortified places consists in putting off the moment of their reduction.' What he meant by this was that fortification could never be the total solution to the problem of winning a war, and that offensive action was required both to relieve such places

---

* See J. France, *Victory in the East: A Military History of the First Crusade*, London, 1994, pp. 24–6.

and to defeat the enemy. In the selection of his offensive action, Hasan had to look at the resources he had available and at the enemy he was fighting – when both were taken into account, assassination would have emerged as the appropriate and obvious stratagem.

Hasan knew the Saljuqs well: he had worked at their court as an administrator under Nizam al-Mulk before his flight to Egypt. Indeed, some sources suggest that the skill he displayed whilst working on land reform was such that Nizam al-Mulk became jealous of the younger man's talent and started a whispering campaign against him at court – this led to Hasan having to flee from the sultan's suspicions. Hasan would therefore have known that, despite being an empire, the Saljuq state was also very much a 'family firm', like almost every other medieval enterprise. Every family has its petty rivalries and jealousies, but in the case of imperial kin these carry serious political repercussions. The chronicler Al-Zahira relates one of the Saljuq family's spats: 'Gawhar Khatun was the aunt of Sultan Malikshah and sister of Sultan Alp Arslan. She was pious and good. On the death of her brother Alp Arslan, Nizam al-Mulk took away much of her wealth. She therefore went to Rayy to recruit the Mubaraki Guards for a fight against Nizam al-Mulk. The latter hinted to Malikshah to do away with her and she was killed. When the news reached Baghdad, people condemned Nizam al-Mulk for it.'*

It was not only aunts that Malikshah had had trouble with during his reign. Earlier in 1072, upon the unexpected death of his father, Alp Arslan, Malikshah had been compelled to defeat and subsequently execute an uncle, Qavord, who had challenged his reign to succeed. Poor Malikshah's father had been failed by, of all things, his skill in archery when, during his invasion of Qarakhanid territory at the end of 1072, a prisoner brought before him suddenly attacked him with a knife. Alp Arslan, shouting to his attendants to leave the prisoner alone, drew an arrow himself but missed his mark and was mortally wounded.

Under Malikshah, the Saljuq state experienced a unity that it had never previously been able to attain, but even during this period Anatolia had broken away to become independent as the sultanate of Rum. In 1092, following Malikshah's death, the state essentially fractured, with the Syrian provinces seceding and east and west Persia separating. Part of the problem was the fact that the possessions of the chiefs of steppe societies were distributed among all his relatives – in particular to his numerous

---

* Al-Muscati, *Hasan Bin Sabbah*, p. 50. The Mubaraki Guards were the bodyguard of her now-dead brother.

sons, through what has become known as the 'patrimonial share-out'. This was very egalitarian and very much in the nature of tribal society, but it was a political time bomb and, almost without exception, led to internecine fighting and political murder among the beneficiaries of the will. A death, or a few deaths, at the top could bring the whole edifice down, or at the very least bring its leaders into conflict that often escalated into all-out civil war.

There was also the aristocratic nature of Saljuq society. As discussed above, the state was a family firm and Louis XIV's encomium to himself, 'L'État, c'est Moi', was certainly true of medieval sultans. Eliminating the man at the top meant a total loss of *raison d'être* for the state. This also applied to lower lords, as in many ways the Saljuq state was a pyramid of fealty, with emirs of progressively higher ranking supporting the royal house. What this meant, in effect, was that there was only limited allegiance within the state and this was based on loyalty to the person of the sultan and to his family, but not to any great project or ideal. The Saljuq state did not have the religious zeal of the early Fatimid state's *dawa*, nor of the later Syrian *jihad* states of Zangi, Nur al-Din or Saladin to drive it along. It did not have the ideal of Rome, as did Byzantium, nor God's Will, as did the Crusaders. In short, Hasan would have looked at the Saljuq state and seen a state lacking belief – a product his little state had in abundance. Certainly, Nizam al-Mulk had gone a long way in resuscitating the Sunni cause, but Sunnism was really the heritage of the *ulama*, the 'men of the pen', and, to a limited degree, the caliph.

The question that Hasan, therefore, would have posed to himself was a very simple one: would a Saljuq lord be prepared to die in a war of religion? Before the advent of the Crusaders, and the Holy War they inspired among Muslims, this was unlikely. Certainly Saljuq emirs were brave, and concepts such as glory, fighting with and for comrades and simple martial pride were central to their culture – but would they risk their lives off the battlefield for concepts as abstract as right religion? It seems not, given the evidence for later collaboration and coming to terms with the Ismailis by various members of the Saljuq aristocracy. Therefore, Hasan's decision to implement a policy of assassination; of bringing the spectre of death to hearth and home, away from the battlefield; of threatening soldiers with an ignominious death in the bedchamber or in the street, a death bereft of all glory – in short, not a death with your boots on – hit hard at the core of the Saljuq lords' psyche. Hasan was not a military man but he seems to have understood one of the most basic rules of warfare – you must empathise with your enemy and understand what makes him act and what will make him detract from action.

As discussed earlier, the Saljuq Empire lacked belief in any great project, whereas the citizens of Hasan's state had such belief in abundance. One of Malikshah's accusations against him was that he led simple people to carry out murder and other disastrous acts of self-destruction. Certainly, Hasan would have realised that the religious fervour his preaching and the Ismaili creed imbued in his followers could make up for his lack of numbers. However, even then, taking the field against the Saljuqs was unlikely to be successful, and did not meet a second rule of war – maximising efficiency.

Battle is an uncertain business in the best of circumstances, and it is common sense to avoid it at all costs, at least until every advantage has been gained over an opponent. Hasan would certainly lose many men in any engagement – men he could ill afford to squander. If he only managed to defend territory, he would essentially not have solved his problem of continued aggression from the Saljuq state. Two things are worth noting here. The first is that Hasan's logic was strikingly modern; the simple acquisition of enemy territory is seen now as an immature military strategy. The destruction of the opponent's army is the goal of the modern military approach.* Obviously, eradication of the vast Saljuq army was impossible, but forcing its disintegration through destruction of its leadership was certainly feasible, and what Hasan's forces lacked in numbers, they made up for in devotion to their cause.

This brings us to the second point. It is somewhat ridiculous for Malikshah to accuse Hasan of deluding simple folk, and it is equally farcical to take on the suggestion of Marco Polo and other European writers that the Assassins of the Ismailis were drugged with hashish or even opium before carrying out their political murders.† The requirements of infiltration, and gaining proximity to their targets, despite the large *askari* of any senior emir, and the small army of a bodyguard that surrounded the sultan, meant that the *fidai'in* Assassin groups sent to

---

* For the lack of perception of this key concept among Middle Eastern commanders, even in the recent past, see S. Pelleterie, *The Iran–Iraq War: Chaos in a Vacuum*, New York, 1992.

† One European chronicler even wrote that long-term confinement underground brought about the Assassins' ecstatic visions of the garden of Paradise. See H. Runte, 'A Forgotten Old French Version of the Old Man of the Mountain', *Speculum*, Vol. 49, No 3, 1974, pp. 542–5.

murder the leaders of the Saljuq state had to be made up of intelligent, adaptable and resourceful men. The Ismailis would have known exactly what to look for, because the Shiite cause in general, and the Ismaili cause in particular, had been using *taqiyya* for centuries and were seasoned conspirators. Such men can be selected from among the populace, but are unlikely to be 'simple'. What is more likely is that volunteers were selected on the above criteria of creativity and aptitude, as well as their strong devotion to the faith and Hasan.

It may have been their unswerving commitment to Hasan that led some etymologists, prior to the great orientalist De Sacy, to believe that the Assassins' name originated from the Persian word *hasaniyyun*, or 'followers of Hasan'.* The mistake, given that these men were prepared to die for Hasan, would have been an easy one to make, but in fact the term for these volunteers found in many of the Ismaili sources is *fidai*, which is translated as 'devotee' – also, and perhaps more accurately, deriving from the verb 'to redeem'. This conveys the idea of completing a pledge or delivering oneself from a state of sin, by means of a sacrifice. This may be oversimplifying the case but the self-imposed restriction of the Assassins, to the use of daggers alone in their killings, required them to get so close to their victim that escape was almost certainly impossible after the strike. The fact that escape does not in fact seem to even have been contemplated makes the notion that they were sacrificing their lives for their creed a credible one.

In this respect, and in the recruitment of volunteers, it is interesting to parallel the Assassins with the early Irish Republican Brotherhood and the later Irish Republican Army. Pearse and his compatriots in the Dublin Easter Rising of 1916 identified their hopeless stand against the British, 'as a sacrificing and cleansing thing', that would raise the banners of rebellion all over Ireland. It is certainly more than possible that the *fidai'in*'s self-sacrifice worked in a decidedly similar fashion. Therefore it was not just a religious act, but also established a 'lore' of sacrifice for the cause. In the 1970s, IRA volunteers were forcefully dissuaded from joining the organisation by senior members of the organisation – initiates have stated how they had 'the fear of God' put into them, and how sacrifice, dedication and honour were stressed, whilst the fact

---

* For a fuller discussion on etymology and De Sacy's achievement see Browne, *A Literary History of Persia*, Vol. II, pp. 204–5. It is important to remember that any terms used by the Nizari Ismailis' enemies to describe the sect were, needless to say, slanderous.

of almost guaranteed imprisonment and death was repeated over and over.

The IRA's assault on the British state was carried out with a physical campaign of terror, but it also relied very much on the threat of violence being maintained. The Assassins relied in the same way, on the fear of their blades' strike just as much as on their actual body count. Just one *fidai* being 'turned' by their enemies, or deserting the cause, would have been enough to destroy the atmosphere of fear and intimidation they built up as time went on. Volunteers, therefore, were absolutely not just simple folk, or the medieval equivalent of cannon fodder – they were an elite, and had a distinct place in the Ismaili hierarchy.

This hierarchy ran from the *lasiqs*, or laymen, through to *rafiqs* (companions), *dais*, *dai kabirs* (superior missionaries) and at the top, the *sheik-el-jebel*, or mountain sheik. Ismaili encyclopaedic works have a tendency to make hierarchies out of every aspect of life. A tenth-century survey of arts and crafts even ranked these activities into basic necessities, accessory trades and luxuries; each artificer was also ranked in terms of the 'merit' of the craft he undertook. This merit was related to the craft's indispensability, skill requirement and simple nobility, as in painting and music.* This idea of strict hierarchy would be one of the most important elements of the Ismaili Assassins' strength in times of need, and was consistently reasserted through the evolving religious theory of the sect. Ismaili missionaries also developed a theory affirming both the inequality of men and the necessity of strict discipline within the community, based around religious instruction. This instruction came from only a few inspired individuals simply because the Ismailis believed that the spontaneous impulses of normal human beings would, if left unrestrained, prevent the establishment of a viable society.† The applicability of this to the creation of a military creed is obvious, as is the idea that developed later in the Assassin sect, that its leaders were divinely ordained. The Ismaili writer, Afdal al-Din Kashani, wrote in the twelfth century that such individuals were singled out for power by divine favour, and were owed unremitting loyalty.

The many rankings and levels within Nizari Ismailism also meant that the organisation could embrace the many expectations of its likely followers. We can be sure that not all the adherents of the Nizari cause were particularly interested in its religious dogma per se,

---

* Lewis, *Islam in History*, p. 86.
† H. Gibb (ed.), *The Encyclopaedia of Islam: New Edition*, Leiden, 1960, Vol. II, p. 802.

but Shiism does require that all aspects of life, whether they be legal, social or intellectual, are directed by the follower's faith. For some, the organisation was undoubtedly simply an organisation of protection – for others, a means to attack enemies. There were of course those who were motivated entirely by faith, and those who entered the order as a *fidai* doubtless thought they were creating a new order on earth and carrying out God's plan. By contrast, for the petty statesmen who became involved with the Assassins, the organisation was a vehicle for maintaining their independence from the empire-building Saljuqs. For many more, the creed gave meaning to hard, short lives and a simple promise of salvation.

A further suggestion for the mysterious origins of the word Assassin was that it was derived from the ancient Achaemenid-Persian word *shahanshah*, meaning 'king of kings'. Certainly Persian national pride, that had grown anew under the Buyids and then been dashed down by the Saljuq Turks, was resurrected by the daggers of the Assassins. But the later spread of the creed into Syria, its large native Syrian following, its upholding of the Arab Nizar's claim to the imamate, and the lack of any history of sacrificial-style killings in Persian history, all mean that the organisation's 'patriotism' should perhaps be viewed as a simple nationalistic reaction against the Turkish invasion. This antipathy for the Turks was certainly a feature of eleventh- and twelfth-century Syria too. The king of kings theory is almost certainly no more than the romantic musing of a western orientalist.*

If the murders and the sacrifices of the *fidai'in* were therefore entirely religiously driven, as I believe they were, then what of the myth of the Assassins being *hashshashin*, or addicts of hashish? Certainly, the *fidai'in* were enraptured with the idea of attaining Paradise, perhaps even unnaturally so. But were the exhausted, starving and outnumbered Crusaders at Antioch, who saw, quite distinctly, an army of their own

---

* In fact the only pre-existing models of formulistic religious murderers prior to the Assassins, at least in the Middle East, were in Iraq. These were carried out by the eighth-century followers of Abu Mansur al-Ijli of Kufa, who used only a cord to strangle their victims, and by the followers of another Shiite extremist, Mughira Ibn Said, whose adherents clubbed their victims to death. It has been suggested that both groups felt themselves to be restricted to primitive weapons until the arrival of the *Mahdi*, who would allow them the use of steel. See B. Lewis, *The Assassins: A Radical Sect in Islam*. London, 1967, p. 4. The *shananshah* theory came originally from the pen of the eighteenth-century writer Gébelin.

dead pilgrims and knights rise up and ride with them against the Turkish army of Kerbogha, any less so?

The consumption of hashish was certainly common in the medieval Middle East – a traveller to Persia in the 1920s even suggested that in that period at least 30 per cent of the population was addicted to the drug as well as to opium.* This may be why Marco Polo and other western chroniclers ending up confusing the facts. The Mamluk sultan Baybars had to expressly deny its use to his troops. Tradition records that the first *Sufi* to discover the usefulness of the substance for getting in direct contact with God was Sheikh Haydar of Khurasan, who requested that the plant be grown around his tomb upon his death; he gave his name to a colloquialism for the drug – the wine of Haydar. He left a charming description of his first high: 'I plucked a few leaves and ate them and got into a happy mood in which you find me now.'† The only thing that can be said here is that the sheikh's reaction seems to be a common one to the drug, and that it does little to incite fervour, rather the opposite. Even if it did so, as Shakespeare's porter in *Macbeth* said of the demon drink, 'it provokes and unprovokes: it provokes the desire, but it takes away the performance.'‡

The use of hashish is certainly a misnomer, just one slur among many others made against the *fidai'in* by the Sunni religious propagandists. Later, Marco Polo would have heard the tales of Assassin grand masters corrupting their followers with hashish from the lips of Crusaders and from Sunni lords of the Levant – it is notable that the Crusader writers treat the Nizari Ismailis in much the same manner as the Sunni writers, who placed the sect beyond even that of simple heresy. Another term they used, *mulhid*, grouped the Assassins with the lowest of the infidels, the polytheists. The term was obviously applied universally across the Islamic world, as even William of Rubruck, the pope's envoy, wrote it as *mulidet* in his descriptions of the Assassins, during an account of his journey through the lands of the Mongol Golden Horde of Russia, to the Mongol capital of Qaraqorum in the 1250s. So the *fidai'in* were not chemically controlled and Marco Polo got far closer to the true motivation of the Assassins when he wrote that: 'The chief thereupon addressing

---

* L. Fortescue, 'The Western Elburz and Persian Azerbaijan', *Geographical Journal*, Vol. 63, No 4, 1924, pp. 301–15.

† Al-Muscati, *Hasan Bin Sabbah*, p. 113.

‡ *Macbeth*, Act 2, Scene 2. In fact the porter is referring to lechery rather than the desire for religious murder, but the same problem of loss of performance applies, I am sure.

them, said: "We have the assurances of our Prophet that he who defends his lord shall inherit Paradise, and if you show yourselves devoted to the obedience of my orders, that happy lot awaits you."'*

But was the religious fervour of the adherents merely manipulated by Hasan? After all, he never left the safety of Alamut castle, and in fact only left his room twice during his reign of over thirty years as grand master – yet he managed to direct murders all over the Middle East. It could be argued that this did occur, but equally, matters of religion were central to life in the Middle Ages – men spent more time preparing for the afterlife than any modern man can possibly conceive of.† Life was short and not occupied overmuch by luxury; preparation for Paradise or Hell was a very pressing concern, even for the young. Fatalism also appears to have been a constant aspect of medieval Islamic psychology. Indeed, such was the strength of belief in fate among Muslims, that both De Joinville, the Crusader and chronicler, and his near contemporary, the Arabic soldier Ibn Munqidh, both noted the phenomenon but from different viewpoints:

> They think that no man can die, save on the appointed day; which is a thing no one ought to believe, for God has power to prolong our lives and to shorten them. And this the Bedouins believe, and this is why they will not wear armour when they go into battle.‡

> The hour of one's death is not brought nearer by exposing oneself to danger nor delayed by being over cautious.§

Following his sacrifice, what did the *fidai* have to look forward too? The Quran has enough verses pertaining to Paradise not to require the construction of further propaganda by Hasan. Sura 55 has the following:

> They will recline on Carpets,
> Whose inner linings will be

---

* *The Travels of Marco Polo the Venetian*, London, 1908, p. 76.
† Gibbon eloquently described it thus. 'The ancient Christians were animated by a contempt for their present existence and by a just confidence of immortality, of which the doubtful and imperfect faith of modern ages cannot give us an adequate notion.' Gibbon, *Decline and Fall of the Roman Empire*, Vol. I, p. 452.
‡ E. Wedgwood, *The Memoirs of the Lord of Joinville: A New English Version*, New York, 1906, p. 239. This is in the middle of a passage in which De Joinville is discussing the Assassins. He confuses them with the Syrian Bedouin.
§ P. Hitti, *An Arab-Syrian Gentleman and Warrior in the Period of the Crusades: Memoirs of Usama Ibn Munqidh*, New York, 1929, p. 194.

Of rich brocade: the Fruit
Of the Gardens will be
Near and easy of reach.

In them will be Maidens,
Chaste, restraining their glances,
Whom No man or Jinn
Before them has touched

Like unto rubies and coral.

And besides these two,
There are two other Gardens,

Dark-green in colour
From plentiful watering

In them each will be
Two springs pouring forth water
In continuous abundance

In them will be Fruits,
And dates and pomegranates:

In them will be Fair Maidens, good, beautiful:

Maidens restrained as to glances, in goodly pavilions

Throughout the Sura, the following verse is repeated and interspersed with the listing of Heaven's delights:

Then which of the favours
Of your Lord will ye deny?

The line is decidedly double-edged, as the believer was expected to accept Paradise from God, but equally was expected to do God's bidding on earth. Through carrying out God's will, he would show his obedience; then there was obedience and reverence for the *fidai*'s master here on earth. Hasan reiterated in his writings the permanent need of mankind for a divinely guided teacher. His writings started from the Shiite doctrine of the *talim*, the authoritative teaching of the imams, and described, in very rigid terms how only the imam and his deputy on earth, in this case Hasan himself, was owed total loyalty.

The language of Ismaili treatises on the duty of followers to the teacher is built upon ideas of submission (*islam*), obedience (*taa*) and submissiveness (*dhull*).* Later grand masters would claim to be imams of the line of Nizar to assure such devotion, but Hasan seems not to have needed to do so. Perhaps his personal example was enough – he had sacrificed much for the cause. He could have retained a comfortable position at either the Saljuq or Fatimid court, but had suffered imprisonment, pursuit and exile from family for his faith. He was an example to his men and his prestige must have been immense within the Ismaili world, simply because so many men were prepared to lay down their lives for him and for his creed. As Napoleon said, 'a man does not have himself killed for a half-pence a day or for a petty distinction. You must speak to the soul in order to electrify him.' In terms of the appeal of martyrdom, the words of an Iranian soldier of the Iran–Iraq War of the 1980s speaks volumes about the strength, not only of faith, but of the Persian lore of sacrifice:

> Martyrdom brings us closer to God. We do not seek death but we regard death as a journey from one form of life to another, and to be martyred while opposing God's enemies brings us closer to God. There are two phases to martyrdom: we approach God and we also remove the obstacles that exist between God and the people.†

Assassination, the weapon of offensive-defence, had therefore been selected, but this could not be an immediate riposte to the Saljuq threat. Recruitment, training, target selection and simple opportunity would certainly all delay the planned offensive. Hasan's more immediate concern was with defence. He knew that his planned campaign of terror had enough ideology to sustain it: his preaching, with its emphasis on martyrdom and its promise of divine and human fulfilment, was enough to fill his Assassin soldiers with sufficient pride and courage, and ensure their absolute devotion. He was putting in place the organisation to maintain the planned assault over a protracted period, but first he needed

---

* S. Calderini, 'Alam al-din in Ismailism: World of Obedience or World of Immobility?', *Bulletin of the School of Oriental and African Studies*, Vol. 56, No 3, 1993, pp. 459–69.
† R. Fisk, *The Great War for Civilisation: The Conquest of the Middle East*, London, 2005, p. 249.

a defence plan for the counter-attack that his first killing would certainly provoke from the Saljuqs.

He travelled to the environs of Qazvin, where his operatives had been reconnoitring for suitable 'ready-made' solutions to the problem. Hasan was personally involved in the acquisition of his key stronghold, Alamut.

Hasan's achievement in capturing Alamut is shrouded in a large degree of mystery. It has been suggested variously that he managed to convert the keeper of the fortress, or that he managed to sneak so many of his followers into Alamut's garrison that one morning its constable awoke to find himself the only non-Ismaili left within its walls. A third tale had Hasan simply buying the ruin from an unhappy owner, and there is an additional account that is certainly an historical topos, attached to this last story. It says that Hasan offered the owner of Alamut a large sum of gold for a patch of land in the fortress's environs that could be enclosed only within a cow skin. The greedy owner acquiesced at which point Hasan cut the cowhide into fine strips and completely encircled Alamut's walls with it.

Whatever the case, Hasan occupied Alamut in 1090. His gold or his effort had secured him a very rough gem – Alamut was in poor condition, with crumbling walls and deficiencies in both water supply and local food supply – it would have been unable to withstand any kind of siege. It was the peculiar nature of the nascent Ismaili 'state' that solved both these problems. Canals and waterways in the fortress's environs were repaired and the lands were tilled and sown – both by his followers and by villagers, who saw in the Ismailis an organisation that was more likely to protect them from robbery, and less likely to squeeze them for tax, than the local Saljuq authorities. How many of these individuals actually converted 'fully' to Ismailism is a difficult question, but there were certainly a sizeable number of new supporters of the new rule among the peasantry.

Alamut is usually translated as 'Eagle's Teaching', from a pre-Islamic tale of a Persian lord being led to found the castle on the mountain's inaccessible high peak after seeing an eagle alight there. The castle was rebuilt in 860 by a Shiite missionary, who was also coincidentally called Hasan, and its history extended into the eighteenth century when it became a state prison. It was in fact only one of about fifty fortified places in the mountain district, but it was important because it sat above the shortest road between the Caspian Sea and the city of Qazvin.

It would be wrong to think of Alamut in the sense of a western medieval castle. It did not strategically dominate a large area of fertile land, nor was it built in a greatly 'scientific' manner like the huge concentric castles of the Crusaders in Syria, that, due to their interruption of Muslim communications, also had an offensive role. It seems likely that, because of the highly mobile nature of first Arab and then later Turkish warfare, fortification was never really that highly developed in the medieval Islamic world. However, it did reach a degree of sophistication under the Mamluk sultans of Egypt, in response to the two-front war they fought in Syria against the Crusaders and Mongols.

The Persian word used to describe Alamut is *qal'a* which translates simply as 'fortified place' rather than castle per se. It is perhaps therefore better to view Alamut as a bolt-hole or refuge, not dissimilar to the fortified villages of Umbria, Tuscany and the Marches in Italy. As a bolt-hole, however, Alamut was perfect. The Crusaders of Syria enhanced natural defences by the addition of glacis walls and turrets. For Alamut there was no need to decide on how to manufacture killing zones or how high a curtain wall would need to be, simply because of the forbidding nature of the fortress's environs. The descriptions by a visitor to Hasan's bastion in the early twentieth century describe how the journey up to the mountain stronghold begins with a long passage through gorges, and along narrow and difficult paths that traverse steeply descending and ascending spurs. Well below the mountain on which Alamut sits, there are two rivers forming gorges which are 'quite impassable after heavy rain or snow',* and only after that does the going get very difficult.

The one useable path goes down into a narrow passage, cut through the hills by fast-flowing mountain streams that become rivers in winter. Then there is an easier section of valley that might hearten an assailant, but then he would have to traverse the slopes of the main range, before re-crossing another ravine to arrive in another valley below the Rock of Alamut. Standing below would, however, probably be quite a depressing experience for any erstwhile attacking force, as this rock has almost vertical walls which are about six hundred feet high, having been lifted volcanically into a standing position. They can only be approached on one side, thus immediately limiting the options for encirclement and dispersed attack – staples of medieval siege warfare. Defence of this one viable point of entry would have been easy, even for the undoubtedly limited garrison of about two hundred men that Alamut could have

---

* W. Ivanow 'Alamut', *Geographical Journal*, Vol. 77, No 1, January 1931, p. 42.

accommodated.* At its base, the profusion of smaller rounded hills would have made the placing of mangonels difficult, and any rainfall ensured that the whole area would be flooded by the sudden appearance of streams and rivers. Even in dry weather the uneven surface that was full of ravines would have made it extremely hard to muster and move troops around the area.

Hasan and his predecessors had improved the rock's natural defences with both extensive walls encircling its very top and fortifications below. These walls were simple compared to the masonry work seen in the cut-stone edifices of Crak des Chevaliers or Montfort in Syria, but then mining of the walls of Alamut would have been a near impossible option for any attacker due to the nature of the ground.

The fact that Hasan fortified quickly in response to an imminent threat of attack by Malikshah and Nizam al-Mulk is indicated by the rectangular holes in the upper stones of many of the walls. It seems evident that quickly erected wooden structures were used to improvise higher walls in a reduced time frame. There is no evidence of a natural water supply to Alamut, but the canal construction discussed above was diverted and brought a water supply underground, into the bowels of the castle. The area around the castle boasted orchards, and it seems that the entire mountain region was cultivated quite effectively. Even in the early twentieth century, despite the poverty of the soil, it seems that this area grew rice and other staple crops in relative abundance.†
Contemporary Muslim writers also described the astonishing fertility of the stark mountain valley – it seems likely that it was their descriptions of this improbable lushness, disseminated throughout the East on the tongues of merchants and travellers, that eventually mutated into the gardens of Paradise that Marco Polo described so lyrically, and with such blithe indifference to fact:

> The Old Man was called Alaoddin in their language. In a valley between two mountains he had constructed the largest and most beautiful garden that ever was seen. Every good fruit in the world grows there. And in that place he caused to be built the most beautiful house and palace ever seen, because they were gilded and adorned with all the beautiful things in the world. And furthermore he had conduits built. Through one of these flowed wine, through another milk, through another honey, and through

---

* Ivanow, 'Alamut', p. 45.

† C. Edmonds, 'A Visit to Alamut in 1920', *Geographical Journal*, Vol. 77, No 6, June 1931, p. 555.

another water. And the most beautiful women and girls were there, who knew how to play all instruments and who sang and danced better than any other women. And the Old Man made his people believe that his garden was Paradise. And the reason why he had built it in such a way was that Muhammad had told the Saracens that those who go to Paradise will have as many beautiful women as they want and that there will flow rivers of wine, milk, honey, and water. And so he had ordered that garden to be made according to the way Muhammad had described

Paradise to the Saracens, and the Saracens of that country truly believed the garden to be Paradise.*

It is hard to relate the above to the stark environment in which Alamut sits, and Hasan's lifestyle and those of his adherents was equally spartan. It is also possible that Marco Polo, Odoric of Pordenone and the other Europeans who reported these fantastic tales of the secret oases of rapture to be found in the Old Man of the Mountain's sanctuary here on Earth, had also misunderstood Ismaili doctrine and its stress on the nearness of the Kingdom of God. Those European writers who were churchmen certainly should have understood this idea, simply because it was much akin to one of the driving causes of the Crusading movement – that of there being two Jerusalems: the physical city and the celestial city of God, and the idea that both could be attained in this lifetime.† The following piece from a Sunni 'mole' who claimed to have been initiated into all the *Batinis'* sacraments, describes how Paradise in the next world could only be reached by attaining understanding in this life:

He says: 'If someone does not reach the Garden of Paradise in this world, he will not reach it in the Hereafter, because the Garden of Paradise is exclusively for the masters of understanding and the people of minds, not for the ignorant. The best of things is what is hidden, and that is why the Garden of Paradise is called the *Janna*, because it is *mustajanna* [veiled, concealed]. The *jinn* are so-called because of their concealment from human beings. The grave is called the *majanna*, because it covers the person inside it. The shield is called the *mijann*, because the warrior covers himself with it. In this Garden of Paradise [*janna*] is that which is screened from these degenerate creatures who have no knowledge and no minds.'‡

* Translated from Marco Polo in C. Nowell, 'In the Old Man of the Mountain', *Speculum*, Vol. 22, No 4, October 1947, pp. 497–519. Polo's Aloaddin was Ala al-Din, the seventh and penultimate grand master of the Persian mission.
† S. Menache, *The Vox Dei: Communication in the Middle Ages*, New York, 1990, p. 100.
‡ Al-Yamani, *Disclosure of the Secrets of the Batiniyya*, p. 47.

Hasan's defence plan relied on generating among the local populace an unshakeable fervour and undeviating devotion for the Ismaili faith and himself, as much as it did on fortresses and mountains. His regime was a harsh one. He killed one of his own sons because of a false charge of misconduct, and despite his regret upon learning the truth, he still found it in himself to put his second son to death for drinking wine.* A flute player was expelled from Alamut forever and music was banned by the grand master. Given that the above interdictions on wine and song were for all the adherents of the faith, from the most ordinary members upwards, we can be sure that the training and lifestyle of the elite *fidai'in* was highly, if not severely, disciplined.

The skills of dissimulation and disguise required a considerable education. Learning the language of their foes – in this early period, Turkish – would not have been a requirement, as Islam carried a mix of languages and Arabic remained the lingua franca, but the mannerisms of individuals such as merchants and military men would have been studied and emulated. This was particularly the case later, when 'sleepers' were deployed in royal courts, and even more so once the operation went truly international, as in the attempt on the Great Khan's life and the slaying of Crusader princes. Even with this expansion of the operation, however, the *fidai'in* do not seem to have received any training in languages contrary to what has been suggested in the inventive accounts of occidental chroniclers of the Crusaders, and later European writers, such as Burchard of Strasbourg, who claimed that the *fidai* were taught, 'Latin, Greek, Roman, Saracen as well as many others'.†

The first great test of Hasan's defence plan came in 1092, with Malikshah's launch of a twin offensive against Alamut and Quhistan, a region far to the south-east of Alamut in the central lands of the Saljuq Empire. Hasan's agents had managed to subvert Quhistan almost completely, leading to the capture of its fortified places and an insurrection against its Turkish lords. Such newly acquired territories were designated as *jazira*, or islands, by the Ismaili Assassins and there would be many more such outposts.

---

* The drinking of alcohol in Muslim lands in the Middle Ages was a lot more common than the faith of the population would suggest. Indeed the English word 'booze' almost certainly has a Persian-Turkish origin from *buza*, an alcoholic beverage made from millet, barley or rice. See B. Laufer, 'On the Possible Oriental Origin of Our Word Booze', *Journal of the American Oriental Society*, Vol. 49, 1929, pp. 56–8.

† Burchard of Strasbourg's report is recorded in Arnold of Lubeck's *Chronica Slavorum*. English translation in Lewis, *The Assassins*, p. 3.

A siege of Alamut was started in June by one of Malikshah's emirs and in the early stages it looked likely that Alamut might fall, as Hasan had few supplies and his garrison consisted of only about eighty men – but these few were enough to hold off the besiegers until help started to arrive from Qazvin. Only about three hundred men came to Alamut's rescue but surprisingly this was enough to turn around the situation. According to the Ismaili sources, this small force made a sally from Alamut in October 1092 and routed the Saljuq forces. This seems unlikely – indeed other writers indicate that the Saljuqs saw virtually nothing of the enemy, except for the ominous figure of one white-robed individual, who was often seen in the distant peaks, observing them, but who disappeared into nothingness when approached. What is more probable, therefore, is that Hasan's fortifications, the beginnings of winter and the difficulty of maintaining the Saljuq army's supplies in the high mountains were enough to erode the morale of Malikshah's men.

Hasan's defensive strategy had passed through its baptism of fire, but what really stopped the Saljuq campaign was his first *fidai'in* offensive. Hasan 'spread the snare of artifices in order at the first opportunity to catch some splendid game, such as Nizam al-Mulk, in the net of destruction and increase thereby his own reputation'.* The chosen Assassin was Bu Tahir Arrani, and he timed his attack for a moment when it was obvious that Nizam al-Mulk's guard would be down. The elderly great *wazir* had just completed his work for the day in the audience chamber and was being carried in his litter to the tent of his women when Arrani struck him with his dagger. The Assassin was disguised as a wandering *Sufi*, and no doubt the *wazir*'s mind was distracted with thoughts of the evening's pleasures to be had. The *Sufi* approached the *wazir* with a petition and while Nizam was reading it his killer drove the dagger into his chest. Nizam al-Mulk's bodyguard hacked Arrani to death as he became entangled in the tent-ropes but it was too late – the *wazir* was dead, and with his death the Saljuq Empire began to splinter. Malikshah died shortly after Nizam al-Mulk, as a result the Saljuq assault on Quhistan fizzled out; the sultana followed her husband to the grave soon after, and an almost predictable civil war ensued. The Nizari Ismaili Assassin state had secured its first victory.

This was truly a double victory, in that the physical apparatus of the Saljuq Empire had been stalled by the internecine fighting that followed the death of the great *wazir* and sultan, but there was more to it than that. Mistrust had been sown at the very heart of government, and rumours

---

* Juvaini, *Chinggis Khan*, p. 676.

abounded that Malikshah, in fear of his great *wazir*'s increasing power, had himself arranged for the killing of Nizam al-Mulk. Ibn al-Jawzi went as far as to claim that, 'the beliefs of Sultan Malikshah were corrupted because of his companionship with *Batinis*,' and that the sultan had been seduced by the preaching of the Assassin sect and was a secret convert.

The conspiracy theories really began to spin out of control, however, with the death of the sultan, which was laid at the caliph's door. The story went that Malikshah had ordered Caliph al-Muqtadi to leave Baghdad and he was advancing towards the city when Nizam al-Mulk was murdered. The sultan then called on the caliph:

> to tell him that he should leave Baghdad and go wherever else he liked. The caliph was perplexed. He asked the sultan for a month's respite but the latter refused. The caliph sent for Taj al-Mulk [Nizam al-Mulk's son] who was appointed as *wazir* after the murder of Nizam al-Mulk and told him to ask the sultan to give him ten days. Taj al-Mulk pleaded to the sultan for him saying that anyone who wants to travel from one place to another needs at least ten days for preparation, so why deny that to the caliph? The sultan ultimately granted ten days respite, and within the period of the ten days Malikshah fell ill and died.*

The implication that the caliph and the new wazir were involved in the sultan's death by poison was strengthened by the fact that Taj al-Mulk and the caliph were in cahoots over the succession to the sultanate of the four-year-old son of Malikshah, Mahmud, over the expected heir, Berkyaruq. The subsequent murder of Taj al-Mulk by the former bodyguards of Nizam al-Mulk, despite his attempts to buy off their leaders with two hundred thousand dinars each, only added to the murkiness of the whole affair and the confusion that followed the deaths of the leaders of the state. Taj al-Mulk was torn to pieces by his father's guards and his fingers were sent to Berkyaruq. All in all, this was a very satisfactory result for Hasan, as was the seizing of Berkyaruq by Mahmud's supporters. They had intended to blind him in order to render him useless to his backers in the Nizamiyya bodyguard and were only restrained from doing so when Mahmud caught smallpox and died.

During this period of confusion that his first killing had evoked, Hasan went on the offensive with the seizure of the mountain castle of Girdkuh, in the eastern Elburz Mountains in 1096. Its appropriation was a relatively simple matter, given that the region's governor was a secret convert to

---

* Abu'l-Mahasin in Al-Muscati, *Hasan Bin Sabbah*, pp. 53–5.

Ismailism and had given his loyalty to Hasan's new Nizari Ismailism following the 'official' schism from the Fatimids in 1094. The chronicler Rashid al-Din claims that the fortress was, in fact, occupied by an Ismaili *dai* some two hundred years before the Assassins made their first killing.* The castle's capture brought with it control of the main communication route between Khurasan and the west of Persia. However attempts to push their influence south towards Isfahan, whilst initially successful with the capture of two hill forts outside the city, ended badly with the massacre of all their supporters on the streets of the metropolis by Isfahan's citizens and militia. This was only the first of a series of bitter reprisals against the sect in the cities of Persia. A general slaughter ensued in Nishapur in 1096 and the fate of ringleaders generally did not end with a simple execution but with a more elaborate and agonising death: 'He was paraded on a camel through the streets of Isfahan, a spectacle for thousands, pelted with mud and dirt, and mocked in derisive verses; afterwards he was crucified, and hung on the cross for seven days. Arrows were fired at him as he hung there, helpless and tormented, and finally his body was burned to ashes.'†

The backlash detailed above, however, seems to have been very much a grass roots reaction, since the contenders for the Saljuq throne, for a short time at least, were content to leave the Assassins alone whilst they fought their brothers and half-brothers for the sultanate. The Isfahan operation got underway again and the *dai* Attash was able to get a position as a schoolteacher to the children of the garrison of a castle called Shahdiz to the south of the city. He was then able to convert enough of the troops to bring the fort over to the Nizari cause without the spilling of a drop of blood. At the nearby castle of Khalinjan, an Ismaili carpenter gave a huge banquet in a nearby village for its garrison; the troops enjoyed the party so much that this castle was also captured bloodlessly. The troops woke up the next day, presumably hungover and homeless – perhaps Sherman's affirmation that 'war is cruelty' does not always hold true.

Sultan Berkyaruq involved himself even further than mere partying with the Assassins, and went as far as to enlist the Assassins of Quhistan against his brother's lieutenants in Khurasan. Whilst there are tales of his own near assassination in 1096, the attempt had none of the hallmarks of the *fidai'in* and did not hold him back from a short political alliance with Hasan. It has been calculated that of the fifty assassinations made under

---

* Stern, 'The Early Ismaili Missionaries', pp. 56–90.
† Browne, *A Literary History of Persia*, Vol. II, p. 316.

Hasan's reign as grand master, over half occurred in this early period of the Saljuq civil war, and that many of these were advantageous to Berkyaruq.* The nearest we have to a 'catalogue' of these murders is the recording of Juvaini, who was able to consult the Ismaili library of Alamut before it was consigned to flames by the Mongols. He tells us of Hasan's ongoing campaign against the upper echelons of Saljuq government:

> Some time after the death of Nizam al-Mulk two of his sons were also stabbed, one, whose name was Ahmad, in Baghdad – he became paralysed – and Fakhr al-Mulk in Nishapur. And from then onwards he used to cause the emirs, commanders and any notables to be assassinated by his *fidai'in* one after the other; and anyone who opposed him in any way he would get rid of with this trick. To record the names of all these people would take too long . . .†

The assaults on the sons of Nizam al-Mulk began in October 1100, when an emir of Rayy was stabbed to death in front of Fakhr al-Mulk as he walked in his garden. Under torture, the Assassin claimed that six more men were marked for death and when Fakhr tremulously enquired if he would be one of them, the *fidai* told him that he was too insignificant for their poniards. Fakhr was doubtless relieved, but he was to die later in Nishapur in 1106 as the victim of an Assassin disguised as a beggar. This *fidai* was also interrogated under torture and gave the names of twelve senior courtiers as Ismaili collaborators – all of whom were summarily executed by the Saljuqs. They were later shown to be innocent of all charges. In 1109 Ahmad al-Mulk was crossing the Tigris on his way to the Great Mosque of Baghdad when an Assassin leapt aboard his boat and struck him in the neck with his dagger, paralysing him, as Juvaini relates above.

Berkyaruq was riding a tiger, and soon enough he found that the Ismaili Assassin tiger had begun to devour chunks of his kingdom and his army. Army officers took bodyguards everywhere with them, and wearing mail under one's clothes became highly fashionable. It was usual practice for officers to appear before their lord unarmed, a very obvious safeguard for the monarch in dangerous times, but Berkyaruq had to grant a special dispensation to his senior lieutenants so they could retain their swords in his presence – such was the general fear that others in the court circle had been turned by the Assassins, or were even disguised *fidai'in*.

---

* Lewis, *The Assassins*, p. 51.
† Juvaini, *Chinggis Khan*, p. 678.

By 1101, Berkyaruq had established some degree of control over western Persia, though his half-brother Muhammad still retained a large parcel of lands in the north of Iraq and in the Jazira. Unfortunately the central treasury had been emptied by his predecessor, Mahmud's mother, Turkman Khatun, who had paid off as many of the emirs as she could, in order to ensure their hostility against Berkyaruq. Berkyaruq had to borrow fifty thousand dinars from the caliph in 1101 and before this the chronicler Bundari records how Mahmud could not even afford to buy the daily beer allowance for his officials and had to resort to returning empty beer boxes to the brewer to obtain credit.* Berkyaruq was only able to achieve the stabilisation of the western empire by effectively giving away Khurasan to his young half-brother, Sanjar.

The new sultan of eastern Persia fixed his sights on the reduction of the Ismaili Assassin islands that afflicted his realm. Sanjar sent a force to Quhistan, which laid waste to the countryside around the Assassin strongholds and then applied mangonels to the walls of their castles. The Ismailis were able to bribe off one of the emirs sent to destroy them, which gave them respite for some three years, but the same emir then returned with a force swollen with Sunni *ghazi*, or volunteer fighters. This time the castles, which obviously were not as impregnable as Alamut, were brought down by the mangonels. Ismaili women and children were enslaved and their leaders brought to heel and made to pledge that they would not rebuild their fortresses, rearm themselves or proselytise their faith. The Saljuq forces then retired with only this promise obtained from the Assassins – it proved worthless and Quhistan was soon enough undergoing re-infiltration by the sect. At first glance the Sanjar's 'clemency' seems odd when compared to the absolute obliteration of the Ismailis that might have been expected, but it is very likely that he saw that Berkyaruq's reign was coming to an end. Indeed the sultan died in 1105, and the potential battles between new contenders for the throne of the west were certainly more of a concern than a campaign of extirpation against a foe thought to have been contained.

Berkyaruq's response in the west was equally fitful – it might be suggested that he only acted against the Ismailis at all because it played well with his Sunni subjects, who were now openly accusing him of complicity with the Assassins. Ibn al-Jawzi wrote that, 'Berkyaruq, by his declaration of enmity towards the Nizaris removed the doubts in the minds of people so that the suspicion in which he was held began to melt

---

* Lambton, *Continuity and Change*, p. 255.

away.' He gave free reign to the pogroms against 'fifth-column' Ismailis in the cities of Persia, and Ibn al-Athir recorded that many, many innocents were caught up in the butchery that now extended to the cities of Iraq.

Hasan appears to have been temporarily stymied by the Saljuq response. The senior officers of the regime were on guard against his daggers and he had lost much of his extended power through the persecutions and mass executions in the cities. His response was perceptive, dramatic and inspired. Realising that an extension of the war was the only way to avoid his dominions being effectively surrounded by the more integrated Saljuq forces, he dispatched *dais* to Syria – a possession of the Saljuqs, but also a distracted and fractious province. Its political make-up had been as disturbed by the murder of Nizam al-Mulk, and the break up of the Saljuq Empire, as Persia had been, and it was now perfectly suitable for infiltration by the Ismailis and their Assassins. Of this Syrian campaign we will read more later.

Hasan turned back to more local issues. He was able to improve the defence of the Alamut region by the acquisition of the castle of Lamasar, which lay to the north-west of Alamut but still in the Elburz Mountains. Lamasar guarded an important pass to the Caspian Sea and cut across the main highway from Khurasan to the central cities of Iran. Hasan's lieutenant, and successor as grand master, Buzurg Umid was put in charge of the operation to capture the castle and he achieved this through a stealthy attack upon the fortress in the middle of the night, in which the entire garrison was slain by silent daggers. Other not so silent, but nevertheless consecrated, daggers were sent with *fidai'in* to the Sunni religious leaders who had done so much in recent years to stir up the populace against the Ismailis. By assassinating some of these leaders, Hasan hoped to intimidate all the preachers. Hasan's decision to target the Sunni religious intelligentsia shows an acute understanding of how Berkyaruq was being forced to act against the Ismailis by preachers and the public anger they stirred. By this act, Hasan also allowed his followers to vent their spleens, which could only be good for morale. The Mufti of Isfahan was murdered in his own mosque, thus fulfilling the Quranic prescription of 'the life for the life, and the eye for the eye, and the nose for the nose, and the ear for the ear, and the tooth for the tooth, and for wounds retaliation',* as it avenged the massacres of 1094. In Nishapur, the city of the massacres of 1096, retribution was also inflicted on the head

---

* Sura 5, v. 45.

of the most violent anti-Ismaili faction and again the murder had strong psychological overtones, as it was carried out in the city's main mosque.

Despite these successes, the years from 1105 to 1118 were hard years for Hasan's followers in the west of Persia. As discussed above, Berkyaruq died in 1105 and Sultan Muhammad acceded to the western throne. Ismaili settlements and strongholds in the hills and mountains around Isfahan were raided constantly, as Muhammad would not tolerate their presence so close to his chosen capital. Such was the brutality that the Saljuq troops brought to the campaign and the entire region, that the Nizaris were even joined in their resistance against the sultan by the Jewish congregations of the area.

Shahdiz came under intense attack, so the *dai* Attash, who had been responsible for its acquisition, now arranged its defence and he did so chiefly through the unusual military strategy of religious argument. He sent letters to the sultan, claiming that apart from a few minor points of doctrine, the Ismailis were in fact the same as Sunnis and therefore warranted the protection of the sultan. Hasan had written to Malikshah in this same vein in the past, claiming that the Abbasids and Nizam al-Mulk had misrepresented him and his followers to the sultan for their own ends. It was of course this correspondence that led to the rumours of Malikshah having, at the very least condoned, if not having actually arranged, the murder of his great *wazir*. Attash obviously wished to create the same sort of confusion and mutual suspicion at Muhammad's court, as Hasan's letters had at Malikshah's.

The correspondence also bought time for the *dai* to organise the physical defences of Shahdiz. Muhammad's advisers treated the note seriously and spent weeks debating it. When this debate had finally run its course, the religious jurists decided that annihilation of the heretical sect was acceptable and this resolution was no doubt helped along by the writings of al-Ghazali: 'The meaning of repentance of an apostate is his abandoning of his inner religion. The secret apostate does not give up his inner confessions . . . He may be killed for his unbelief because we are convinced that he stays an unbeliever who sticks to his inner beliefs.'* Doubtless, the fact that an Assassin very nearly took the life of one of the sultan's senior emirs during the deliberations also encouraged their decision to make war on Attash.

---

* F. Griffel, 'Toleration and Exclusion: Al-Shafi and al-Ghazali on the Treatment of Apostates', *Bulletin of the School of Oriental and African Studies*, Vol. 64, No 3, 2001, pp. 339–54.

Attash then started on a new stalling tactic. He offered to withdraw from the Isfahan environs, but demanded another fortress further away, citing the massacres of Nizaris in the 1090s as his need for a safe haven. This was agreed to and arrangements were made for the Nizaris of Shahdiz to be allowed to go to Alamut and to another stronghold in the southern Zagros Mountains. Ismailis had been living relatively peacefully there since 1092, when a *dai* who had come to the region as a shoemaker had converted an enclave of former followers of the Fatimids to the Nizari faith, and had secured the area for Hasan's sect by obtaining the fortress of Arrajan.

The party for Arrajan left and arrived safely at their home, but then Attash and the remaining garrison at Shahdiz broke the accord and decided on resistance. He concentrated all his efforts on defence in one wing of the castle, but having only eighty men meant he still had to leave one wall undefended, with only shields and spears propped up against the battlements as a somewhat hopeful ruse against an attack on that part of the castle. It was soon pointed out to the sultan that one part of the ramparts was suspiciously quiet and the Saljuqs soon broke in through the undefended sector. There was a general slaughter of the garrison, although it is hard to see how it could have been otherwise, as Nizari Ismaili Assassins almost always fought to the death. Attash's wife, wearing her finest jewellery and clothes, completed the horror show by flinging herself from the high ramparts on to the stony ground below. Attash himself was captured and after being shown living to the populace of Isfahan, he was flayed alive. His skin was then stuffed with straw, presumably so that his body would not putrefy too badly as it was sent on tour around the cities of Persia while his head travelled to Baghdad. As he was being stretched out to be flayed, a member of the crowd mockingly called out that astrology – the understanding of which all Assassin masters were supposed to be adept – had surely not predicted this end. Attash is said to have replied that he had, through the stars, portended a ceremonial parade through the streets of Isfahan for himself, but not of this kind.

Attash's fate, the ongoing massacres and the unremitting fanaticism of the Nizari Ismailis in defending their masters and their homes, seems to give the lie to the second half of Sherman's axiom on the nature of war – 'The crueller it is, the sooner it will be over' – because this war would continue with just such barbarism and with new foes for the Nizaris, for the next century and a half.

Muhammad instructed his brother Sanjar in the east to begin attacks on the Assassin strongholds in his lands. In the west, Arrajan fell to Muhammad and the smaller castle-community of Takrit in Iraq was evacuated by the Nizaris, as the western Saljuq offensive began to show more success. In 1107 Sultan Muhammad then seems to have settled on the destruction of Hasan's headquarters as the key to the war. Whilst the immediate storming of Alamut was not possible, due to its near-impregnable position, the sultan's troops attempted, by a process of bringing down the forts surrounding Alamut, and destruction of its croplands, to both isolate and to starve out Hasan's followers. The campaign went on for eight years, with the Saljuq troopers returning every autumn to burn crops and slay villagers. It was Hasan's cold determination and fierce discipline that ensured the survival of the Ismaili sect during this period, although many of its adherents did not. Juvaini writes of the inhabitants of Alamut eating grass to stave off hunger. The grand master sent his wife and daughters to Girdkuh, as if their presence might cause him some weakness of will. He wrote to the castle's governor, 'since these women work the spindle on behalf of our propaganda, give them their needs as wages therefore.'*

During these eight years the regime pushed itself beyond human pity and weakness – it was during this time that Hasan killed both of his sons. The first, Husain, had assumed that he would reign when his father died, but Hasan allowed no special status for kin. For him the hierarchy was all, and when Husain was accused of murdering one of his competitors for the succession, Hasan was quick – almost certainly too quick – to bring him to trial and execution. Perhaps wine was solace for the loss of a brother, but one goatskin of wine was enough to seal the fate of the second son. Hasan's wife and daughters never returned and he was now devoid of family having either effectively banished or killed them all. His adamantine spirit was impervious to worldly needs, and yet a Byzantine mission to Alamut reported the following about Hasan:

> His natural dignity, his distinguished manner, his smile, which is always courteous and pleasant but never familiar or casual, the grace of his attitudes, the striking firmness of his movements, all combine to produce an undeniable superiority, which is magnetic in its domination. There is no pride or arrogance, he emanates calm and good will.†

---

* Juvaini, *Chinggis Khan*, p. 680.
† From the Ecumenical Patriarchate of Constantinople, in E. Franzius, *History of the Order of the Assassins*, New York, 1969, p. 60.

It was perhaps only the character of Hasan that saw the Nizaris survive the eight-year war, although the *fidai'in* must have also boosted the castle garrison's morale with the killing of the religious judge, or *qadi*, of Nishapur at the end of Ramadan (during the very celebrations that marked the end of the fast) in 1109. Similarly, in 1108 they had managed to kill the *qadi* of Isfahan, despite his large bodyguard and body armour, in the middle of Friday prayers in one of the city's main mosques. By this point the *fidai'in* and their deeds were becoming the stuff of legend in Persia's great cities, and at home mothers of Assassins would weep with joy at news of their sons' success in murder and subsequent sacrifice. Indeed, it is recorded that a Syrian mother who learned of her son's successful mission and death, 'anointed her eyelids with kohl, and was full of joy; then after a few days her son returned unharmed, and she was grieved and tore her hair and blackened her face'.* The *fidai'in* also appear to have adopted a uniform at this time for domestic guard duties, comprising a simple white robe with red cords to secure it, red turbans and red boots. The uniform may have been created as a visible sign of resistance, designed to boost the morale of the lower orders of the sect – white was chosen simply because it was the complete opposite of the black of the Abbasids' ceremonial robes. It seems that the *fidai'in* also carried large axes when guarding the grand master; the immense size of these weapons may have been more ceremonial than anything else. Their impressive size, and the white-robed guards bearing them, gave prestige appropriate to Hasan's position as an uncrowned king and created the image of strength at the heart of the movement.

Such strength was certainly required in 1117 as mangonels were brought, laboriously, up to the walls of both Alamut and Lamasar. As described earlier, siege artillery in the twelfth century was generally poorly developed. The manual of warfare that al-Tarsusi produced for Saladin tells us that the Persian or Turkish mangonel could only throw stones of 'more or less' fifty pounds, although he goes on to discuss a traction-driven catapult that must have been capable of more than this. Therefore, the physical impact of these devices could not have been that great, given the height of the rock on which Alamut sat, but the psychological effect must have been vast, and this time the Turks seemed determined to drive the siege to its full conclusion.

However, in April 1118, news of Muhammad's death in Isfahan was heard, and true to form, the Saljuq emirs packed up their war against the

---

* From the Zabda of Kamal al-Din in Lewis, *The Assassins*, p. 105.

Assassins and ran back to the capital, to ensure first place for themselves in the reframing of power that attended the death of every sultan. Rumours abounded that the Assassins of Shahdiz, who of course had lost their fortress and leader Attash, to the Saljuqs, had bribed and threatened a barber or surgeon to use a poisoned blade on Sultan Muhammad. The tale seems unlikely, simply because it is out of character with the Assassins' ethos of death by the dagger, followed by the sacrifice of the Assassin's own life, but it proves how the psychological fallout of the assassination campaign was just as important as the killings themselves. It was also suggested that the *wazir* at the court of Muhammad was a secret Ismaili, and that he had hobbled the operation of 1118 by making accusations against the expedition's leading emir – causing his downfall and execution once Muhammad was dead.*

The death of Muhammad brought a respite to the Nizaris; it also brought Sanjar, the thirty-two-year-old sultan of the east to the top of the Saljuq pile, where he would remain for the next thirty-nine years. The new Great Sultan faced three major problems. Politically, the Saljuq Empire was still a loose confederation of semi-independent kingdoms, over which he exercised only nominal sovereignty – this made concerted action difficult. Unfortunately, concerted action was exactly what was required to face his second problem in the north-east of the empire: the Ghuzz Turk tribes – the very tribes from whom the Saljuqs had come – had always been troublesome neighbours, ever since the Arab defeat of the Chinese in 751 and the extension of Islamic power into the region that followed this victory. They were, however, now beginning to raid Islamic lands with impunity, and were also being pushed further west by events beyond the River Oxus.

The Khitai Liao Dynasty of China had fallen and the Khitai were pushed from western China by the new lords of China, the Jin. The Khitai were still a powerful force, however, and they displaced the Ghuzz Turks, who, having nowhere else to go, had started to enter the *Dar al-Islam* en masse, once again, from 1100 onwards. All this would give rise to the myth of Prester John in the west and the hopes of the Crusader kingdoms that a great Christian king would ride from the east to destroy Islam. What it meant for Sanjar was that his presence in the east was required more than in the west of his lands. He therefore settled his capital at Marv, and tried to deal with the Ghuzz migration, through military confrontation and partly through meeting their needs for pasture and attempting to pacify

---

* Lewis, *The Assassins*, p. 57.

them, using officers called *shahnas*. These officers treated the Ghuzz as special subjects and whilst they collected dues of sheep for the sultan's table, they also ensured there was enough grassland and water for each tribe. This appeasement of the Ghuzz worked for a while, but the unruly tribesmen, and the problem of maintaining his superiority in the highly chaotic world of Saljuq politics, distracted Sanjar to a great extent from his third problem – the need to destroy the Nizari Assassins.

Sanjar did, however, manage to campaign on and off against the Assassins of Alamut in person and his emirs worked away against Quhistan for years, burning cropland and denuding the area of its population. The Saljuq troops were told once again that the enslavement of Ismaili women and children was acceptable. This was totally against Islamic law but the Nizaris' status as *mulhid* meant they were outside of the *umma* and this fine point of theology allowed the Saljuqs to put them into bondage.

The sultan's first brief campaign against Hasan's stronghold was brought to a sudden halt by the grand master's imaginative correspondence, which was effectively the medieval equivalent of a letter-bomb campaign:

> Hasan-i-Sabbah would send ambassadors to seek peace but his offers were not accepted. He then by all manner of wiles bribed certain of the sultan's courtiers to defend him before the sultan; and he suborned one of his eunuchs with a large sum of money and sent him a dagger, which was struck in the ground beside the sultan's bed one night when he lay in a drunken sleep. When the sultan awoke and saw the dagger he was filled with alarm but not knowing who to suspect he ordered the matter to be kept secret. Hasan-i-Sabbah then sent a messenger with the following message: 'Did I not wish the sultan well that dagger which was struck into the hard ground would have been planted in his soft breast'. The sultan took fright and from then on inclined towards peace with them. In short because of this imposture the sultan refrained from attacking them and during his reign their cause prospered.*

Juvaini has the story half right. In fact the Nizaris did not prosper in this period but they did consolidate what they had. After Sanjar's emissaries had witnessed one *fidai* cutting his own throat and another leaping from Alamut's battlements to his death upon a mere nod from Hasan, there was a tacit agreement made between Sanjar and the grand master that the Nizaris should retain their lands and most of the revenue they drew from it, as long

---

* Juvaini, *Chinggis Khan*, pp. 681–2.

as they remained 'good' subjects of the sultan. Sanjar also appears to have gained from this accord the opportunity to have *fidai'in* deployed against mutual enemies, and a promise that the *dais* would not proselytise in his lands. Hasan seemed to have secured a great deal with Sanjar and, given the relentless Saljuq assaults of the last few years, he may have needed just such an agreement, if only to repair the physical fabric of his state. However, in many ways the agreement was the beginning of the end of the Nizari Assassins as a real force in Persian life. Their *dawa* was the state's *raison d'être* and it demanded that conversion to Ismailism and destruction of the upholders of wrong religion must continue. By voluntarily denying themselves the right to preach everywhere, they effectively gave up the ends for which their killings were the means – the Ismaili faith's eventual victory in the lands of Islam. Without that goal, the faith was little more than an increasingly ossified exercise in religious conservatism, and without a cause they were little more than common murderers. It would take another great religious revolution, and the leadership of another remarkable leader in Syria, to at least partially revive its soul.

Hasan died in 1124, certainly of natural causes, and perhaps even comfortably in his bed. Given the landscape of blood and murder that medieval Persian politics was, this in itself was quite a feat, but his achievement was much more than that. He had created the oddest of things – a dictatorship that individuals entered into freely. There was no free thinking for adherents of the grand master – acceptance of his teaching as the representative of the imam and a total rejection of free choice was the only path to Paradise. To modern eyes, such devotion might seem to be a suffocation of all things human, but for creating an army of God on earth it was ideal and it would maintain the Nizari Assassin cause through another century and a half of struggle.

The struggle with the Saljuqs reignited in 1126, with assaults by Sanjar's emirs against both Quhistan and Alamut. Hasan had selected Buzurg Umid as his successor – the choice was not surprising: Umid had been a child page in the castle of Alamut before its capture by Hasan, and had been taken under the grand master's wing from an early age. He had also led the assault that had captured the castle of Lamasar. The fact that he and his comrades had moved so calmly and methodically around the castle, slitting the throats of all of its inhabitants surely proved that he was just the man of steel to follow the man of ice.

Initially Sanjar's men were successful, with an entire Ismaili village being put to the sword in Quhistan. The denouement of this slaughter was the village head leaping to his death from the highest minaret in the town. There was also the partial destruction and burning of another settlement, from which a great deal of booty was taken. Then, however, the campaign started to unravel, as the emirs headed north to the environs of Alamut. They were roundly beaten in a pair of pitched battles that included local forces fighting for each side. The Saljuqs lost both booty and territory and had one commander captured. With such a dismal end to the campaign, revenge scarcely seemed necessary but Umid exacted it through his *fidai'in* anyway. This time, however, there was a new development in the methodology of killing. Sanjar's *wazir* was the victim and he was killed by two trusted servants. His two favourite grooms had been in his service for just over a year when they revealed themselves to be *fidai'in* and killed him among his prize Arab horses, as he discussed which steed to give to the sultan for a New Year gift. They had hidden the dagger in a horse's mane – from stroking the horse's neck to the killing stroke was achieved in one swift movement. The audacious murder stopped the planning of any more attacks by the sultan and showed that Umid had absorbed all of Hasan's understanding of human frailty and the psychology of terror.

Umid also followed Hasan's policy with the building of further fortifications. The new castle of Maymundiz was founded to the north-west of Alamut. This apparent renaissance in the fortunes of the Nizaris brought Mahmud, the junior sultan of the west, to the conclusion that negotiation with the sect was a better option than confrontation, especially as he was now having difficulties with his own emirs. His plans, however, unravelled when two Nizari envoys from Alamut were torn to pieces by the Isfahan mob, before they could even begin talks with the sultan's men. Umid then showed that he was also capable of fighting 'classical' warfare as well as a war of terror, by attacking the city of Qazvin, killing four hundred people and robbing the treasury. The death of one Saljuq emir in this confrontation was enough to send the rest of the garrison into a precipitate flight.

Perhaps the Nizaris on the battlefield were just as indifferent to personal safety as their Assassins were in their consecrated killings, and such an ideology would have been truly terrifying to soldiers trained in the Turkish tradition of avoiding direct confrontation. Indeed, Islamic war manuals of this period state that the ability to protect oneself, and not to throw away one's life, is a duty of the soldier to the army. The Turks' abrupt flight when confronted by a foe quite ready to die also brings Herodotus's thoughts on the Persian defeat at Marathon to mind: he says they failed because of 'that most dangerous tendency in war: a wish to kill but not to die in the process'. Dealing with an enemy who is prepared to fight to the death has been a problem for many armies at different times throughout history. The Turko-Mongolic method of warfare, as described by John of Plano Carpini, 'if they can avoid it, the Mongols do not like to fight hand to hand but they wound and kill men and horses with their arrows; they only come to close quarters when men and horses have been weakened by arrows', was fine for keeping such dangerous individuals at more than a weapon's length away on an open battlefield, but in urban combat, as at Qazvin, closing in on the enemy with a death wish was unavoidable.

Mahmud responded to the debacle of Qazvin with an assault on Alamut, but this was easily beaten off, and his failure against the Assassins was complete by the time of his death in 1131. His and Sanjar's failed campaigns had actually left the Nizaris stronger than before, as the populace were attracted by the resistance of these Persians to the oppressive Turks. Mahmud's death also saw the usual infighting among his relatives and emirs for control of western Persia. His son, Masud, won the initial stages of the contest and was proclaimed sultan, but then many of his senior emirs connived with the caliph to depose him. The caliph's interest in further disturbing the Saljuq polity was probably based around his territorial ambitions. The caliphs had always retained personally sponsored religious college lands around Baghdad. Now with the splintering of the Saljuq Empire into petty principalities, and Sanjar's preoccupation with the east, Caliph al-Mustarshid was attempting, like the renaissance pope Julius II against the French, to extend his temporal empire and free himself of the Saljuqs.

It has long been a subject of dispute just how much involvement Sanjar and Masud had in the subsequent slaying of the Abbasid caliph by Assassins, but it certainly worked to the advantage of Masud. In 1135, the caliph took his small Baghdad army into the sultan's lands, but half of his force quickly deserted him, and Masud captured him easily and took him to the city of Maragha in north-west Persia, enticingly close to Nizari territory. Masud's problem now was what to do with his illustrious prisoner – the caliph, by involving himself with matters of this earth, had become a political embarrassment. Acts of lèse majesté such as this normally called for execution of the miscreant and extirpation of his family, but the caliph was the titular head of the Sunni world and really belonged to the spiritual world. Masud's solution seems to have been not to lift a finger to end the caliph's life, but not to stir himself to its defence either. Sanjar attempted to keep himself clear of the deed with a message to Masud:

> When my child Masud Ghiyas-ad-Din has seen this edict let him at once proceed to the Commander of the Faithful and after kissing the dust of the audience hall, which is the asylum of all the world, let him crave fair pardon for the crimes and misdemeanours which are the result of desertion [by God] and seek forgiveness for the faults he has committed; and let him know that the falling of so many thunderbolts and the blowing of violent winds such as no one has experienced the like of in this age and which have now continued for twenty days - these things I consider to have been caused by that event and I fear lest from this disturbance the armies and the people be thrown into confusion. By God! Let him see fit to make amends, let him regard it as his bounden duty!*

Certainly there had been earthquakes and thunderstorms all over the empire for the last month and the last thunderclap came when Masud left the palace he had given over to the caliph, unattended and unguarded. He took his entire retinue with him to greet mere messengers from his brother on the road outside Maragha. Such was the ease of murdering the caliph that a large band of Assassins was able to virtually walk into Maragha and stab the Commander of the Faithful to death. Celebrations erupted inside Alamut and lasted for seven days and nights.

Umid's Assassins had previously murdered the governor of Maragha and the prefect of Isfahan; in Tabriz and Qazvin the prefect and mufti also fell to the *fidai'in*'s daggers. In 1138 they bagged their second caliph. Although in truth, Caliph al-Rashid had been 'retired' from the post by a panel of religious judges at Sultan Masud's express orders, because he had been playing the same empire-building games of his predecessor. The ex-caliph was marching on Alamut with a small force to revenge the killing of al-Mustarshid, but he fell sick on the way and was resting in Isfahan when *fidai'in* entered his audience chamber and stabbed him to death. Juvaini tells us that, 'from that time onwards the Abbasid Caliphs went into hiding and concealed themselves from the people,'† which was all fine for Sultan Masud and brought another seven-day celebration to Alamut. This apparently included the beating of kettledrums and blowing of trumpets from the ramparts of the fortress. Evidently Hasan's

---

* Juvaini, *Chinggis Khan*, pp. 684–5.
† Juvaini, *Chinggis Khan*, p. 686.

interdiction on music had been allowed to lapse, or was at least ignored on very special occasions. The Nizaris also deployed regular forces to capture a Shiite preacher, a certain Abu Hashim, who had tried to set up an alternative radical religion to Ismailism in the villages at the edge of the Nizari domains. The Nizaris read the proofs of their religion to Hashim while they burned him.

It was business as usual for the Assassins despite Umid's death from natural causes in February 1138, but normal business was becoming more and more difficult for Sanjar. Just to the south of the Aral Sea, a dynasty grew up from Turkish emirs who had stayed loyal to Malikshah but who upon his death began a quick march towards independence from the Saljuqs. These petty kings, perhaps somewhat pretentiously, took the title of Khwarazm shahs, and by the late 1130s they had become a discernable threat to the far north-east of Sanjar's lands, just at a time when direct confrontation with the Khitai also seemed unavoidable. In 1141, Sanjar was totally defeated by the Khitai on the Qatwan steppe near Samarqand. He bravely rode into the Khitai lines at the head of his personal bodyguard of three hundred men and emerged with only fifteen remaining; a similar rate of attrition was applied to the rest of his army by the Khitai archers. It was to be only the first taste of the disasters that would come to Islam from Central Asia. The Khitai army was decidedly similar to the Mongol hordes of steppe archers that Chinggis Khan and his successors would later unleash on Persia.

With one battle, Sanjar lost lands across the Oxus River that Islam had held since 751, but even then his problems were not over – his chastisement at the hands of the Khitai just seemed to make the Ghuzz Turks within the *Dar al-Islam* more truculent. The Ghuzz killed a dues collector and refused to send meat to the sultan's table. The *shahna* was sent to investigate and to bring the Ghuzz back into line, but they claimed the special rights of appeal to the sultan given to them in the reign of Malikshah. When the *shahna* returned with troops to back up his refusal to call the sultan into the affair, he and his son were killed by the Ghuzz. Sanjar reluctantly, and chiefly at the behest of his emirs, went to war with the Ghuzz – battle was joined in 1153 and Sanjar was defeated. His great cities of Marv and Nishapur were sacked and, worse still, he was captured.

The Ghuzz held him for three years in a cage, although oddly enough they still recognised him as their sultan and placed him on a throne during the day, and then returned him to his coop at night. He did eventually manage to escape his royal captivity, but died, broken by his experiences, soon after in 1157. The Ghuzz may have needed to have a sultan, even if they were his jailers, simply because they were unable to produce a government of their own. Ghuzz tribes overran Khurasan and Kirman but, unlike the Saljuqs, these tribes never accepted Islam or its cultural institutions. There was to be no order at all, to speak of, until the rise of the Khwarazm shahs from their regional obscurity, at the end of the century.

With the death of Sanjar, the eastern Saljuq Empire was effectively at an end – its demise had essentially been brought about by the knife stroke of one Assassin in 1092. The Assassins had acquired a new leader in 1138, in the form of Umid's son, Muhammad, and the early part of his reign shows an odd provincialism in the Ismaili chronicles. Successful cattle-rustling raids are recorded proudly, as is the failed and half-hearted attack by Sultan Masud on Alamut in 1143. However, most of the warfare recorded in the chronicles was related to a vicious local contest with the Saljuq governor of Rayy, who built towers out of the skulls of those whom he merely suspected of being Ismaili. The governor was eventually bought to heel on the orders of Sanjar, who also found him to be a problem, and he was later murdered in Sultan Masud's court in Baghdad. Sanjar received his head in a box; perhaps it cheered him a little after the events of 1141.

In a rare break from the narrow local politics and murder described above, in 1143 the minor Saljuq sultan in control of Baghdad, Daud, was assassinated. He was far from his realm and visiting Tabriz, when four Syrian *fidai'in* took his life. The Assassins involved in the killing were listed in the roll of honour kept in Alamut, which recorded both the victims of the Assassins and the *fidai'in* who carried out the murders. This was indeed odd, as the men had most definitely come from Syria, not from Persia, and had acted at the very least in connivance with, and at the worst in direct collaboration with, Zangi, the ruler of Mosul and leading light of the Syrian *jihad* against the Crusaders.

To discover why Zangi wished Daud dead, why he was fighting a counter-Crusade, and even how the Crusaders had ever managed to take most of Syria and threaten Egypt with their dominion in the first place, we have to go back once again to the Assassins' daggers, the death they brought and the fear they inspired.

4

NEW BLOOD IN A NEW LAND

THE ASSASSINS IN SYRIA

In this year also news was received from Homs that its lord, the emir Jana al-Dawla Husain Atabeg on descending from the citadel to the mosque for the Friday prayer, surrounded by his principal officers with full armour, and occupying his place of prayer, according to custom, was set upon by three Persians belonging to the *Batini*. They were accompanied by a sheikh, to whom they owed allegiance and obedience, and all of them were dressed in the garb of ascetics. When the sheikh gave the signal they attacked the emir with their knives and killed him and a number of his officers. There were in the mosque at the time ten Sufis, Persians and others; they were suspected of complicity in the crime, and were straightaway executed in cold blood, every man of them, although they were innocent. The people of Homs were greatly perturbed at this event, and at once dispersed in panic. Most of the Turks amongst the inhabitants fled to Damascus . . .

*From the Damascus Chronicle of Ibn al-Qalanasi for the year 1102–3**

THE TACTICS USED IN Persia were repeated in Syria to good effect. Political murder was followed by political chaos and this allowed the Nizari Assassins to extend their control over both the territory and the loyalties of petty rulers and people. What was different in Syria was that there was a political wild card, in that Crusaders had entered the region in 1095. Despite their near destruction at both the Battle of Dorylaeum and the siege of Antioch, the Crusaders had completed the political fragmentation of the Levant by carving out, by the beginning of the twelfth century, a strong position on the Syrian coast, and around Jerusalem. They had also gained outposts as far inland as Edessa. In his chronicle, the *Historia Hierosolymitana*, Fulcher of Chartres asked why the many kingdoms of Islam feared to attack this little occidental colony and its people, and why Egypt, Persia, Mesopotamia and Syria did not

---

* H. Gibb, *The Damascus Chronicles of the Crusades*, London, 1932, pp. 56–7.

send 'at least a hundred times a hundred thousand fighters' into the field to destroy the Frankish Kingdom of Jerusalem. The pious historian attributed the miracle of the survival of the Crusaders to God's will. Certainly religion had something to do with it, but it was the faith and *dawa* of, first the Fatimids, and then the Nizari Assassins, that called into existence the exhausted and distracted state of Syria that the Crusaders entered in 1097. They had also ensured that the Crusaders would never face the full power of the Islamic world.

From as early as the tenth century, there had been Fatimid Ismaili religious missions operating in Syria. They had been sent to cultivate the peoples before the expected push of the Fatimid armies through Syria and on to Baghdad. But as we have seen, the Fatimid Islamic world-domination project effectively ran out of steam after the disappearance of Caliph Hakim in 1021, stalled in Syria and subsequently went into reverse once the Saljuqs had reinvigorated the Sunni cause, following their taking of Baghdad in 1055. The Fatimid *dawa* had, however, made successful inroads into much of Syria and left behind pockets of Mustali Ismailis.

The Sunni renaissance in Syria under their new champions began with the first Turkish invasions of 1063. In 1077 an attempt was made to invade Egypt itself, and by 1079 the Turks had lieutenants in both Damascus and Jerusalem, with Nizamiyya *madrasas* propagating the Sunni creed all over northern Syria. During this push west, the Turks met, almost inadvertently, the Byzantines in battle. The Saljuq sultan, Alp Arslan, had tried through parley to avoid a confrontation with the Byzantines, but the problem was that the sultan did not have total control of the Turcomen who had been raiding Byzantine lands. Indeed these Turcomen had been sent to the west of the sultanate, partly to fight the Fatimids, but also to remove their destructive tendencies from the heart of the Saljuq empire. The sultan therefore could not give a cast-iron guarantee that they would not continue their assaults against the Greeks in Anatolia. Meanwhile, the Greek emperor, Romanus, was spoiling for a fight. He had brought his army into Anatolia to secure the border, but the exercise had not gone well. His army was constantly harassed by Turks using hit-and-run raids, which even extended into the night. He was under political pressure at home to get a result, and his army, particularly the Turkish mercenary component, was deserting at an alarming rate. He rushed into battle with the sultan, without really thinking about what he was doing.

The emperor's army met the sultan's forces near Manzikert on 19 August in 1071, in one of history's most significant battles, and the Greek army was annihilated. Or at least those who stood with the emperor were. Many of the Greek nobles deserted their leader early on in the fight. The capture and subsequent ransoming of Romanus was enough to end his reign and the panicking Byzantines, fearing that the Turks would follow up their victory by crossing the Bosporus, sent missives to the pope asking for a western army to come to their aid. The Turks were, however, looking south, not north, and began again their war with the Fatimids. By 1092 only the Syrian coastline remained in the hands of the Fatimids and they were only able to hold on to these cities because the Egyptian navy maintained supplies to their besieged garrisons.

The killing of Nizam al-Mulk brought all this Saljuq success to an end. The fragmentation of Persia and its polity brought about by this one assassination, and the death of Sultan Malikshah soon after, has been discussed above, but the situation was even worse in Syria. Tutush, the brother of Sultan Malikshah and ruler of Damascus, upon hearing of Malikshah's death began his preparations for taking over the entire Saljuq Empire. He mustered his army and began occupying the territories of Syria one after another. Between 1092 and 1095, he conducted bloody campaigns that brought Syria's infrastructure close to collapse. His objective was to take Aleppo and Antioch and other minor dependencies, before challenging his nephew Berkyaruq in 1095. He managed to take the cities, but failed in his larger enterprise. Berkyaruq, despite his youth, defeated his uncle and Tutush died in battle. Shortly after, an Assassin made an attempt on Berkyaruq's life and it took the new sultan some considerable time to recover from his wounds.

If Berkyaruq had died, the western Saljuq Empire would probably have disintegrated in just the way that the eastern part did, only sixty years later under Sultan Sanjar. As it was, the death of Tutush meant that Saljuq Syria fractured into a collection of city-states without any bond to one another. This was the favourable political situation that faced the Crusaders as they began their march into Syria in 1097. Furthermore, each of these city-states was governed by men mutually suspicious of each other's motives. It also meant that the two most important cities of Syria, Damascus and Aleppo, fell to the inexperienced sons of Tutush to govern. Neither of these sons was capable of dealing with the ongoing economic, political and agricultural crisis that the long Fatimid–Saljuq confrontation in Syria had brought about. The power vacuum that Tutush's sudden death left in the countryside also allowed opportunistic and independent-minded Bedouin regimes to take control. Their nomadic pastoralism particularly damaged the agricultural resources of Damascus and Aleppo, and also limited safe communications between all the cities of Syria.

There followed plague that affected the area in 1097, 1099 and 1100. All of this meant that, for Aleppo and Damascus, a long war against the Crusaders was not economically sustainable. This, however, did not stop the two brothers, Ridwan of Aleppo and Duqaq of Damascus, from undertaking short wars against each other in 1096 and 1097. The conflicts between the two were brief because neither Aleppo nor Damascus had many troops – another impediment to challenging the Crusaders. Many Saljuq emirs and their troopers were simply deserting Syria for the lucrative business of the Saljuq civil war in Persia. Baghdad changed hands some thirty times between October 1099 and April 1101, and both sides were paying well for more troops. The emirs also returned to Persia to ensure the safety of their *iqtas*, compared to which, their Syrian possessions were worthless.

Syria was therefore of little value to the Saljuqs, now that the Nizari Assassins had caused Persia to teeter on the brink of collapse, following their murder of Nizam al-Mulk, but it was really very attractive to the Nizaris themselves. Hasan-i-Sabbah had sent *dais* to the region probably as early as 1100 and he must have known that he was throwing seeds into fertile land. Syria was a heterogeneous mix of Arabs, Greeks and Armenians in the cities, and the populace viewed their Turkish masters as tax-hungry tyrannical aliens. The Saljuq invasions had caused enormous social upheaval, overthrowing Arab landowners, traders and bureaucrats, who had been the dominating element in earlier times.

The people of Syria were also renowned for being politically and religiously militant, and the Turkish rulers of cities often had cause to fear the mob. Unpopular leaders like Ridwan of Aleppo had particular dread of a popular revolt. There was also a very free mix of religions in Syria, despite the Saljuqs' attempts to bring orthodoxy to the region. Large minorities of Maronite Christians and Druze and Nusayri Muslims existed, as well as the 'left over' Fatimid Mustali Ismailis discussed above.* Many of these Mustali Ismailis converted to the Nizari branch once the

---

* Even in recent times, Lebanon, which effectively made up much of the coast of medieval Syria, nicely reflected this mix of creeds. When forming its first independent government in 1943, it had to assure a 6:5 fixed ratio of Christian to Muslim seats and cabinet-level positions for every sect's representatives, including Shiites of various

New Preaching was established. The Nizari *dais* could then expect, at the least, more tolerance from these groups than they had received from the Sunnis of Persia – perhaps even assistance in what might be called a religious 'popular front' against persecution by local Sunni Turkish rulers and Sunni clerics.

The first readily identifiable Assassin leader in Syria was al-Hakim al-Munajjim, 'the physician-astrologer', and it seems that he followed the Nizari blueprint for acquiring fortified places, but with a new twist. Ridwan of Aleppo was easily identified as a leader with a particularly weak powerbase, an ambition to take his brother's dominions and a large Shiite population in his city, of which he was afraid. A few years earlier he had even proclaimed Fatimid allegiance as a means to shore up his domestic approval. Al-Munajjim seems to have presented himself and his followers to Ridwan as 'fixers', who could take care of all his political and population concerns, in return for the free use of Aleppo as a base for propagating their faith, and the chance to obtain the highly desired fortresses.

The physician-astrologer quickly organised the killing of al-Dawla of Homs, as described by al-Qalanasi at the head of this chapter. This removal of one of Ridwan's political enemies, who was also an ally of his brother in Damascus, pleased the prince enough for him to grant the Nizaris a house of propaganda in the city. It was al-Munajjim's last killing, after which he died of natural causes – a common achievement of Assassin chiefs at this time, it would seem. He was succeeded by Abu Tahir al-Saigh, a goldsmith, who made it his business to attempt the capture of a series of mountain strongholds to the south of Aleppo, which the killing of al-Dawla had left without an effective overlord. Their first attack was on the castle of Afamiya, which Ridwan had lost to a lord called Khalaf, who had made his living by banditry some years earlier.

The Aleppan Assassins' approach to the castle's capture was highly ingenious. They first made contact with Ismailis inside the castle, who, like the robber lord, were devotees of the Fatimid creed, but who, unlike him, were now about to change their colours. Then six of them obtained, perhaps through the medieval equivalent of car-jacking, a Crusader's horse, mule and armour and proceeded to the castle's front gate There they hailed the lord and claimed that they wished to enter his service and had brought these goods as proof of their fighting worth and as a gift to

---

leanings and the Druze, in order to form a nation-state. Medieval Syria's religious politics would have been just as complex.

their new potential master. Khalaf took the men into his service and into the citadel of his castle, where they wasted no time in tunnelling through the wall to allow their new converts in the castle's lower town to slip into the citadel. There they gathered slowly until their force was large enough to be able to move through the castle killing all Khalaf's guards and the robber lord, along with his entire family. As Khalaf woke to find a *fidai* at his bedside, he is said to have stuttered out the question, 'Who are you?' The reply cannot have lessened his fear, 'I am the Angel of Death come to take your soul.'

In early 1106, Abu Tahir came down from Aleppo to assume control of the Assassins' first castle in Syria. He was not to be allowed to enjoy it for long. The Crusader lord, Tancred of Antioch, was campaigning nearby and evidently saw an opportunity for mischief.* He quickly captured the brother of one of the senior Afamiya Ismaili converts and marched on the castle. At first, he simply besieged the castle until the Assassins agreed to pay tribute, but after a few months he tightened the siege and forced Abu Tahir and his men into capitulation. They first had to arrange for their own ransoms to be paid by their compatriots in Aleppo, they were then packed off once again to do the dirty work of Ridwan, in the hope of being granted a second chance at obtaining a useable headquarters.

In 1111, the Saljuq sultan of Persia, Muhammad, had managed to calm things enough in his own lands to contemplate trying to bring the Syrian provinces back under Isfahan's control. This was presented as a *jihad* against the Crusaders, but it was obvious to the petty princes of the Levant and the Assassins what this invasion really meant. Ridwan closed Aleppo's gates to the sultan's 1111 expedition and the sultan's army destroyed the countryside surrounding Aleppo to a far greater extent than Crusaders had ever done. The expedition's leaders had evidently expected much, much more of the lord of Aleppo:

> They had expected that either the king, Fakhr al-Muluk Ridwan, lord of Aleppo, would himself come out to join them, or else his officers would join them by his command. But he paid no heed to any of them, and shut the gates of Aleppo, took hostages from the townsmen into the citadel, and organised his troops with the armed bands of the *Batinis* and the loyal citizens for garrison duty to guard the city wall and to prevent the citizens

---

* Tancred fully embraced oriental politics, despite being a Norman knight who had only arrived in the Levant with the First Crusade. He titled himself Grand Emir of Antioch and in 1108 even fought with Islamic allies against Baldwin le Bourg over Edessa in the Battle of Tel Bashir.

1.	Bukhara was left virtually bereft of life by Chinggis Khan in 1220. It was only a foretaste of what the Mongols would bring to Persia in their campaigns against the Assassins.

2.	Isfahan was the site of a massacre by the city's Sunni populace of supporters of the Assassins. Many were crucified and the Assassins' riposte was to start a systematic campaign of murder against Sunni religious leaders. The Assassins' first great enemy and victim, Nizam al-Mulk, is also buried in the city's main mosque compound.

3.	The classic novel *Alamut* by Vladimir Bartol, first published in 1938, is based on the story of the Assassin grand master Hasan-i-Sabbah. The novel's central theme is that, 'nothing is real, everything is allowed'. In fact such sentiments belong more correctly in the reigns of later grand masters. Hasan was a strict disciplinarian and even put his own sons to death for breaking the rules of the order.

4. The caliph before Hulegu. Hulegu is about to have the caliph executed and extinguish the Abbasid caliphate. The Assassins had fought the caliphs for over one hundred and fifty years but were soon to share its fate at the hands of the Mongols.

5. Rustam slaying the White Div from the Persian classic *Shahnama* (Book of kings). The ongoing influence of ancient Persian culture was enough to ensure that Persian nationalism, a major factor in the initial formation of the Assassins Order, survived the Arab conquest of the seventh century *Freer Gallery*.

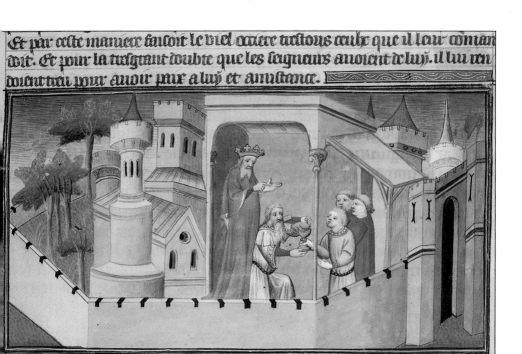

Et par ceste maniere faisoit le viel acroire trestous ceulx que il leur coman doit. Et pour la tresgrant doubte que les seigneurs auoient deluy. il lui ven doient trieu pour auoir paix a luy et amistance.

. Ala al-Din Muhammad drugging his disciples before they set off to assassinate his nemies. From *Le Livre des Merveilles* (1410–12), recounting the travels of Marco Polo 1254–1324). *Bibliotheque Nationale Paris.*

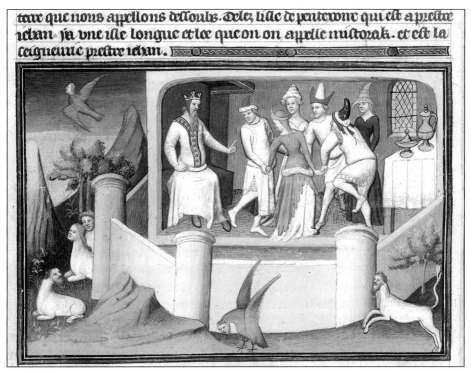

terre que nous appellons dessoubs. Delez liste de prestreiehan ja vne isle longue et lee que on on apelle multorak. et est la seigneurie prestre iehan.

. The garden of the Old Man of the Mountain with his boy Assassins from *Le Livre es Merveilles* (1410–12), recounting the travels of Marco Polo (1254–1324). *Bibliotheque Nationale Paris.*

8. The siege of a Turanian stronghold by the forces of Kai Khusraw from a *Shahnama* (Book of kings) by Firdawsi in the fifteenth-century Turkoman dynasty. Saljuq sieges of the Assassins' castles nearly all ended in failure. It wa only with the arrival of the Mongols in the Middle East with their Chinese siege engineers that the fortresses began to fall. *Freer Gallery*.

9. Bird-shaped vessel, twelfth century, Saljuq Dynasty, Persia. Beautiful metalwork of this kind was commonly produced in Persia by guilds. These guilds were strong sources of support and finance for the Assassins. *Freer Gallery*.

10. The Prophet enthroned and the four orthodox caliphs from a *Shahnama* by Firdawsi in the early fourteenth-century Ilkhanid dynasty, Shiraz, Iran. Three of the four caliphs would be murdered and Ali's slaying heralded the schism within Islam that would, in time, lead to the creation of the Assassins Order. *Freer Gallery*.

بجائی که او دارد آرام گاه
نشست سپید چون باده بر دو لب
جو آتش بدید آذرکیان شد

بنا بد بپا بندۀ داد خواه
دمان تا در خان آذرکشیب
جو بر آتش نیر بریان شد

برین راز کشیدند مر دو یکی
برفتند با جامهای سپید
مرا اینجا یکه زار دکریان دو

کنگر یدک تن زر آهن از
پر از تن دل یک یک پکر او
بپیش خدا وند خورشید و

جهان آفرین را همی خواندند
یک مهره برپش ایشان
که خجست اندیشه کرد و درا

بر آن موبدان کوم افشاندند
میدارک آتش برپشان بد
هم از پاک نو بی بناز

جو چهر و بآب مژده گشت
که آتش بد الکا محراب
یک آه درآ ذرابا کان

برافتند دینار برزنده
پرسپنده را دیده پر آب او
بود ند نذ شاهان وازاد کان

که سرکه نغار از جهان نسود
بغار اندرون جا باب آلای با
زکرده بیشیان و دل پر

نبر دکیک برد ع یکی خار بود
ی ساخت
خورش برد و ازم پیم جان جان
سمی بود جندی نجانه در ولن

که باشد یگان ایمن وتن در
نه زیرپش بی سترو جای کران
جو خانه همی کسدی افرا آسیا

همی از جهان جای کلالحنت
نديد ازيرش جاى پرواز نا
زسرشهرو درو تبر دیک آ

11.   Kay Kavus and Kay Khusraw approach the Fire Temple. From a manuscript of the *Shahnama* by Firdawsi [d. 1020], dated 1482, Turkoman dynasty, Persia. Zoroastrianism, the pre-Islamic faith of Persia, was among many pre-Islamic belief systems in Persia that may have influenced the beliefs of the Assassins. *Freer Gallery.*

12. A *Sufi* riding a leopard, from a copy of the *Bustan* (The Orchard) by Sa'di, 1525, Safavid Dynasty, Afghanistan. The picture indicates the level of esoteric belief prevalent in Persia in the Middle Ages. Such mysticism was a major component of the belief systems of the Assassins. *Freer Gallery.*

13.   A page from the Mughal emperor Akbar's copy of the *Chinghiz-nama* (The History of Genghis), a portion of the *Jami al-Tawarikh* (History of the World) by the Islamic statesman and historian Rashid al-Din (1247–1318). The illustration shows Hulegu standing on a rampart above the gates of Alamut after its surrender on 15 December 1256. *Virginia Museum of Fine Arts*.

14. An *iwan* of the city of Qazvin's main mosque. Men, women and children were slaughtered in the concentration camps that the Mongols set up outside the city in their final destruction of the Assassins Order. Even babes in their cradles were murdered.

15. The mausoleum of Sultan Sanjar. The sultan had two major preoccupations in his reign – the Assassins and the continual pressure of the Turco-Mongolian tribes to the east of Persia. He concluded a *modus vivendi* with the Assassins but could not stem the advance of the Steppe peoples into Islam.

16. The Assassins have returned to our culture as the central characters of the computer game *Assassins Creed*©. The game emphasises the Assassins' code of secrecy, their ability to penetrate even the closest of bodyguards and the massive political implications of their killings. *Image by very kind courtesy of Ubisoft.*

1. With the fall of Jerusalem to Saladin in 1187 the fate of the Assassins and the Crusaders in Syria seemed sealed. Upon Saladin's death, however, Muslim Syria fractured once more and the Assassins thrived, as they always did in times of political discord.

2. The founder and first master of the Assassins, Hasan-i-Sabbah, is depicted here in an eighteenth-century sketch, purportedly 'drawn from witnesses' descriptions'.

3. Whilst there is no truth in the tale of the famous mathematician and poet Omar Khayyam being a schoolfellow of Hasan-i-Sabbah, the first Assassin grand master, his twelfth-century poems reflect a desperation within Persian society that would have driven young men towards radical groups such as the Assassins.

4. The tomb of Saladin. Despite three attempts on his life by the Assassins, Saladin managed to die of natural causes. He may even have conspired with the Assassins to secure the murder of Conrad of Montferrat, Jerusalem's king in waiting.

5. *Sufis* from the late Ottoman Empire. Such men were responsible for the conversion of Saljuq Turks to Sunnism in eleventh-century Persia. This would lead to the Sunni Turks contesting northern Persian with the Shiite Ismaili Assassins, and bloody massacres of Ismailis in Persia's cities.

6. The Aqsa Mosque in Jerusalem was redecorated by the Shiite Fatimids after their conquest of Jerusalem and Syria. Their war with the Sunni Saljuqs over Syria, however, left the region distracted and weak. An ideal state for the Assassins to thrive in.

7. The citadel of Aleppo. In 1113 followers of the Assassin creed were hurled from its walls by a Sunni mob as the *jihad* against both the Assassins and the Crusaders began to crystallise.

Below, left:
8. The minaret of Aleppo's Great Mosque. The bazaar that was situated in front of the mosque was burned down by Assassin commandos as a reprisal for the seizure of one of their villages.

Below, right:
9. The gateway of Aleppo's citadel showing interlaced snakes. There was a similar intertwining of the Turkish 'men of the sword' and the Syrian Sunni clerics or 'men of the pen' against the Assassins that was the genesis for the Syrian Sunni *jihad* aimed at the destruction of both the Assassins and the Crusaders.

10.   The retaking of Jerusalem from the Crusaders by Islam also meant that the city and its holy places returned to the Sunni division of the faith from the Shiite Fatimids. This is the *minbar* of the Sunni champion Nur al-Din.

11.   The minaret of the Great Mosque in Mosul. The Sunni *jihad* that would eventually clear Syria of both the Assassins and the Crusaders began among the princes of Mosul and the Jazira.

12.   The Mosque of the Barber in Kairouan was said to have held three hairs from the Prophet Muhammad's beard. Perhaps this was why it was the starting point for the Fatimid Shiite Revolution. The Fatimids were in many ways the parents of the Assassins but their dynasty later fell as a victim to the daggers of their estranged offspring.

13. The Great Mosque of Mecca with the Kaaba. In 930 the Qarmatians, radical Shiites and forerunners to the Assassins, slaughtered 13,000 pilgrims here and stole the holy black stone from the Kaaba.

14. The Kaaba in Mecca [See above].

Above and right:
15a and 15b.   The great college mosque of al-Azhar was built by the Fatimids in Cairo to produce religious agents and missionaries. This policy would rebound on them, however, as many of their later enemies among the Assassins underwent their original training here. *15a courtesy of Bean Edge.*

16.   The Syrian Assassin castle of Maysaf. The Ismaili Assassins began to infiltrate Syria in the late eleventh century but it was at the end of the twelfth century, under the charismatic leader Rashid al-Din, that they pulled off their greatest coup with the murder of Conrad of Montferrat, the king-elect of Outremer. *The Taylor Library.*

7a–c.   The forbidding nature of the
Ilburz Mountains was enough to put
off a besieging army even before they
reached the walls of the Assassins'
castles.

18. The murder of Nizam al-Mulk in 1092. This killing was a huge coup for the Assassins and a disaster for the Saljuq Empire, which splintered upon the death of its chief minister. *Topkapi Sarai Treasury.*

19. In the courtyard of the Great Mosque of Damascus the Assassins killed the emir Mawdud who was leading an expedition against the Crusaders. Despite the emir's large bodyguard one *fidai* was able to strike him down. By this act the Crusaders and the emir of Damascus were saved from the Sultan of Iraq's army. Spectacular and very public killings such as this also increased the fear of the Assassins' blades among Syria and Persia's nobility. *Photo Courtesy of Bean Edge.*

from ascending it. Besides this he gave a free hand to the brigands to seize whosoever they could from the fringes of the army.*

It is obvious that the 'brigands' were Assassins. Only the *fidai'in* of the Nizari *Batinis* would have had the skill to snatch individuals from the expedition's camp. Their murder and abduction of troops from the army's camp made Ridwan a wanted man among the Saljuqs of Persia. Their other role of guarding the citadel and taking hostages from the populace made them unpopular with the Sunnis of Aleppo. The expedition's leader, Mawdud, the emir of Mosul, returned two years later with orders from the sultan to bring all the Saljuq emirs of Syria together to launch an assault on the *Franj* – the Franks – but the order deliberately excluded Aleppo from this hopeful union of Muslims.

Mawdud established himself in Damascus, which had fallen into the care of Tughtigin. Tughtigin had been the *atabeg*, or guardian, of the son of Duqaq of Damascus but when both Duqaq and his son died, this had left him effectively as the prince of the city, but without a crown. It was this lack of legitimacy that may have required him to allow the sultan's forces into Damascus since he needed a caliphal diploma to rule lawfully and the caliph was under the sultan's power. In fact, Tughtigin feared that Mawdud might use his forces to take Damascus away from him. He would have taken warning from the fact that Mawdud had become emir of Mosul by virtue of having led an expedition that the sultan of Baghdad had sponsored against its independent ruler in 1108.

The subsequent assassination of Mawdud in Damascus was almost certainly instigated by Ridwan, but Tughtigin's complicity cannot be ruled out; following a victory for the joint Damascus–Mosul forces over the Kingdom of Jerusalem at al-Sinnabrah, the forces of Damascus did not march on with the army of Mosul to attempt the capture of any towns, but rather concentrated on plundering the environs of Jerusalem and Jaffa. The lord of Damascus appears to have been happy to see the Franks 'reined in', since they had been raiding the lands of Damascus with increasing frequency, but he was reluctant to see Mawdud gain a foothold in the region by taking fortified towns from the Franks. He was also keen for the Franks to remain an effective deterrent to the Great Saljuqs' ambitions in Syria. The *atabeg* therefore had to show some decidedly neat footwork in order to survive as Damascus's prince, both politically and in a very real sense:

---

* Gibb, *The Damascus Chronicles*, p. 115.

On the last Friday of the Second Rabi of the year 507 [2 October 1113] the emir Mawdud came as was his custom from the encampment at the meadow outside the Iron Gate to the Cathedral Mosque, in the company of the *atabeg*. When the prayers were completed and Mawdud had performed some supplementary prostrations, they went out together, the *atabeg* walking in front by way of showing respect for him. Surrounding them both were Daylamites, Turks, Khurasanis, [militiamen] and armour bearers, with weapons of all kinds, fine tempered blades and keen thrusting swords, rapiers of various sorts and unsheathed poniards, so that they were walking as if in the midst of a tangled thicket of intertwined spikes, while the people stood round them to witness their pomp and the magnificence of their state. When they entered the court of the mosque, a man leapt out of the crowd, without exciting the attention of anyone, and approaching the emir Mawdud as though to call down a blessing on him and beg alms of him, seized the belt of his riding cloak and smote him twice with his poniard below the navel. One of the blows penetrated his flank and the other his thigh. As the Assassin struck his second blow swords fell upon him on every side and he was struck with every kind of weapon. His head was cut off that it might be known who it was but he could not be recognised, so a fire was kindled for him and he was thrown upon it. The *atabeg* had moved on some paces during the occurrence and was surrounded by his own officers, while Mawdud, controlling himself, walked on till he was close to the north gate of the mosque. There he collapsed, and was carried to the residence of the *atabeg* who walked alongside him. The people were at first cast into a great commotion and confusion, but afterwards calmed down on seeing the emir walking on. The surgeon was called for and sewed up part of the wounds, but he died, may God have mercy upon him, a few hours later on the same day.*

The fact that Mawdud was killed in such a public manner and in the mosque courtyard is not that surprising. The Assassins needed the maximum public exposure for their killings in Syria if they were to achieve their secondary aim of intimidation. Also medieval killings often required absolute proof of death for any murder or execution to have political value. The Mongols, for example, would distribute heads and even body parts around all parts of the dominions, in order to prove to everyone that a wrong-doer had been done away with and that equal punishment could be expected by all other miscreants. The Assassins had to rely on word of mouth to achieve the same effect.

There was, however, a downside to such sensational killings. In his chronicle, Ibn al-Athir claims that even the king of the Franks, Baldwin,

* Gibb, *The Damascus Chronicles*, pp. 139–41. The 'Cathedral Mosque' is the Great Mosque of Damascus, erected under the Umayyads in 706.

was incensed by such an ungodly murder in a place of worship. But this did not stop him and Roger, who had succeeded Tancred as lord of Antioch, from allying themselves with Damascus, Aleppo and Prince Il-Ghazi of Mardin in 1115, after Sultan Muhammad sent yet another expedition into Syria in order to bring *jihad* to the *Franj*, and doubtless also to punish Tughtigin. With religion put to one side, the union made perfect sense. On the Muslim side, there was simply no advantage to the Syrian leaders in the complete expulsion of the Franks from the Levant, if this meant a loss of their independence to Isfahan and Baghdad, and the Crusaders had to look for local and temporary allies to face a powerful foe.

Realpolitik was by now becoming the standard form of earthly endeavour for both the Knights of the Holy Crusade and for the Islamic princes of Syria. The Nizari Assassins, as always when political confusion was rife, prospered. Only a few months later, the Persian Saljuq army withdrew after being heavily defeated by Roger's forces at the Battle of Danith. This was to be their last attempt to bring Syria back into the Great Saljuq fold. The Assassins had, therefore, effectively seen off their fierce opponents from Persia in this, their new land, but their patron Ridwan had died in 1113, and his death had brought them new and deadlier enemies much closer to home.

As Ridwan lay dying in December 1113, Ibn al-Khashab, the Sunni *qadi* of Aleppo, and Ibn Badi, the leader of the city militia, gathered supporters and as many of the city's militiamen as they could trust, together. During the night, they spread out through the city, seizing and killing as many of the Nizari Ismailis as they could find. The *qadi* knew that he did not have the manpower to take on his Turkish overlords, but he hoped to deprive Ridwan's son and heir, Alp Arslan, of the support base his father had relied on and by virtue of this, to force the young prince, who was only sixteen, to depend on the Sunni body politic.

The *qadi's* policy seemed initially to be a success and Alp Arslan, perhaps sensing which way the wind was blowing, added his support to the anti-Nizari campaign. Abu Tahir was killed and about two hundred of his followers were also executed. Under the prince's guidance, the purge quickly became a bloodbath, as these things are wont to do, and was used as a cloak for the destruction of all possible opposition to the new reign. Certainly, several more Nizaris were executed, by being thrown off the citadel, but two of Alp Arslan's brothers were also executed and officers and palace functionaries were included in the indiscriminate slaughter.

Alp Arslan was eventually killed by one of his close servants named Lu Lu, in September 1114, as he slept. One of Ridwan's infant sons was then placed on the throne.

As discussed earlier, the city aligned itself with Damascus and Baldwin, against the sultan's forces, in 1115, but this did not stop Roger of Antioch from occupying the major fortresses ringing the city, in preparation for its reduction in the same year. In response to this threat Lu Lu, now the *atabeg*, called on Il-Ghazi of Mardin for support. Il-Ghazi quickly occupied Aleppo and was supported by the Sunni *ulama* of the city, who had been strengthened by the witch hunt of 1113 against the Nizaris. These same Sunni clerics had been the most voluble of all in their calls for *jihad* against the Franks, ever since the first refugees from the coastal cities, taken over the last few years by the Crusaders, had flooded into Aleppo. Indeed it was the same men who had started the pogrom against the Nizaris of Aleppo, that had taken their call for Holy War to Baghdad, as early as 1111. In a concerted campaign of protest against the sultan's inactivity, they disturbed the Friday prayers and broke the pulpit of the city's main mosque. This was a forceful political statement, as the pulpit symbolised the authority of the sultan. Contemporary Syrian literature also kept up the calls for *jihad*:

> Ungodliness has brought to Syria a blow from which Islam will resound endlessly
> Truth is ignored, crime is justified . . . and blood flows freely
> How many Muslims fatally wounded
> And Muslim women violated in the heart of the harem
> How many mosques changed into convents?
> The crucifix stands in the middle of the mihrab *

The phrases 'truth is ignored' and 'crime is justified', might well have been aimed at the Nizaris. Their deeds were seen by the Sunni populations of Aleppo and other cities as hampering the *jihad*. Certainly their unsuccessful attempt on the life of a Persian visitor to the city, who was either popular because of his fervent Sunnism or because of the way he threw his money around, was noted among their crimes by the local populace. In truth, however, to single out the Assassins was far from fair. The ineffective Muslim response to the Crusaders had as much to do with the desire among the petty princes of Syria to preserve their independence

---

* From an anonymous Syrian poet in E. Sivan, *L'Islam et la Croisade: Ideologie et Propagande dans le Reactions Musulmanes aux Croisades*, trans. M. McCrystall, Paris, 1968, p. 30.

as it did with the Nizaris. In fact, the Assassins were a target for the Sunni jurists calling for *jihad* simply because the Sunni concept of *jihad* involved far more than simple Holy War. It required just rule and Ridwan's use of the *Batinis* against his own people was in opposition to this. It also required a union between the men of the pen and Quran and the men of the sword which could not take place whilst heretics had the ear of the military men.

Al-Khashab, the *qadi* of Aleppo who had helped organise the anti-Nizari persecutions of 1113, had therefore apparently won another victory over them by securing Il-Ghazi's attachment to the Sunni factions of Aleppo. Before the Battle of *Ager Sainguinis*, or Field of Blood, in 1119, he preached to Il-Ghazi's troops whilst holding a spear, before they rode forward to assault Roger of Antioch's army. The incongruity of a religious judge on the field of battle is reflected in the disdain of some of the prince's troops for the presence of a 'turban' in their ranks. At the end of the battle, Roger was dead and his men and horses, according to Ibn al-Qalanasi, looked like stretched-out hedgehogs, such was the volume of arrows the men of Il-Ghazi had poured into them.

It was a great victory and it seemed to herald the emergence of the kind of union between faith and military action that had brought Islam its early conquests. The Sunni world had lost this union during its subjugation by professional Turkish military men. After the Fatimids fell under the power of their own *wazirs*, the Assassins were effectively the only political group to retain a direct link between military action and religious belief. Now the Assassins of Aleppo found themselves under pressure from just such a union, between the Sunni *ulama* and the Turkish prince Il-Ghazi. The organisation therefore went underground in Aleppo, but it was far from ready to cede the city to the Sunnis, and far from inactive in other arenas.

Many of the Nizari Assassins had to take refuge in Frankish lands during Il-Ghazi's reign and the lack of mountain refuges was evidently impairing the movement's success in Syria. A lifeline to Alamut was therefore vital in maintaining the continued flow of both Persian organisers and *fidai'in* to Syria. Whilst it is a matter of some controversy, it can be said with reasonable confidence that the Nizari Assassins of Alamut were, in this period, responsible for a number of killings in Christian Georgia, perhaps also in Azerbaijan, in order to keep open a corridor of communication with Syria. It also made sense for the Alamut Assassins to try to extend their influence in this region. Islam's

Georgian border was not well protected in this period as a result of the Saljuq civil wars that the Assassins themselves had started with their murder of Nizam al-Mulk. The Georgians took advantage of this to take territory from the Saljuq Empire and this, of course, placed pressure on the nearby Nizari state based around Alamut, and on communications between Alamut and the Syrian mission. In 1121, David IV of Georgia defeated Sultan Mahmud's army and took Tiflis. The Georgians refused to continue paying tribute to the Saljuqs from this point and attempted further expansion. Assassinations of Georgian lords, however, impeded any further push into the *Dar al-Islam*.

Through the corridor that the Assassins kept open between Alamut and Syria, Persian *dais* and *fidai'in* did manage to keep infiltrating Syria. From 1113 they cultivated the towns and villages around Aleppo, especially to its east where there was a significant Shiite population. By 1114 their renaissance in the region was so complete that they were able to send a force of one hundred men to take the castle of Shaizar, which had been conveniently abandoned by its Muslim lord and his men, as they had all been invited to watch a tourney celebrate Easter at a nearby Christian town. Upon their return, the now ex-tenants found the gates closed to them, but they rallied the townspeople of the castle's settlements and villages to their side, hastily formed an attack and after overwhelming the Nizaris, they killed them all. The lords of this castle were the family of Usama Ibn Munqidh, an Arab warrior who has left us a record of the period and of the action of the day:

> On that day I had an encounter with an Ismaili who had a dagger in his hand while I had my sword. He rushed on me with the dagger and I hit him in the middle of his forearm as he held the grip of the dagger in his hand with the blade close to his forearm. My blow cut off about four finger-lengths of the blade and cut his forearm in two in the middle. The mark of the edge of the dagger was left on the edge of my sword and the trace of it is there to this day . . .*

Usama's memoirs also show how the Assassins' blades were not just aimed at 'great' men. There was a low-level war between minor lords and the sect also taking place, over patches of territory, water sources and, of course, fortified places. The governor of a castle close to Shaizar told Usama how he was attacked by four *fidai'in*. The governor recalled how, after the attack, he said to a servant:

---

* Hitti, *An Arab-Syrian Gentleman and Warrior*, p. 146.

'The back of my shoulder is itching in a place I can't reach', and he called one of his attendants to see what had bitten him. The attendant looked and behold, there was a cut in which was lodged the point of a dagger which had broken in his back and which he had not known about . . .*

So the Assassins were up against tough men in this turf war, as Usama's next reminiscence makes clear:

One of our comrades, named Hammam al-Hajj had an encounter with one of the Ismailis when they attacked the Castle of Shaizar in a portico of my uncle's house . . . the Ismaili had in his hand a dagger while al-Hajj held a sword. The *Batinite* rushed on him with the knife but al-Hajj struck him with the sword above his eyes. The blow broke his skull and his brains fell out and were scattered over the ground. Al-Hajj laying his sword from his hand vomited all that he had in his stomach on account of the sickening he felt at the sight of those brains . . .†

The brains and chief organiser of the Assassins in Syria, now that Abu Tahir was dead, was named Bahram, and he had to wait some time before he could score a real success. Even then it was only an act of revenge and not the hoped-for gaining of a real foothold. Ibn Badi, the militia leader of Aleppo, who had been a joint organiser of the massacre of Nizaris in Aleppo in 1113, was expelled from the city by Il-Ghazi in 1119. The Sunnis had had their great victory over Roger of Antioch in the same year, but the Assassins had to make do with a much smaller triumph at a ford on the River Euphrates, where Ibn Badi and his two sons were crossing to take refuge in the city of Mardin; they were ambushed and knifed to death.

It was small recompense for all that they had lost, but the psychological impact of the killing was enough for the Assassins to be able now to make threats against Il-Ghazi, and everyone knew such threats were never empty. In 1120, they demanded a fortress from the prince of Aleppo – he acquiesced, but then very rapidly had the castle destroyed. He rather disingenuously excused himself from the Assassins' wrath by claiming that he had ordered the demolition but then revoked the order. He claimed that by the time his second message had got to the emir of the castle, the orders for its knocking down had already been carried out. No doubt a vengeance killing was planned against Il-Ghazi, but the prince died in 1122 of natural causes. Of course, someone had to pay and the

---

* Hitti, *An Arab-Syrian Gentleman and Warrior*, p. 148.
† Hitti, *An Arab-Syrian Gentleman and Warrior*, p. 146.

emir who had carried out the demolition was killed some years later when he had no doubt forgotten all about the incident. The Assassins had very long memories.

Il-Ghazi's death brought his son, Suleiman, to the throne of Aleppo, but his cousin Balak quickly usurped the crown after a whirlwind campaign of blockades and crop burning. In fact, this was to be a propitious regime change for the Sunni Aleppans, as Balak was strongly anti-Ismaili. He expelled all known and suspected Nizari sympathisers from the city after forcing them to sell their property and then proceeded to arrest a man suspected of being the representative of Bahram. The history of the sect as a real force in Aleppan politics ends with Balak's persecutions in 1122. The new prince of Aleppo was also a superb soldier, as well as a good Sunni, and he defeated and captured King Baldwin II in battle at Manzara in the same year. Unfortunately for the Sunni Aleppans, he was killed in 1124 at Manbj whilst besieging a rebel emir. He had just received an appeal for aid against the Crusaders from Tyre, and was making a last inspection of his mangonels surrounding the emir's castle before leaving for the coastal city, but he was hit by an arrow shot from the walls of the fortress. He pulled the arrow from his neck and with the words, 'that blow will be fatal for all the Muslims,' he then fell dead.

Once again the *realpolitik* of Syrian politics had reared its head. Turkish princes had to spend as much time fighting their peers and other pretenders as they did the Franks, but Balak's brief career as a *ghazi*, waging *jihad* against the King of Jerusalem, was enough to gain him a perhaps slightly exaggerated inscription on his tomb to this effect. It read, 'Sword of those who fight the Holy War, leader of the armies of the Muslims, vanquisher of the infidels and polytheists.'* It is evident from this that, by this time, a tradition of the Turkish princes from the house of Il-Ghazi fighting the Sunni *jihad* was certainly beginning to evolve. Al–Adim had written of Il-Ghazi's followers, '[They] bravely make it their duty to fight with heroism . . . they spill their blood for the holy war.'† The kind of harsh discipline that Hasan-i-Sabbah had used to form the cohesive and seemingly unbreakable strength of the Nizari Assassins was not present in the Sunni leaders of this embryonic *jihad*, but Balak seems to have maintained a strong adherence to the precepts of Islamic justice, '[He] would impale a Turk for taking a bit of meat from a

---

* S. Blair, *Islamic Inscriptions*, Edinburgh, 1988, p. 57.

† Sivan, *L'Islam et la Croisade*, p. 41.

poor man and he would not let anyone harm the [local] Christians even by word.'*

The Assassins seem to have realised that this Sunni *jihad* was not just aimed at the Crusaders and that the complete union of the Turkish military men and the Sunni *ulama* spelt danger for their mission in Syria. Other 'dissident' groups, such as native Christians in Aleppo, were already feeling the weight of this hardening of Sunni sentiment after Balak's death left them without a protector:

> A Muslim judge in Aleppo, Abu'l Hasan son of Khashab, told the Christians to rebuild the two mosques. Two bishops were in the town, an orthodox Edessene named Gregory and Samson, a Melkite. The church treasurers would not agree but said. 'We will not do this for we should open a door against ourselves that whenever a mosque is destroyed we must rebuild it out of church funds'. On the Friday at the judge's order thousands of Muslims with carpenters axes rushed to the churches, to Saint Jacob's, broke the pulpit and the angels of the altar, defaced the pictures, made an opening in the south wall of the sanctuary, prayed there, and made it a mosque. The same with the Greek church . . .†

The Assassins would therefore have been horrified to see the 'turban' Ibn al-Khashab, once again involving himself in military affairs and organizing the defence of Aleppo against a renewed Frankish threat, following the death of Balak. Il-Ghazi's son, Timurtash, had released King Baldwin II in exchange for a ransom of twenty thousand dinars. He also presented him with a gold helmet, but this chivalry was poorly repaid by Baldwin, who made another attempt on Aleppo.

Ibn al-Khashab did not waste time calling on Timurtash for assistance, since he was out of the city and did not seem to show much interest in returning to break the siege, but instead sent to al-Bursuqi, the emir of Mosul. He came at once and broke through the Franks' lines. It might be cynical to suggest that the chance of controlling both Mosul and Aleppo was too good an opportunity to miss for al-Bursuqi, but that is certainly not how the Islamic chroniclers saw it, and he certainly saved the city as its supplies were almost exhausted when he arrived. He then chased the Franks all the way back to Antioch according to Ibn al-Qalanasi, and

> By this Aq-Sunqur al-Bursuqi acquired great merit and renown, and having entered Aleppo, he governed it with uprightness and protected the interests

* H. Gibb, 'The First and Second Crusades from an Anonymous Syriac Chronicle', trans. A. Tritton, *Journal of the Royal Asiatic Society*, 1933, p. 92.

† Gibb, 'The First and Second Crusades', p. 94.

of its people, and made every effort to defend the city and keep the enemy at a distance from it. Thus its affairs were set in order, its districts restored to prosperity, its roads made safe, and caravans frequented it with their merchandise and objects of trade.*

This all sounds extremely pleasant and above all, ordered, and there was no place for the Nizari preaching in a well-ordered and 'just' society.

It was as if al-Bursuqi was following what might be called the first 'anti-terror guide' as written by Ibn Zafar al-Siqilli in the twelfth century. In his guide for rulers wishing to avoid rebellion in their lands, Ibn Zafar identifies the methods and philosophy a prince needs to employ: paternal affection for all subjects, vigilance over the populace, courage to defend the people, sagacity to delude foes and prudence to take advantage of every opportunity. If terrorism came to the prince's lands, he was advised to have patience and not give way to depression, execute strict justice, secure the roads and protect people seeking refuge, conciliate alienated subjects and show generosity and clemency.† This seems like good advice, even for governments today, and such actions completely stymied the Assassins' attempts to regain Aleppo.

The movement did best, as we have seen, in times of turmoil and when chaos reigned. They attempted to re-create just such conditions in Aleppo, by the murder of Ibn al-Khashab in the summer of 1125, as he left the great Mosque of the city. The *qadi* was fatally stabbed in the chest by a *fidai* disguised as an ascetic, but the political order of Aleppo could not now be smashed by just one killing. Later, in November 1127, al-Bursuqi saw himself in a dream, being torn apart by eleven dogs. He had his dream interpreted and was warned not to attend prayers the next day. He ignored the advice and was set upon by some eight *fidai'in* as he left the Friday Mosque.‡ His murder, however, did little more than vent Bahram's spleen and Ibn al-Qalanasi's chronicle tells us why: 'Al-Bursuqi was succeeded by his son, the emir Masud, who was noted for the nobility and purity of his character . . . and he maintained the laudable conduct and aims of his father; his power was thus firmly established and his affairs rightly and excellently ordered.'§

---

* Gibb, *The Damascus Chronicles*, p. 178.
† H. Dekmejian and A. Thabit, 'Machiavelli's Arab Precursor: Ibn Zafar al-Siqilli', *British Journal of Middle Eastern Studies*, Vol. 27, No 2, November 2000, pp. 125–37.
‡ Gibb, 'The First and Second Crusades', p. 96.
§ Gibb, *The Damascus Chronicles*, p. 178.

There was no chance against such 'excellently ordered affairs' and the Nizari Assassins headed away from Aleppo and towards the south. Bahram, apparently, was a master of disguise and he did not appear openly in Damascus until the end of 1126. By this time Tughtigin, who was already suspected of secret collusion with the Assassins back in 1113 with the killing of Mawdud, had accepted the bolstering of his forces by one hundred Nizari fighters. He took the Nizaris with him when he went out to meet the Franks in battle in January 1126. His army was routed by a furious and well-delivered Crusader charge, but the fact remains that the emir of Damascus was in cahoots with Bahram long before the *dai* revealed himself, and already so indebted to the Nizaris that when they asked for a castle he gave them one.

The fortress of Banyas was on the border with the Latin Kingdom, so perhaps Tughtigin thought he might make use of the Assassins' skills against the Franks. However, assassinations of Occidentals was a little way in the future yet, and the emir's granting of the fortress and an Ismaili house of propaganda in the city to Bahram may say more about his fear of the sect than any great defence planning on his part.

Bahram set about improving the fortifications of Banyas, aided by his 'rabble of varlets, half-wits, peasants, low fellows, and vile scum',* and at last, the Assassins had their bolt-hole. They soon needed it as they began a campaign of banditry in the region and attempted to extend their influence to the west around the river Jordan. The area was an enclave for Druze and Nusayri Muslims. Bahram's aim, therefore, may have been either to seek an alliance with these other persecuted sects, or to convert them. In order to achieve this, it was decided that the most powerful clan leader in the area should be killed – he was quickly captured, placed in fetters and then put to death in cold blood. This, however, caused a huge backlash among the very people the Assassins had wished to impress by their deed, and Bahram had to retreat to Banyas.

The Nizaris marched out of their new castle, later the same year, in order to crush a union of villagers and tribesmen that had formed around the dead man's clan, but as Bahram and his men camped ready for battle the next day, the tribesmen

> ...rose to meet him in a body like lions rising from their lairs to defend their cubs, and flew at them as mountain-hawks at partridges. On approaching his broken faction and god-forsaken host they charged upon them when

---

* Gibb, *The Damascus Chronicles*, p. 180.

they were in their camp and took them off their guard. Shouting the battle cry, they took them unawares, and ere the horseman could mount his steed or the foot soldier could seize his weapons death overtook the greater part of the *Batinis*, by smiting with the sword, abrading with the poniards of fate, sprinkling with the arrows of destruction, and stoning with the rocks of predestination . . .

Bahram's head and hand was cut off, after he had been dissected by swords and knives, and one of the slayers who took these along with his ring, to Egypt, carrying the joyful tidings of his death and destruction, was vested with a robe of honour and rewarded.*

Bahram's body parts were received with joy at the court of Cairo. This is not surprising considering that Syria was still seen as the rightful property of the caliphate of Egypt by Fatimids. The propaganda of the Nizaris against the Fatimids had also been so widespread and apparently so effective, in both Syria and even Egypt, that Caliph al-Amir felt compelled in 1122 to lay out 'once and for all' his family's legitimacy and claim to be the true imams. It perhaps seems churlish of the caliph to be refuting the claims of his now long-dead uncle Nizar, but the Fatimids were still technically at war with the Saljuqs, and very much at war with the Crusaders. The continued adherence of their followers in Syria was therefore vital to their war aims. The *sijill*, or epistle, was drafted by the theologians of the Cairo court and distributed all over Egypt and Syria.

The Fatimids were certainly at war with the Assassins. Al-Afdal, the *wazir* responsible for Nizar's dispossession and death had been assassinated in 1121 by Assassins sent from Aleppo. After this, the new *wazir* al-Mamun set his militia the task of rooting out any other *fidai'in*, and also tried to seal the border with Syria with road-blocks and stop-and-search policies. The remaining family of Nizar were also put under surveillance and his sister was made to listen to the first public proclamation of the caliph's anti-Nizar epistle.†

The first thing that should be noted about the Fatimids' war with the Crusaders was that, following the death of Tutush and the splintering of the Saljuq government in Syria, the Fatimids had been able to retake Jerusalem and other towns of the interior from the Turks, but they had not had sufficient time to consolidate their position before the

---

* Gibb, *The Damascus Chronicles*, pp. 189–91.
† S. Stern, 'The Epistle of the Fatimid Caliph al-Emir [al-Hidaya al-Amiriyya] – Its Date and Its Purpose', *Journal of the Royal Asiatic Society*, 1950, pp. 20–31.

Franks' arrival in Palestine. They were also still, in 1095, playing the 'Great Game' against the Saljuqs over the whole of the Levant, and it is feasible that the Fatimids would have not been entirely displeased by the formation of a Latin state in northern Syria. A contemporary writer, Al-Azimi, states that in 1095 the Byzantine emperor wrote to the Fatimids about the Crusade's arrival in Asia Minor.* The Fatimids may well have tried to utilise this outside force in their strategy to meet the Saljuq threat.

The Fatimids were accustomed to accounting for the presence of a third force in Syria: Byzantine operations in northern Syria were not uncommon in the late eleventh century. There is even, albeit tenuous, evidence of collusion between the Crusaders and Fatimids over northern Syria. The contemporary Arab writer al-Athir wrote that when 'the master of Egypt saw the expansion of the Saljuq Empire they took fright and asked the *Franj* to march on Syria.'† It is notable, however, that there is no other contemporary textual evidence for this complicity. What seems more likely is that al-Afdal had not colluded in the Crusader invasion, but when it took place he hoped that the diversion in the north would impair Saljuq attempts to recover in Syria. He therefore stood aside as the Crusaders conquered Antioch, but when the Crusade began its march south to Jerusalem, he reversed his policy, even imprisoning Frankish envoys sent to Cairo in 1098.

The Fatimid response to the Franks' invasion of the south was initially concerted, but ultimately unsuccessful. Their *jihad* failed on the battlefield, chiefly because of the fiscal exhaustion of Egypt and Frankish superiority at sea. The Crusaders were often engaged by the Fatimid army between 1099 and 1105. Due to the state reforms that al-Afdal had introduced, Egypt had, by this point, developed a medium-sized, well-developed army that was composed of various ethnic units. Fulcher of Chartres records the presence of Ethiopians in the Fatimid Jerusalem garrison, and how a wing of Arab cavalry encircled the Frankish rear at the Battle of Ascalon. This army brought defeat to the Franks at Ramla in 1103, but the Fatimids were unable to press their advantage to take Jaffa, as their naval blockade was cut short by the arrival of a pilgrim fleet. Any victories could also not be followed up by prolonged military deployment, simply because of lack of finance and overstretched

---

* C. Hillenbrand, *The Crusades: Islamic Perspectives*, Edinburgh, 1999, p. 44.
† A. Maalouf, *The Crusades through Arab Eyes*, trans. J. Rothschild, London, 1983, p. 44.

resources. Egypt, despite relief measures, had not fully recovered from the famine and virtual civil war that had afflicted the state between 1066 and 1073. The Nile valley remained under-populated and under-cultivated, and Syria had become largely independent of Egypt during the civil wars incited by the Turkish and Black troops, causing a further loss of revenue to the caliphate.

There was also the problem of western naval superiority, based around a new ship-building technology available in the docks of the Italian maritime republics. The depleted resources of Egypt did not allow it to match the volume of ships produced by Venice, Genoa and Pisa in this period. The loss of twenty-five ships in a storm, in 1105, was a heavy blow to the Fatimids' naval resources, but they enjoyed success at Sidon in 1108. The fleet, however, failed to save Tripoli in 1109 from the Genoese, and was trapped and badly mauled at Beirut in 1110. The coastal cities of Syria did not have their own warships, and the Byzantines had almost completely contained the Turkish naval threat by 1092. Egypt, therefore, fought the naval war single-handed, but despite this, and the obvious superiority of the Latins at sea, its *wazirs* managed to supply the Muslim cities of the Syrian coast until Tyre eventually fell in 1124.

Al-Afdal was, as has been discussed earlier, a soldier and not an ideologue. He wrote to the leaders, both military and religious, of Damascus in 1102, requesting 'the help of its army in the Holy War for Muslim land and Muslim folk'. The ideological opposition between the Sunni Turks and the Fatimids did therefore not preclude cooperation between the Egyptian caliphate and the local rulers of Syria – sometimes the need for alliance against the Franks prevailed over such ideals. A policy of cooperation was shown by Sunni Damascus's assistance to the Fatimid Syrian ports, which the Egyptian fleet was also defending, and by Damascene troops assisting the Fatimids at the battle of Ascalon in 1118 – from which their leaders earned Fatimid robes of honour.

Despite all this effort, the Fatimids were, however, effectively defeated by the Franks in Palestine. Poor battlefield leadership and low army morale may have been partly to blame. Lack of organisation at the higher levels of the state also ensured that it took up to two months for the Fatimids to mobilise and establish an army in Palestine. This ensured that the Franks had plenty of opportunity to reinforce their resources for each assault. Furthermore, the Fatimid army was always operating at a distance from its bases, whilst the Franks were operating within an area already consolidated by them. Al-Afdal was effectively robbed of victory many times, simply by bizarre occurrences that also hint at the poor condition of Fatimid military leadership. At one point, there was even a mini war between the Egyptian navy and the land forces. On another occasion the commander of the land forces was accidentally killed, and this was enough to break the army's will to continue. Ibn al-Athir wrote of how this superstitious general had received a prediction that he would die as the result of a fall from his horse, and how, when he became governor of Beirut, he ordered all the paving-stones removed from the streets, for fear that his horse might stumble. Then, just as battle with the Franks was commencing, his horse reared without having been attacked, and the general fell dead among his troops.

The Fatimids' withdrawal from the war for Syria was, however, not a direct result of Frankish victories per se. Egyptian 'isolationism' in the period immediately after 1125 was a result of sustained political crises. The slaying of al-Afdal by the Assassins in 1121 may well have been achieved with the connivance of the caliph – indeed in Syria it was believed that the Assassins were not even involved in the killing:

> In this year news arrived of the assassination of al-Afdal by the *Batinis* but this statement is not true. On the contrary it is an empty pretence and an insubstantial calumny. The real cause, upon which all accurate and indisputable narratives concerning this affair are agreed, was an estrangement between him and his lord, the Caliph al-Amir, arising out of al-Afdal's constraint upon him and restraining him from following out his inclinations, and the aversion which he had shown to him on several occasions . . . When he was killed al-Amir manifested unconcealed joy before all the courtiers and men of rank in Misr and Cairo. It is said also that the place of his assassination was in Misr on the middle of the bridge at the head of al-Suwaiqataon the last day of Ramadan. He was fifty-seven years of age at this time, having been born at Akka [Acre] in the year 458 [1066]. He was a firm believer in the doctrines of the Sunna, upright in conduct, a lover of justice. All eyes wept and all hearts sorrowed for him; time did not produce his like after him, and after his loss the government fell into disrepute.*

Al-Afdal's death began a veritable procession of nearly continuous infighting as *wazirs* and caliphs competed for the allegiances of army factions. Then in 1130 al-Amir, the tenth caliph, fell victim to the poniards of the *fidai'in*. The Arabic historian, Ibn Khaldun, tells us that:

---

* Gibb, *The Damascus Chronicles*, p. 163.

On Tuesday, the 3rd of the month, the caliph proceeded to Fustat and thence to the Island of Eoda, where he had built a pleasure house for a favourite Bedouin concubine. Some persons who were plotting his death were lying there concealed with their arms ready. As he was going by them, they sprang out and fell upon him with their swords. He had then crossed the bridge, and had no other escort than a few pages, courtiers, and attendants. They bore him in a boat across the Nile and brought him still living into Cairo. That night he was taken to the castle and there he died.*

This was enough to virtually kill the Fatimids as a political force to be reckoned with. Before this point, they had at least attempted to compete with the Franks for Syria. Indeed, the focus of the Fatimid resistance, Ascalon, was a Muslim shrine, and the Fatimid response to the Crusaders was *jihad*. Many historians have overlooked this, maybe because *jihad* was not, in this period, a discrete action in Shiism as it was for Sunnis. It was rather a consistent presence in the religion as we have seen with the continuing war of the Nizari Ismailis. The assassination of the caliph exhausted even this small flame of *jihad* and the ideological drive in the Fatimid dynasty completely died. The last four Fatimid caliphs in Cairo were not recognised as imams, and did not even attempt to claim the title. Even the Ismailis, who had remained faithful to the Fatimids, broke away from the Mustalian branch and many joined the Nizari Assassins. Egypt folded in on itself and awaited extinction – the only question now being who would claim the corpse.

Revolutions, according to Vergniaud, devour their own children, but in this case the Nizari Assassin rebels had brought destruction to an estranged parent. They continued the war against those they were not so closely related to in Syria. They were now under a new leader, another Persian named Ismail, who despite his propitious name and strong start to his rule, was to end his days in failure. Despite Bahram's death and the seizure of Banyas, the compliance of Tughtigin and the active assistance of his *wazir* seemed to herald great things for the Nizaris in Damascus. But Tughtigin died in 1128, and, as at Aleppo, the Assassins were undone by the actions of members of the Sunni *ulama*, who plotted with Tughtigin's heir Buri to kill his father's *wazir* and purge the city.

Ibn al-Athir reported in his later chronicle of the events of Syria that, 'al-Mazdaghani [the *wazir*] had written to the *Franj* proposing to hand over Damascus to them if they would give him the city of Tyre in return. Agreement had been reached. They had even set a date, a Friday.' This

---

* Ibn Khaldun, *Muqaddimah*, p. 467.

would explain the speed with which Buri and his comrades moved against the *wazir* and his Nizari supporters, but the Sunni chronicler was writing in the 1200s, when the notion of *jihad* against the Crusaders was well developed and he was undoubtedly biased. The Sunni chronicler Ibn al-Qalanasi had family who actually took part in the massacre of the Nizaris in Damascus. His contemporary account mentions nothing of any such conspiracy, but does talk of the boiling hatred of the people of Damascus towards both the *wazir* and the Nizaris. The Nizaris' arrogance, overconfidence and overt violence were perhaps their undoing:

> Their hands and tongues were lengthened by slander and abuse against the men of repute among the subjects, and with greed and spoliation against lonely travellers on the highway, whom they seized with violence and used despitefully, and with the slaying of men outrageously and unjustly . . .*

Their ruin came suddenly and without warning:

> On Wednesday 17th Ramadan 523 [4 September 1129] the *wazir* presented himself as usual with all the emirs and commanders in the Rose Pavilion at the Palace of the Citadel at Damascus, and various matters were transacted and discussed in the council with Buri and those present, until the hour of their withdrawal and return to their houses. The *wazir* rose to withdraw after them, according to his custom, and at that moment Buri gave the signal to his bodyguard, who struck the *wazir*'s head several blows with his sword and killed him. His head was then cut off, carried with his dead body to the ash heap at the Iron Gate, and thrown upon it, that all the people might see the act of God upon one who plotted and sought helpers other than Him [God]. His body was burned with fire some days later, and reduced to ashes strewn by the winds. 'This is the reward for that which his hands wrought, and God is not unjust towards His creatures.'
>
> The report of this spread immediately, and the militia of Damascus, assisted by the mob and the refuse of the city, rose with swords and naked poniards and put to death all the *Batinis* and their adherents upon whom they could lay hands, and every person connected with them or related to them. They pursued them into their dwellings, fetched them out of their houses, and dispatched them all either by dismemberment with swords or slaughter with poniards, and they were thrown out upon the dung heaps like abandoned carrion. A large number of individuals among them who had taken refuge in various high quarters in order to protect themselves, and who hoped for safety through their intercession, were forcibly seized and their blood was shed without fear of consequences. By the next morning the quarters and streets of the city were cleared of the *Batinis* and the dogs

---

* Gibb. *The Damascus Chronicles* 1932. p. 190.

were yelping and quarrelling over their limbs and corpses. 'Verily in this is a sign to men of intelligence.'

Amongst those who were captured was the man known as Shadhi the freedman, the pupil of Abu Tahir the *Batini* goldsmith who was formerly at Aleppo. This accursed freedman was the root of all the trouble and evil, and was repaid with the severest punishment, at which the hearts of many of the Believers were comforted. He was crucified, along with a few others of the sect, on the battlements of the wall of Damascus, in order that it might be seen how God had dealt with the oppressors and brought signal chastisement upon the infidels.

As for Ismail the missionary, who was living at Banyas, and those who were with him, when they heard the report of this disaster they were filled with despair and humiliation and began to lay the blame upon one another, while their supporters dispersed throughout the country. Ismail himself, knowing that disaster threatened him if he remained at Banyas and being unable to put up an obstinate resistance, sent to the Franks, promising to deliver up Banyas to them, in order to seek safety with them. He surrendered it to them accordingly, and he with a number of others came into their hands and slunk away from Banyas into the Frankish territories in the utmost abasement and wretchedness. Ismail was smitten by the disease of dysentery, and dying of it was buried in Banyas at the beginning of the year 524 [1130]. So this district was rid of them and purified from their uncleanliness.*

The nemesis experienced by the Assassins after their hubris at Damascus was almost classical in its exaction of its due, and the sect was never able to re-establish itself in the city. Damascus would, soon enough, become the centre of the fully formed Sunni *jihad* that would, in time, retake Jerusalem from the Franks and push the Assassins to the margins of Syrian politics. The device of *taqiyya* was used in desperation by those who remained within the Muslim zone and, as recorded above, many fled to Frankish areas. They attempted to exact revenge on Damascus through the Franks, by their gifting of Banyas to King Baldwin II, who realised that its strategic position close to Damascus, and on the road that linked the city with Jerusalem, effectively made it an offensive fortification for the Latin Kingdom. Using it as his base, he brought a large force, which included contingents from Edessa, Antioch and the coastal cities, close to Damascus's walls.

Buri acted quickly to meet this threat and after gathering allies from the nomadic Turcomen of the region, as well as Arab bands, he struck the Crusader force as it was in the act of foraging and destroying the environs

---

* Gibb, *The Damascus Chronicles*, pp. 192–5.

of Damascus. Spread out and unready for pitched battle, the Crusaders were scattered by the sudden attacks. They quit the area the next day after setting fire to their camps and Buri returned to Damascus in triumph. He was not to be allowed to bask in glory for long – Baldwin returned later the same year, but his war plans were wrecked by appalling weather. However, it would not be the King of the Franks, with his knights and lances, that would finish Buri – once again, it would be the Assassins' daggers.

Two Turcomen arrived in Damascus one day seeking employment. Their pay demands were no more than the normal fixed rate and they were hired on the spot, as Buri's vetting procedures were evidently non-existent. Within only a few months he brought the pair into his close bodyguard.* Then, on 7 May 1131, as he was riding back from the baths, these Turks attacked him. He had reached the gate of his palace and his bodyguard of Khurasanis, Daylamites and Turks were preparing to leave him, when the new guards came at him with their daggers. The first blow only grazed his neck and the second is recorded as striking him in the flank. Buri saved himself from further injury by throwing himself from his horse, then his loyal bodyguards rushed upon the Assassins and killed them. More and more troops of the prince's *askari* appeared and continued hacking at the Assassins' bodies, cutting them to pieces.

Buri had survived and it seemed for a short time that he would recover from the attack and his wounds. Certainly, Muslim medical facilities were at this time among the best in the world; the work of Dioscorides, the famous Byzantine physician, had been translated into Arabic, complete with diagrams, in the early Islamic period, and such was the size of the trading network of Islam, that Indian medicine and even Chinese remedies were known to Muslim physicians. Skilled treatment of wounds by Muslim physicians is attested to by Usama Ibn Munqidh, who had opportunities through Crusader friends of comparing this to what he recounts as being 'the barbaric treatment of patients' by Latin doctors. He recalls how a servant of his, who was stabbed by a drunken Turk, received an abdominal wound that was about four fingers deep:

---

* Saladin, like Buri, was also fairly cavalier about his choice of bodyguards. During the siege of Acre (1188–90) the sultan tried to attract into his *askari* a Sicilian knight, the 'Green Knight', whose abilities he admired. See J. Richard, 'An Account of the Battle of Hattin Referring to the Frankish Mercenaries in Oriental Moslem States', *Speculum*, Vol. 27, No 2, 1952, pp. 168–77.

The *jarrahun* [surgeon] made frequent visits to my servant until he was better, could walk and do his work, but the wound would not close up completely. For two months it continued to excrete something like scabs and yellow water then the cut at last closed up, the abdomen of the man resumed its normal condition and he returned to perfect health.*

But such healing took time:

I once witnessed, in an encounter between us and the Franks, one of our horsemen named Badi Ibn Tahl al-Qushayri, who was one of our brave men, receive in his chest a lance thrust from a Frankish knight while clothed only in two cloth garments. The lance cut his breast-bone and came out of his side. He turned back right away but we never thought he would make his home alive. But as Allah, worthy of admiration is He, had predestined, he survived and his wound was healed. But for one year after that he could not sit up if he was lying on his back unless someone held his shoulders and helped him. At last his suffering entirely disappeared and he reverted to his old ways . . .†

It may have been either Buri's character, or the fact that politically things always deteriorated when a prince was incapacitated, that made him leave his bed early and continue with the business of government. His flank wound became a running sore and almost certainly became infected. He died just over a year after the attack. Stories like this, of a lingering death after an Assassin had struck, may have leant credence to the notion that the *fidai'in* used poison on their daggers, but this seems unlikely given the sacred nature of their killing method. If poison was to be used, why not charge a glass of wine with it or use arrows and spears? In short, the method of bringing death was as important, and in some ways, more important than the mere political worth of each victim. Arnold of Lubeck, writing in the twelfth century said of the *fidai'in* that: 'When therefore any of them have chosen to die in this way the Chief hands them knives which are, so to speak, consecrated.'‡ The holiness of the act of murder is therefore evident.

The political worth of the murder of Buri was small, given the continued Sunni revival that was taking place in the Syrian cities and the Nizaris' much less spectacular activity of obtaining castles. Many of these were obtained through simple purchase during the period following the Nizaris' expulsion from Damascus, but would prove to be of enormous

---

* Hitti. *An Arab-Syrian Gentleman and Warrior*, pp. 88–9.
† Hitti. *An Arab-Syrian Gentleman and Warrior*, p. 70.
‡ Lewis, *The Assassins*, p. 4.

value to the sect's future in Syria. They concentrated their efforts on the Jabal Bahra out to the west of the Orontes River, as well as the hinterland between the Muslims and Franks. They bought the mountain fortress of Qadmus in 1132, and they were able to obtain the nearby and larger castle of al-Kahf from its owner, when they interceded in a dispute between him and his cousins. They took direct action against the Franks, for the first time since 1126, and forced out the Crusader garrison from the castle of Khariba in 1137. Then in 1140, they took the fortress of Masyaf from a governor of Usama Ibn Munqidh's clan, and also took the castle of Khawabi that lay just south of al-Kahf. This small chain of castles, Masyaf, al-Kahf and Khawabi, would become the core command centre and refuge of the Assassins in Syria just as Alamut, Maymundiz and Lamasar were in Persia.

Such was the degree of secrecy that the Assassins' *taqiyya* engendered in this period, that the names of the key Nizari players are unknown to, or at least unrecorded by, the contemporary chroniclers. It is only with the brief appearance of Nizari irregulars in the army of Raymond of Antioch in 1149, and the disclosure of his identity as chief *dai* in Syria to all his followers in 1162 by Rashid al-Din, that the history of the sect surfaces in the general Syrian histories of the period. Indeed, so quiet were the *fidai'in*, that their assassination in 1149 of the leader of the resistance to Bahram (when the Nizaris had tried to extend their influence west of the Jordan in 1128), went virtually unrecorded by the chroniclers. Most writers from the 1120s onwards were more interested in writing about the house of Zangi and its rise to power in the region.

Only a few months before the Assassins' attack on him, Buri had received letters from Zangi, who was in theory only an *atabeg*, but was effectively the lord of Mosul, and from 1128, of Aleppo too, following the assassination of Ibn al-Khashab. Zangi wrote requesting the assistance of Damascus against the Franks. Five hundred men were sent under the command of Buri's son, but Zangi treacherously imprisoned these men, seized the city of Hama and then demanded ransom which Buri, realising that he was now dealing with the region's new strong man, eventually paid. Zangi had married the daughter of Ridwan – the unfortunate lady was already the widow of Il-Ghazi and Balak. He had also transferred his father's remains to the city and had obtained diplomas from the sultan of Iraq, giving him undisputed authority over the whole of Syria and northern Iraq. The Syrian Assassins must have realised that, with the union of Mosul and Aleppo under Zangi, they were witnessing the renaissance of Turkish ambitions for a united Syria, reconnected to the eastern Sunni world. There was also the unpleasant fact that Zangi's domain of Mosul cut right across their lifeline to Alamut.

However, there was not always complete enmity between the Assassins and Zangi – as recorded at the end of chapter three, Zangi would have at the very least smiled at the murder of the Iraqi Saljuq sultan, Daud. The death of Zangi's main political rival in the Jazira freed him for operations in Syria. The fact the Assassins came from Syria meant that they would have travelled across Zangi's territories – perhaps they were given safe passage, or maybe Zangi's complicity in their mission was even greater than this.

So Zangi was not above cutting cards with the Devil, but he was also a brilliant leader of men and had the perseverance to travel the length and breadth of Syria and Iraq for eighteen years on campaigns. His charismatic leadership was vital to the maintenance of a Turcoman army in the field, particularly at the successful siege of Edessa, which he took from the Crusader Joscelin II in 1144. Al-Qalanasi described how Zangi called on the tribes of Turcomen to carry out the obligation of Holy War, but he also controlled these Turcoman forces through iron discipline. He crucified transgressors of his laws – this, as well as his call for *jihad* and the booty his successes accrued, was enough to hold his army together. From the very outset of the Crusades, no Muslim leader, excepting the Nizari Ismaili masters, had managed to achieve such a prolonged union of his forces as Zangi did. The Turcomen, in the past, had always dispersed at harvest time and showed no supra-tribal loyalty. Any unity that was achieved by a Muslim army had been ephemeral. The achievement of Zangi was to realise that the Sunni revival and an alliance between the Sunni *ulama* and himself could be an effective stalking horse for his ambition to build a dynasty in Syria. If he also brought Holy War to the *Franj* then that was an added bonus and could only help his cause. In fact he had a lot to thank the Nizaris for, as they had called this alliance into existence by their bloody acts in Aleppo and Damascus.

Zangi was even able to utilise *jihad* during his assaults on the dominions of Damascus in the early 1140s. The city had passed through a turbulent period that had included the killing of a prince by his own mother, and the death of another in a palace conspiracy. Zangi began a siege of Damascus in 1139–40. When the leaders of Damascus called on the Crusaders for help and allied themselves with King Fulk, Zangi's religious propaganda machine went into overtime. An inscription of 1142 at Aleppo, written in a period when most of Zangi's actions had in fact been against Muslims, describes him as the 'tamer of the infidels and polytheists, leader in the holy war, helper of the armies, protector of the Muslims'.

It perhaps seemed fortunate for the Crusaders, the Damascenes and every other group, including the Assassins, that he was killed in September 1146, by a Christian slave as he lay drunk in his tent, but Zangi's capture of Edessa had already effectively made him a *shahid*, or martyr. Upon his death, his army plundered and then rapidly dispersed in time-honoured fashion and the counter–crusade looked likely to collapse before Zangi's son, Nur al–Din, could consolidate his position. This did not happen, however, because by this time there was a lore of *jihad* evolving in northern Syria – Zangi's martyrdom was elemental to the maturing of this tradition.

5

THE GATHERING TEMPEST
NEW ENEMIES FOR THE PERSIAN MISSION

If the people of the world whom Chinggis Khan and his followers killed
had remained, they would be cramped for room in the world.

*Anonymous Persian writer, c.1347**

THE ASSASSINS HAD MURDERED one of the princes of the Khwarazm
shahs back in the early 1150s, but the dynasty, at that time, had
not been a real force to be reckoned with. It was with the death
of Sultan Sanjar in 1157 that it came into its own, and the shah Il-Arslan
consequently emerged as the most powerful ruler in eastern Persia. He
was still paying tribute to the Khitai, whose steppe empire held a strong
position between the *Dar al-Islam* and China, and was unable to fully
assert his authority over the Ghuzz.

As a result of the prosperity of his lands around the Aral Sea, he was,
however, able to recruit heavily for his army among the Turkish tribes,
and it therefore grew quickly. Il-Arslan's troopers had a reputation for
viciousness, and are recorded as having carried off Muslim children
into slavery and of depriving local farms of the herds they needed to
survive. Il-Arslan's death in 1172 was followed by civil war, but his son
Tekish, after finally establishing himself as shah, was able to throw off his
allegiance to the rapidly ailing Khitai at the end of the twelfth century. He
was also able to involve himself, to his own profit, in the war between the
last Saljuq sultan of Iraq, Toghril, and Caliph al-Nasir, who was trying,
like the earlier caliph, al-Mustarshid, to take advantage of the collapse of
the Saljuq Empire to extend his lands.

Tekish backed the caliph, and in 1194 he defeated and killed Toghril
near Rayy. However, he then found himself at loggerheads with the
caliph over the inclusion of his name in the *khutba* at Friday prayers in

* Lambton, *Continuity and Change*, p. 20.

Baghdad. This would have been tantamount to the caliph accepting the dominion of yet another secular, albeit Sunni, lord, and al-Nasir was more ambitious than that. The caliph went to war, but was poorly equipped to deal with Tekish's vast army of one hundred and seventy thousand cavalry – he was defeated in 1196.

Tekish died in 1200, but this feud and the brutality of their troops had already alienated grass-root Sunni Muslim opinion from the Khwarazm shahs. Tekish's son, Ala al-Din Muhammad, only worsened matters by continuing the dispute with the caliph, and making western Iraq a war zone in a conflict with a minor Saljuq emir, Mengli, who had managed to remain independent of the shah. Contemporary writers recorded that the crimes committed by the shah's army, 'were greater than the irregularities committed by the Ghuzz in Khurasan and were not less than those committed by the Christians of the Caucasus, the Georgians, the Khitai Turks and the Franks of Syria'.* Muhammad made another error by continuing his attacks on the Khitai. This made the Mongols' work of dismembering the Khitai steppe empire far easier, and so removed a powerful buffer state – Juvaini called them a 'great wall' between the Muslims and fierce enemies – from between himself and the new power in Asia.

From the end of the twelfth century, this was then an obvious new foe for the Nizari Ismailis, since the shah now controlled vast areas of Persia. Furthermore, he was ostensibly Sunni, though alienated from the *ulama*, and most of all, he was Turkish. His capture of Rayy had also brought his forces dangerously close to Alamut.

Doubtless the Nizari Ismailis would have to look for ways of bringing down this nascent empire as they had that of the Saljuqs, but before they faced this new threat, they had perplexing internal matters to deal with. Muhammad, the grand master, had shown a great deal of provincialism in his outlook and the murders he ordered. By 1143 there was a general dissatisfaction inside the organisation with the apparent abandonment of the project to convert the whole of Islam.

Muhammad might have pointed to the difficulties currently being experienced by the Syrian mission in its attempts to extend the *dawa*, and to the fact that agreements made between Hasan-i-Sabbah and Sanjar effectively restricted the sect's missionary work in Persia. Such arguments would however have found little sympathy among Nizari firebrands, and a radical faction formed around Muhammad's son Hasan, who at this time was about seventeen years old. Perhaps Muhammad later regretted

---

* Lambton, *Continuity and Change*, p. 33.

having given his son the same name as the great Hasan-i-Sabbah, as it certainly seemed to assist him in his demagoguery. He drank wine openly, thus implying he was above the law, and devoured the writings of the first Hasan, whose copious works were stored in Alamut's library.

Hasan also had eloquence on his side, and at this time a tale began to emerge that Hasan himself was the awaited imam and a direct descendant of Nizar. This doubtless grew out of much earlier propaganda that Hasan-i-Sabbah had disseminated, about the smuggling out of Egypt of an infant grandson of Nizar. Muhammad saw how Hasan was using this story and acted quickly to stop the usurpation of his powers by his son:

> He denounced him roundly and having assembled the people spoke as follows: 'This Hasan is my son, and I am not the imam but one of his *dais*. Whoever listens to these words and believes them is an infidel and atheist.' And on these grounds he punished some who had believed in his son's Imamate with all manner of tortures and torments, and on one occasion put two-hundred and fifty persons to death in Alamut and then binding their corpses on the backs of two-hundred and fifty others condemned on the same charge, he expelled these latter from the castle.*

Hasan was frightened enough by his father's actions to write a series of treatises, denying that he had ever believed himself to be the imam and he managed to survive the remaining years of his father's reign and then succeed him. Hasan II maintained the rudiments of his father's rule for the first two years, but was certainly not as harsh in enforcing discipline as Muhammad had been.

Then in 1164 he very literally made a complete volte-face, by changing the direction of worship away from Mecca, and declaring during Ramadan that the Millennium was beginning. He strode up to the pulpit that he had had built outside Alamut and addressed his followers in Arabic, as if he were receiving the words directly from a heavenly messenger. He claimed to be acting as the mouthpiece for a hidden imam and that the imam told the people to obey Hasan as the *Qaim*, the bringer of the *Qiyama*, or Resurrection, as a *hujja* and as a *dai*. He then invited his people to break the feast of Ramadan, as the Holy Law had now fulfilled its purpose in maintaining mankind until the Millennium, which had now, of course, come to pass.

In the Festival of the Resurrection that followed, the Sunni chroniclers tell us that widespread debauchery, playing of harps and drinking of

---

* Juvaini, *Chinggis Khan*, p. 687.

wine took place, as well as the stoning to death of individuals who continued to follow the *sharia*. Hasan's message was subsequently received enthusiastically in all the enclaves of Ismailism in Persia. In Syria, most leaders of the sect seem to have allowed the new directive to run a little while, but then put an end to it and returned to the *sharia*'s interdiction on wine and re-instigation of the rules of chastity. This may have had as much to do with the splitting away of the Syrian mission under its impressive leader Rashid al-Din, who controlled the mission from 1160, as much as for any of the finer details of theology.

Hasan II may well have believed that the Millennium and the end of the Holy Law was at hand, but it cannot be denied that his announcement was also an attempt to politically re-invigorate the movement, after the safe but stale years of Muhammad's stewardship. As we have seen above, the sect was as nothing without the fervour of *dawa*. Hasan II also perhaps hoped to strengthen his position at the organisation's head, by his proclamation of the Resurrection and by being 'appointed' *Qaim* by the hidden imam. Among the adherents of Ismailism, he was called *Ala dhikrhi's Salam*, meaning 'peace be on his mention', and a personality cult seems to have been the basis of his rule, in rather the opposite fashion to that of his father, who relied on hierarchy and the chain of command to manage the movement.

Nizar Ismailism was a radical sect but this was only reflected in its dealings with other Muslims and in the methods it used to ensure its survival. There was also, however, a broad streak of conformism and conservatism that ran through Ismailism, that could not accept Hasan II's sweeping changes. The conservative elements in the organisation thought they had found a champion in Hasan's brother-in-law and they backed his revolt against the *Qaim*. Hasan was stabbed to death by his brother-in-law in January 1166, but the killing was swiftly avenged by Hasan's son, Muhammad. Muhammad, despite being only nineteen years old, obviously had enough experience of, and stomach for, bloody statecraft to not only torture and eliminate his uncle, but also to extend his revenge to the entire household of the murderer, including women and children.

Muhammad II let the Resurrection run on, and seems to have sought to more fully understand it and explain it through his many writings. He certainly had a long enough reign to undertake such a project. He also went on to proclaim himself imam, claiming to be descended from the mysterious smuggled grandson of Nizar. Yet despite this attempt to re-energise the movement, there was little political action undertaken in these years. The reforms seem rather to have eroded the strict hierarchy of the movement that had earlier made it a real force to be reckoned with – it was more like a religion of personal salvation than a revolutionary movement.

The *wazir* of the Caliph of Baghdad was murdered by *fidai'in* and the Sunni theologian Fakhr al-Din Razi of Rayy was silenced, but little else was achieved. Razi seems to have particularly enjoyed destroying the arguments of the Ismailis in his seminary and filling his students with contempt and hatred for the sect. He was an obvious candidate for assassination, but the Assassins' response was in fact a lot more inventive than mere elimination. A *fidai* enrolled in Razi's seminary and studiously attended lectures for seven months, and doubtless had to bite his tongue to stop himself launching into argument with his teacher. One day, he sought out Razi in a quiet part of the college, ostensibly to question him over a difficult theological question. In fact, the question turned out to be very simple – did the teacher wish to have his belly slit from navel to throat, or would he rather accept a small bag of gold and some fine Yemeni garments as the first of a series of payments the imam Muhammad was prepared to give him as a stipend? The chroniclers give Razi the witty reply that the argument was too pointed for him to refuse such a kind offer. Razi remained silent on the Ismailis and their doctrines until he died in 1209 and his story stands as a perfect example for George Bernard Shaw's quip that, 'assassination is the extreme form of censorship.'*

The first clash with the Khwarazm shah came in 1199, probably by chance. There is no evidence that the shah had decided on a policy of persecution of the Ismailis at this point; indeed there had been a leaning towards Shiism by the shah, in an attempt to find a new legitimacy after his attacks on the caliph. The attack on the Assassin castle of Arslan-Gushai near Qazvin, therefore had as much to do with the Khwarazmians' desire to control all of Persia, following their humbling of the minor Saljuq sultans and the caliph, than any policy of direct attack on the Ismailis. The Khwarazmians were satisfied with the withdrawal of the castle's garrison under treaty, and the fact that they were able to achieve this says a lot about their military power at this point. Arslan-Gushai was described as being, 'a strong castle built of solid rock upon a lofty mountain top, which seizes Heaven by the forelock and butts Orion;

---

* From *The Shewing-Up of Blanco Posnet* (1911).

and it was crammed with men eager to give their lives and supported by every manner of arms'.*

As a background to this small conflict, there was also an ongoing war of words between the caliph, al-Nasir, and the Khwarazmians, who had beaten the caliph on the battlefield but could not drag him from the pulpit. In a particularly clever move, al-Nasir called on both Twelver Shiites and the Ismailis to rejoin mainstream Islam. His call perhaps seems somewhat hopeful, given the history of violence between the Abbasids and the Shiites, but the response from the two divisions of Shiism was more enthusiastic than could possibly have been expected. This surprising unity may have been due to the ongoing chaos and misery that the Khwarazmians were bringing to just about everyone in Persia. The Assassins were particularly affected, as the campaign against them in Quhistan had been picked up by Tekish's son, the new shah, Ala al-Din Muhammad. Standing together was the only form of action anyone who was not a Khwarazmian Turk, and thereby employed in wrecking the country, could take.

The caliph's appeal was also the cause of yet another strange change in the faith of the Assassins in 1210. Muhammad II died in September and it has been suggested that his heir, Hasan III, had a hand in the old man's demise. There is certainly mention in the chronicles of Muhammad wearing armour in his son's presence and surrounding himself with axe-wielding *fidai'in*. The irony of an assassination of the Assassins' master was not to be contemplated.

Upon his accession, Hasan moved with some speed to stop the 'heresy' of the Resurrection and reintroduce the *sharia* to Alamut and the other Ismaili settlements. He also sent to the caliph and to the Khwarazm shah to inform them both of the return of *sharia* law, and the re-adoption of Islamic practice in his lands. *Fatwas* were sent from Baghdad and other major centres of the Sunni world, stating that the Ismailis were no longer heretics and that Hasan III and his followers were 'neo-Muslims'. Sunni teachers were sent to Alamut and the other settlements, employed as *qadis*, and it was almost as if the Nizari creed had never existed – although Hasan III did organise tours of the library of Alamut for interested Sunni officials. The sect's history was there for all to see in copious volumes.

Hasan's mother went on pilgrimage via Baghdad, where she was the guest of the caliph in 1212, but the trip nearly went very badly wrong. The Sharif of Mecca's cousin was murdered during her stay at the holy city,

---

* Sadr al-Din quoted by Juvaini, *Chinggis Khan*, p. 312.

and suspicion naturally fell on the entourage of the mother of the Lord of the Assassins. The fact that the sharif's cousin was almost his twin in looks only made the matter worse as the sharif was sure the *fidai'in* had been after him and killed his cousin in error. He was also certain that the caliph was involved. The sharif fined the *hajj* party and exacted his penalty by basically robbing them of all they had as they returned home. The incident did not, however, affect Hasan's relationship with the caliph. Perhaps the sharif's unfortunate cousin had succumbed to a *fidai*'s blade after all – a later sharif was certainly killed by an Assassin, at the caliph's behest.

Hasan was invited to spend some time in Baghdad as an honoured guest – by travelling to Baghdad he became the first grand master to leave Alamut. He went even further afield, to Azerbaijan, to secure treaties with the leaders there, and to Gilan, the densely forested area surrounding the south of the Caspian Sea, to claim four brides from the emirs there. He took a personal letter of recommendation from the caliph to bolster his qualification as a son-in-law.

Hasan III had effectively made the Assassin state respectable. He had normal relations with his neighbours, and made and broke treaties with them, just as any other prince might. He assisted in a league of emirs against Mengli, the sultan of western Iraq, and after Mengli's defeat in 1215, he obtained more districts for his little state from his Sunni allies. His diplomacy extended well beyond the parochialism of his immediate predecessors and he sent emissaries to the new power in the East. Chinggis Khan was fairly well advanced on his career of conquest by this point, but had not reached towards Islam yet. Hasan's informants and agents in the eastern Muslim lands must have been sending information back on the new empire-builder at a very early stage, as Hasan, wisely as it later transpired, offered duty and allegiance to the Khan.

Hasan III died at the beginning of November 1221 and his only son, Ala al-Din, succeeded him. Hasan's death serves, perhaps, as a warning against polygamy:

> The disease of which Jalal al-Din [Hasan III] died was dysentery and it was suspected hat he had been poisoned by his wives in connivance with his sister and some of his kinsmen. The *wazir*, who by virtue of his will was administrator of the kingdom and tutor of his son, Ala al-Din, put to death a great number of his relations, his sister, wives and intimates and confidants on this suspicion. And some he burnt.*

---

* Juvaini, *Chinggis Khan*, p. 704.

Poisoning by a wife is certainly not that uncommon, but to be poisoned by *wives* marks Hasan out as being fairly remarkable, and in many ways he was. His 'conversion' to orthodoxy in 1210 and relations with the caliph take some explaining and may ultimately have been what led to his death, despite obvious successes for the Ismaili state. It could be suggested that it was all done under the philosophy of *taqiyya*, the time-honoured tradition of Shiites disavowing their true beliefs, so that they might survive and continue to propagate their faith in times of danger. Certainly Hasan's accommodation took place at a time when the ravages of the Khwarazmians were a menace to every polity in Persia, but there may be more to Hasan's union with the caliph than just this.

The Xi Xia, the kingdom lying to the west of China and to the east of the Khitai, had just been conquered by Chinggis Khan in 1209, and by 1218 the Mongols would be occupying the lands of the Khitai. Could it be that Hasan saw further than anyone and portended the storm that would come from the east? This is certainly possible, especially if we believe in the Ismailis' skills in astrology, but what is more likely is that Hasan III could see that a clash between the Khwarazm shah and Chinggis Khan was inevitable. Hasan, with his intellect, contacts with the Mongols, and first-hand experience of the Khwarazm shah, knew who the victor of such an outcome would be. Given the past experience of the Saljuq invasion, an alignment with the Sunni caliph made perfect sense for the Assassins if they were to survive. What is also likely is that Hasan undertook the change to strengthen his own position, as the Resurrection, with its lawlessness, had, over time, actually eroded the position of the grand master through its denial of all laws.

Ala al-Din was only nine when he succeeded his father, under the control of a *wazir*, who maintained the policies of his father. From the peripheries of the Persian-Ismaili state there were growing defections from the policy of accommodation with the Sunnis and some adherents were even reverting back to the practices of the Millennium – perhaps the joys of wine-drinking and harp-playing were too much to go without. Ala al-Din, despite his youth, seems to have shrugged off his *wazir*'s tutelage, and moved the organisation to an ideological 'half-way' position. The period of active Neo-Islam was certainly over, but the Resurrection and Millennium were not re-proclaimed. What Ala al-Din and his close advisers seem to have aimed for was the extension of the personality cult surrounding the imam, who was now of course, Ala al-Din himself. Ala al-Din therefore ruled more like a heaven-anointed king than a grand master – whilst there were some advantages to this form of rule in this period, there were dangers too.

In the larger scheme of things, what Ala al-Din and the Assassins did at this point did not really matter however. They had proved in the past that their daggers could change the course of events, but now events were moving so fast that any such disruption would have only a slim chance of changing anything. The Assassins were now up against the proclaimed destiny of Chinggis Khan and that destiny was to conquer the entirety of the known world. After the Mongol conquest of the Khitai Empire, which was pretty much completed by 1218, there was almost immediate friction between the Mongols and the Khwarazm shah. In the same year, Chinggis Khan sent an embassy to the shah. In this he was responding tardily to an earlier delegation, sent by the Khwarazmians in 1215, which may have been requesting an alliance and a commercial treaty. This was certainly what the Khan suggested in his letters of 1218, and it was agreed to. At this point, Chinggis may well have been wary of engaging the shah. As we know, the Khwarazmians could, in theory, call one hundred and seventy thousand cavalry to the field and the Khan still had his Chinese project going on – Beijing had only fallen in 1215, and the remnants of the Jin Empire and of the Xi Xia were not fully subjugated yet.

The Mongols subsequently sent four hundred merchants to Utrar, on the borders of the two empires, which lay on the Jaxartes River in modern day Kazakhstan. The merchants were plundered by ill-disciplined Turcoman troops. The shah had said of the Turcoman in the past that even he found it impossible to control them because he was beholden to their tribal leaders. Perhaps he should have tried this excuse on Chinggis, but instead, when the Khan sent ambassadors to demand the arrest of the governor of Utrar the shah murdered one envoy and sent the others back with their heads shaved. In response, in 1219, Chinggis Khan crossed the Jaxartes with an army of between one hundred and fifty to two hundred thousand men.

The shah should, in theory, have been able to match this invading force, but he had a number of problems. First, as we have seen, his army was ill-disciplined and he had not had time to put in place reforms suggested by his *wazir*. The minister had suggested that one thousand of the Turcomen should be taken into direct service of the shah to act as his bodyguard, and this number should be increased over time to ten thousand. Around this core, the rest of the army could then gain order and discipline. This was certainly a pattern the Saljuqs had used effectively, which would find its fullest development in the Ottoman armies of the fourteenth and fifteenth centuries.

So the shah could not be sure of his troops, and he could not be sure of his generals either. His mother had been plotting against him, in disappointment that her favourite son had not succeeded to the throne, and many of the leaders of Ala al-Din Muhammad's army had tribal associations with his mother's family. He attempted, therefore, to avoid the risk of a coup d'état by dispersing his forces around Khurasan, and so was at the head of a decidedly reduced army as he faced up to Chinggis Khan. Finally, of course, the shah had estranged many of his Persian troops by virtue of his conflict with the caliph and his cruelties against the Persian people.

At Utrar, Chinggis Khan's army faced a force of about sixty thousand men, and the walls of the town, which were already strong, had been re-fortified. Leaving a force to surround the city, the Khan then divided his remaining forces. He set out for Bukhara and his son, Jochi, was sent to form the northern limb of a three-pronged assault on the shah's empire. Another army, probably led by the generals Jebe and Subedei, formed the southern prong. The siege of Utrar went on for five months and even after the Mongols had broken into the city, the governor retired to the citadel where he put up further resistance for another month. He was doubtless in fear of his life and in fear of the likely manner of his death – he was after all the *casus belli* of the whole affair.

Jochi's northern forces witnessed the pleasant sight of the Khwaraz-mians deserting their assigned task of defending the city of Jand and the city fell easily enough to the Mongols in April 1219. The same occurred on the southern approach, as the shah's army simply fell away. Bukhara and Samarqand, the shah's capital, were approached by Chinggis Khan's central army. It also seems that the Khan picked up a great many Ghuzz Turks on the way to Bukhara and added them to his force, so his advance was 'accompanied by a host of fearless Turks that knew not clean from unclean, and considered the bowl of war to be a basin of rich soup and held a mouthful of the sword to be a beaker of wine'.*

He approached Bukhara in March 1220, and at last, the sultan's army made a response. A force of twenty thousand men came out from the city to engage the Mongol army, but was destroyed rapidly and totally, in a battle that the chroniclers were able to record in only a few lines.

---

* Juvaini, *Chinggis Khan*, p. 98.

The gates of Bukhara were then immediately opened to the Mongols. The Khan sat down in the main mosque and asked if it was the sultan's palace. He then ordered his horses' bellies to be filled and his troopers flung Qurans from caskets to make troughs for their mounts. The city's singing girls were sent for and a wine party began in the main mosque. The Muslims could now see how their new masters would behave. The pages of the Quran were trampled under horses' hooves, as the Khan and his men retired for the night.

The next day, the Khan mounted the mosque's pulpit and addressed the people. 'O people, know that you have committed great sins, and that the great ones among you have committed these sins. If you had not committed great sins, God would not have sent a punishment like me upon you.'* He sent Mongols with each nobleman to collect all their gold and then, in order to save Mongol troops from danger, the Khan set the people of Bukhara the task of reducing their own citadel. Some of the shah's men were still holed up in the citadel and fired arrows at the townspeople as they approached the citadel's walls. The Mongols then set fire to the city to push the townspeople towards the citadel. The citizen attackers were therefore caught between the arrows from the citadel and the flames at their backs:

> And on either side the furnace of battle was heated. On the outside, mangonels were erected, bows bent and stones and arrows discharged; and on the inside, ballistas and pots of naphtha were set in motion. It was like a red hot furnace fed from without with hard sticks thrust into the recess . . . for days they fought in this manner; the garrison made sorties against the besiegers . . . but finally they were reduced to the last extremity; resistance was no longer in their power and they stood excused before God and man. The moat had been filed with animate and inanimate objects and raised up with levies and by people of Bukhara; the outworks had been captured and fire hurled into the citadel; and their leaders and notables, who were the chief men of the age and the favourites of the sultan and who in their glory would set their feet on the head of Heaven, now became the captives of abasement and were drowned in the Sea of annihilation.†

The populace was sent into the fields by the Khan, while the city's walls were levelled. He took every able-bodied man and boy with him as a levy, and moved on to Samarqand, where he was met by his son's detachment, with the civilians of Utrar also formed into a levy. News

---

* Juvaini, *Chinggis Khan*, p. 105.
† Juvaini, *Chinggis Khan*, p. 106.

came at this point of the shah's flight from the war and the Khan sent the two generals, Subedei and Jebe, to pursue Ala al-Din Muhammad. Chinggis then spent two days just encircling the walls of Samarqand, at this time one of the greatest cities in the world. On the third day, his army was engaged by the Khwarazmians of the city's garrison, and in a great battle of mounted archers the Khwarazmians may even have won the day. This was not, however, enough to dislodge the Mongols from their siege, and by the next day the encirclement of the city was complete.

The Mongols attempted to stop further sallies from the city by placing extra forces at each of its gates, but the Khwarazmians came out again, showing much more stomach for battle than their shah had. They deployed elephants against the Mongol troopers, who, after initial difficulties, managed to pour so many arrows in to them that the poor beasts turned tail and trampled their own infantry in a dash back to the city. The battle continued until nightfall when the Khwarazmians retired and closed the city's gates.

The Mongols gained entrance to the city the next day, through a secret meeting with the *qadi* of the city and other members of the *ulama*. The Mongols began flattening the walls of the city after gaining entrance, but otherwise the populace was unharmed by their entry and the Khwarazmians withdrew to the citadel where they were encircled by the Mongols just as they had been at Bukhara. The people and the elephants were then rudely ejected from the city. The chroniclers tell us that the elephants starved to death, but say little else about the people, except that their possessions were pillaged by the Khan's men.

The citadel was broken into, following a heavy bombardment from the Mongols' Chinese siege engineers. The Khwarazmians staged a last stand in the Friday mosque, but the Mongols threw naphtha at the mosque until all the defenders inside were burned alive. The survivors of the citadel's garrison were then separated and the Ghuzz Turks had the front of their heads shaved in the Mongol fashion and joined the Mongol army. The Qipchaq Turks, from the steppes of the Caucasus, who formed the elite of the shah's army, were however immediately executed.

The conquest of Khwarazm was handed on to Chinggis's sons, Ogedei and Chaghatai, and the now leaderless Khwarazmians elected one of the kinsmen of the shah's mother as sultan to defend their homeland by the Aral Sea. Juvaini mockingly called him the *nauruz* king, or 'king for a day', and such was the speed with which the entire area east of the

Oxus was conquered by the Mongols that the name seems apt. At the end of this destruction, Juvaini records the one-day sultan as drinking 'the wine of adversity', and of having his heart cut in two after viewing the Mongol destruction of his homeland. The devastation was so complete that Juvaini, normally so fastidious about numbers stated, 'I have heard of such a quantity of slain that I did not believe the report and so have not recorded it.'* Artisans, as noted below, escaped the general holocaust only to be deported to Mongolia as slave labour.

A flavour of the kind of warfare and genocide the Mongols employed all over eastern Persia is given by Juvaini:

> The Tartar army planted a standard on top of the wall, and warriors climbed up and caused the earth to ring with their shouts, cries, yelps and uproar. The inhabitants opposed them in all the streets and quarters of the town: in every lane they engaged in battle and in every cul-de-sac they resisted stoutly. The Mongols meanwhile were setting fire to their houses and quarters with pots of naphtha and sewing the people to one another with arrows and mangonels . . . In the morning the people of the town for a while applied themselves to battle in the same manner and bared the claw of conflict with sword, arrow and banner. By now the greater part of the town was destroyed; the houses with their goods and treasures were but mounds of earth; and the Mongols despaired of benefiting from the stores of their wealth. They therefore agreed among themselves to abandon the use of fire and rather to withhold from the people the water of the Oxus, across which a bridge had been built inside the town. Three thousand men from the Mongol army put themselves in readiness and struck at the centre of the bridge; but the inhabitants entrapped them there so no one was able to return.
>
> On this account the townspeople became more energetic in their action and more stubborn in their resistance. On the outside also, the weapons of war became more furious, the sea of battle more raging and the winds of confusion more tumultuous, on earth and in the heavens. Quarter by quarter, house by house, the Mongols took the town, destroying the buildings and slaughtering the inhabitants, until finally the whole town was in their hands. Then they drove the people out into the open; those that were artisans or craftsmen, of whom there were more than one-hundred thousand, were separated from the rest; the children and young women were reduced to slavery and borne off into captivity; and the men that remained were divided among the army, and to each fighting man fell the execution of twenty-four persons . . .†

---

* Juvaini, *Chinggis Khan*, pp. 126–8.
† Juvaini, *Chinggis Khan*, pp. 126–7.

Such stories of rampant destruction were, however, generally limited to towns that resisted occupation. A number of points are worth noting here. First, extirpation and the crushing of all resistance were obvious sequelae to the Mongol policy of requiring total submission or *il* from all peoples. Negotiation for terms with the Mongols was really a non-starter, until the world-conquest project got into trouble in the 1260s because of the stubborn resistance of the Mamluk sultanate of Egypt and warfare between the descendants of Chinggis Khan. Only at this point was negotiation and parley with likely allies, such as the western Europeans, undertaken as near equals.

Second, in this early stage, the Mongols were quite happy to wreck the entire world and kill all of its inhabitants, if this was what was required for world domination. They had no interest in the life of cities, and, because they practised nomadic pastoralism, no interest in agriculture either. Indeed, depopulating may even have been a deliberate policy, as it opened new pasture for their vast flocks. Their total wreckage of the ancient *qanat* system of underground canals that maintained Persia's fragile agrarian fertility meant that those who survived the initial killing and the burning down of granaries faced slow starvation as the soil turned to dust. Thirdly, news of such wanton killing spread fast – indeed, later in the 1240s the English herring fleet lost a fortune as no one from Scandinavia would dare cross the sea to buy their catch for fear of the Mongols.*

A review of Mongol policy then makes it seem odd that the Assassins are often accused of being the first terrorists, when their attacks were almost entirely limited to men of power and influence. There were rarely any indiscriminate killings, nor were there female victims or the striking down of children by the *fidai'in*, even though child sovereigns were not uncommon in the medieval world. The real war of terror in the Middle Ages was brought to Eurasia by the Mongol superpower, during their war *on* terror against the Assassins. They used the simple volume of killings as coercion, whereas the killings of the Assassins caused intimidation and 'terror' through their highly public nature and the way in which they sowed distrust among the guarded and their guards, and between those vying for power. The ordinary citizen usually appears in history only as a voiceless statistic – 'Old one hundred names', as the Chinese would call

---

* Edward Gibbon found it 'whimsical' that the actions of a Khan in distant Asia should affect such things, but as one of my university tutors, Dr David Morgan, once pointed out, it just goes to prove that history really is all about the price of fish.

such ordinary people, are missing from a history of the Assassins simply because the Assassins did not slay such individuals.

The real number of deaths directly attributable to the Mongol genocide in the *Dar al-Islam* will be disputed over and over by historians. In the past, some have even gone as far as to suggest that millions died in Herat and Nishapur, and to accept verbatim the chroniclers' undoubtedly over-inflated numbers for the carnage in Persia. However, there is no reason to completely dismiss the accounts and accounting of contemporaries of the events – they resonate with the enormity of the devastation, as it presented itself to the people of the time. Refusing to sail from Sweden to England just for some fish does not seem so ridiculous when we consider that such horrors were whispered across Islam and through Europe. The later Assassins' policy towards the Mongols was born of this terror.

The massacre and destruction of Transoxania, and south of the Aral Sea, was mild compared with the fate of Khurasan over the next few years. Tolui, Chinggis's youngest son, was placed in charge of this phase of the operation, and the previous deaths of cities were used to encourage surrender by the great metropolises of Balkh, Herat and Nishapur. These cities were soon enough razed to the ground, however, after minor rebellions and their populations were slaughtered. Tolui's reign of terror continued until 1223, and the message eventually spread throughout the region that the Mongols meant what they said – that only total submission equalled survival. The Ismaili grand master, Hasan, so Juvaini tells us, had sent couriers to make submission to Chinggis Khan, even before the Mongols had reached Khwarazmian territory. This and the fact that the Ismailis were enemies of the shah, seems to have given the Assassins immunity from the destruction wreaked on Khurasan by the Khan's men as they extinguished the Khwarazmian state.

Chinggis Khan's determination to totally destroy eastern Islam may simply have been related to a fear, similar to that of Rome's fear of Carthage, that Ala al-Din Muhammad's armies were a direct threat to the Mongol lands, and likely to impinge on the main Chinggisid project of conquering China. But, as we have seen, the shah's army soon enough fell apart and his son, Jalal al-Din, was only really able to form any resistance once the main Mongol forces had quit the *Dar al-Islam* with Chinggis Khan in 1223 to campaign once again against the Xi Xia.

The Great Khan died in 1227, and this effectively put Persia on the back boiler for the Mongols, as they struggled to decide on the succession to the World Conqueror. During this lull in the storm, what was left of

Persia began to take stock. The shah had died on an island in the Caspian, after being chased right across northern Persia by Jebe and Subedei, who had burnt and pillaged their way across Manzandaran. The two Mongol generals had passed close to the Assassin castles, where many notables sought refuge, but left them unharmed. They did, however, carry out a hurried massacre of the towns around Rayy before moving on. Their armies then crossed the Caucasus, defeated the Russians on the River Kalka and butchered the Turks of the Qipchaq steppes of southern Russia on their way home to Mongolia.

This left Jalal al-Din, having broken through the Mongol lines, and after several desperate adventures that included having to swim the Indus, returning in 1226 to try to restore his rule in the mountains of western Persia. The west, unlike many parts of the east of Persia, was not at this point being ruled directly by Mongol viceroys.

The Assassins had meanwhile taken the opportunity of the destruction of the shah's empire to extend their lands. They had seized Damghan, and attacked Rayy. Jalal al-Din's return threatened to call a halt to this expansion, and this, in addition to raids undertaken by the new shah's *wazir* against Quhistan, was enough to bring three *fidai'in* to the city of Ganja, where they murdered one of the shah's officers in the middle of the night. Evidently disappointed that there were no guards to kill them, they then forced the issue by brandishing their bloody daggers and running towards the residence of the *wazir* whilst shouting the name of Ala al-Din as loudly as they could. Unfortunately the *wazir* was not at home, and after lightly wounding a servant, who was the herald of this disappointing news, they rushed into the town. The whole thing became entirely bathetic – the trio rushed into the town centre, still shouting at the top of their lungs until enough townsmen gathered to stone them to death from the rooftops above. The sacrifice had, at last, been made.

The Assassins followed up on their daggers with words, and an envoy was sent to the shah from Alamut. The *wazir*, perhaps thinking of what might have occurred had he been at home that night, readily invited the envoy to parley. It seems that the Assassin envoy, Ahmad, was good company. Soon enough, he and the *wazir* were enjoying wine and conversation, and the Assassins agreed to pay Jalal al-Din a stipend for their possession of Damghan. The conversation even grew amicable enough for the *wazir* to ask Ahmad about the presence of any hidden *fidai'in* in his own Khwarazmians. To this end the envoy replied that there were *fidai'in* throughout the shah's army, in his stables and even among the shah's bodyguard. The *wazir* attempted to call Ahmad's bluff by guaranteeing the safety of any *fidai'in* if he could produce just one. Ahmad briefly left the table and returned with five. One, an Indian, told the *wazir* that he could have murdered him on many occasions, but had not done so because he had not yet received the order. The *wazir* was so frightened by this that he sent a message back to Ala al-Din with Ahmad, that he was merely the shah's functionary and only obeyed his lord's orders. Jalal al-Din got word of the bizarre dinner party and insisted that the *wazir* burn the five *fidai'in* alive, in front of the *wazir*'s own tent. The *wazir* now realised what a difficult situation he had put himself in, and he had to work hard to stay alive. He carried out the shah's orders, and as the *fidai'in* were hurled into the fire they cried out their devotion to Ala al-Din. He then negotiated a fine for himself with the Assassins of fifty thousand gold dinars for the incinerated men and also reduced the annual tribute of thirty thousand dinars for Damghan by a third for five years.

The truce did not last between the shah and the Assassins, chiefly because Ala al-Din's policy was to maintain friendly relations with both the caliph and the Mongols, the shah's enemies. Ahmad, the envoy who had visited the *wazir*, was sent east to the Mongol capital, Qaraqorum, to maintain a presence for Alamut at a court that was rapidly filling with envoys from all over Asia. As Ahmad's embassy returned to Persia in 1228, the Khwarazmians attacked its caravan train and slew seventy Assassins, because they suspected that there were Mongolian envoys among them. Even this was not enough, however, to turn what had become a low-level war, of occasional assassination followed by Khwarazmian reprisal, into the kind of all-out-siege war that the conflict with the Saljuqs had been.

Ala al-Din was keen for the peace, however phoney it might be, to be maintained and he even over-paid the tribute he sent the shah. He also showered gifts on the envoy sent to collect the tribute. Perhaps conversion through theological argument was not enough in this time. Certainly, the envoy was mightily impressed by the satin cloaks and Chinese crepe that were piled into his outstretched hands and by the camels and horses waiting outside for him. Ala al-Din needed peace with the shah because he was contesting a nasty little border war with his neighbours, the Gilanis. Hostilities had begun ostensibly over the four brides Ala al-Din's father had obtained from Gilan, since all four had been executed after Hasan III's poisoning. However, the conflict had just as much to do with the exaction of payment from travellers on the road below the Elburz Mountains that led from the sea to the major cities of the region.

Ala al-Din, despite being only in his teens during his contest with Jalal al-Din, effectively outlasted the shah, who was killed in 1231 by a Kurdish bandit. The shah's death was enough to cause the final disintegration of the Khwarazmian state. Many of its soldiers left for mercenary employment in the Levant, where we will meet them later. The grand master sent missionaries during this period into India, where the faith flourished without the attendant need of political murder – this of course is where the Ismaili sect's headquarters and its head, the Aga Khan, are resident today.

Despite the statements of Sunni historians that he was brain-addled and melancholic as a result of excessive blood loss during a surgical procedure undertaken when he was a small child, Ala al-Din maintained an effective foreign policy – this included having almost permanent emissaries at the court of the new Great Khan, Ogedei. His representatives would, however, have been competing for the attentions of the Mongols with numerous emissaries from all over Europe, from the Christian states of Georgia and Armenia, as well as envoys from the still unconquered Chinese southern Song. Ala al-Din's men evidently did a good job in their diplomacy, as the Assassins were simple onlookers of the Mongol offensive into western Islam of 1230. Western Persia was conquered and northern Mesopotamia was taken. Georgia and Armenia took vassalage to the Mongols, and in 1241 the army of the Golden Horde moved out of Asia and into Europe, where they inflicted a crushing defeat on the cream of Polish chivalry and of the Teutonic Knights at the Battle of Leignitz.

Something very odd then happened, that must have caught the attention of the Assassins. Ogedei died, and though the whole of central Europe lay open to them, the Mongols retired from their march on Vienna and all offensive operations ceased, on every front. Upon the death of the Khan, all roads were closed to trade and war traffic, and the entire state seemed to hold its breath while its leaders returned to Qaraqorum for a *quriltai*, or tribal meeting, to select the new Khan. Europe was saved by the natural passing-away of Ogedei, and Ala al-Din may have considered that even an unnatural death of a Khan might one day do the same for his kingdom.

The Mongols squabbled over the accession for five years, whilst the regency was held by Ogedei's widow. Even then, Batu Khan of the Golden Horde in Russia would not accept the new Khan, Guyuk, and it seems reasonable to mark the beginning of the Mongol superpower's break-up from 1241. Certainly, the tendency for internecine fighting, that would become a dominant feature of the Mongol world empire from the 1260s onwards, started in the short reign of Guyuk, which ended with his death in 1248, as the Khan was on his way to challenge Batu. This hostility within the Chingisid family would certainly have reminded the Assassins of the Saljuq family feuds following the assassination of Nizam al-Mulk and death of Malikshah – and may have led them more and more to the conclusion that just one dagger could solve their Mongol problem.

Despite the above interregnum, the Mongols did, however, subdue Anatolia in this period, following the total defeat of the last Saljuq sultan of Rum at the Battle of Kose Dagh, in 1243. This left the rump of the Abbasid caliph's state of southern Iraq and the Assassins statelets effectively surrounded. The invasion of Eastern Europe did not raise the western Christian states to any response. Indeed, the courts of France and England sent a mission requesting aid home empty-handed and the Bishop of Winchester is recorded as having said to Henry III of England that he should, 'Let those dogs devour each other and be utterly wiped out, and then we shall see, founded on their ruins, the universal Catholic Church, and there shall truly be one shepherd and one flock.'*

Perhaps it was the long-hoped-for coming of Prester John to save the now desperate Crusader states from the Muslim *jihad*, an event the West had been waiting for since first news of him in 1157,† that made the invasion of Eastern Europe only a secondary concern of the western kings and of the pope. Certainly, they redoubled their efforts to convert and befriend the Mongol Khans. Pope Innocent IV sent his envoy, John of Plano Carpini to the enthronement of Guyuk Khan, whilst the Abbasid caliph and the Assassins sent a joint delegation. Carpini's friends described him as being so enormously fat that a particularly strong ass had to be found to transport him across Asia, to Qaraqorum, to discuss an alliance over the Holy Land. It seems likely that the Khans were already concerned over the Assassins' reputation, as Friar John tells us about the security arrangements that Guyuk employed, as well as the host of states vying for Mongol favour:

---

* See Matthew Paris, *Chronica Majora*, ed. H. Luard, London, 1872, Vol. III, pp. 488–9.

† The myth of Prester John was so pervasive that Marco Polo even recorded passing though his lands and wrote of Tenduk, his seat of government (*The Travels of Marco Polo*, p. 141). The defeat of Jalal al-Din in 1231 had, of course, added fuel to the fire, as the Mongols then advanced to the upper Tigris which was exactly where Europeans expected to find the empire of the legendary king.

In the wall of boards about the tent were two great gates, by one of these, the emperor only was to enter, and at that gate there was no guard of men appointed to stand, although it stood continually open, because no one dared go in or come out by it. All that were admitted entered by another gate at which there stood watchmen with bows, swords, and arrows. And whosoever approached the tent beyond the bounds and limit assigned, and, being caught, was beaten, but if he fled, he was shot at with arrows. Without the door stood Duke Jeroslav of Susdal, in Russia, and a great many dukes of the Cathayans, and of the Solangs. The two sons also of the King of Georgia, an ambassador of the Caliph of Baghdad, who was a sultan and, we think, more than ten other sultans of the Saracens beside. And as it was told us by the agents, there were more than four thousand ambassadors, partly, of such as paid tribute and such as presented gifts, and other sultans and dukes, which came to present themselves, and such as the Tartars had sent for, and such as were governors of lands. All these were placed without the enclosure, and had drink given to them.*

The friar also intimates that he realises such parleying and kowtowing by all these envoys would be of little avail in the long run:

Their intent and purpose is to subdue the whole world, as they had been commanded by Chinggis Khan. Hence it is that the emperor in his letters writes after this manner: 'The power of God, and emperor of all men'. Also upon his seal, there is engraved: 'God in heaven and Guyuk Khan upon earth, the power of God: the seal of the emperor of all men.'†

The security arrangements continued inside the Khan's *yurt*:

Then each one of us bowed his left knee four times, and they gave us warning not to touch the threshold. And after they had searched us most diligently for knives, and could not find any about us, we entered in at the door upon the east side; because no man dare presume to enter at the west door, but the emperor only.‡

King Louis IX of France sent the next envoy to the Mongols, a rather thinner Franciscan called William of Rubruck, in 1248. William carried a portable altar in the hope of making converts of the ruling house, and

---

* M. Komroff (ed.), *The Contemporaries of Marco Polo: Consisting of the Travel Records to the Eastern Parts of the World of William of Rubruck [1253–1255]; The Journey of John of Piano de Carpini [1245–1247] and the Journey of Friar Odoric [1318–1350]*, London, 1929, p. 41.

† Komroff, *The Contemporaries of Marco Polo*, p. 41.

‡ Komroff, *The Contemporaries of Marco Polo*, p. 41.

in this he was competing for the Mongols' attentions with the Nestorian Christians and Muslims:

> Then the priests of idols arrive and they do the same. The monk told me that the Khan believes only the Christians, but that he wants everybody to pray for him. The monk lied, for the Khan believes in no one, as you shall soon learn. Every one seeks the court as flies seek honey and they leave it satisfied, each imagining he has the prince's favours, and showering blessings on him . . .*

Despite William's acerbic view, there was a confidence in Europe that newly baptised Mongols would become the instrument of Outremer's salvation. This meant that there was absolutely no sympathy for embassies that had been sent as early as 1238 to the courts of France and of England by the Syrian-Ismaili mission. The envoys were, in fact, sent in the names of both Ala al-Din and of the Abbasid caliph to seek alliances against the Mongols. Ala al-Din's foreign policy was limited simply by the fact that the Mongols had little need of alliances and allies, and the Europeans thought they did not either. His only ally at this juncture was ironically the Abbasid caliph, the original enemy of the Assassins but now a friend of convenience. Ala al-Din, simply by virtue of being an Assassin grand master, had always found friends in short supply, and now had a new enemy very close to home, in the form of his son, Rukn al-Din, or 'Pillar of the Faith'.

It seems that with advancing years, Ala al-Din had become, to put it mildly, eccentric and dangerously contrary. Anyone venturing to contradict him or question his policies, risked mutilation, amputation of limbs and death by torture. This, in addition to the natural tendency of courtiers to seek the favour of the heir apparent, encouraged many within Alamut to look to Rukn al-Din for instructions, rather than to the grand master. This strained the relationship between father and son, and Ala al-Din tried to change the succession to a younger son. However, he was frustrated in this by his own following, who could only accept the eldest son as the new imam – the grand masters were becoming more and more like kings, less and less like first ministers.

Ala al-Din next confined his son to the harem and spent more and more time with his companion, Hasan of Mazandaran. Hasan had been abducted as a child from his home by the Mongols; he had then escaped and fled to Alamut. The relationship of this attractive youth with Ala

---

* Komroff, *The Contemporaries of Marco Polo*, p. 139.

al-Din seems to have become dangerously sado-masochistic, and whilst he accrued great wealth and influence as the grand master's favourite, he also suffered the torments of broken teeth and the severing of half of his penis at his master's hands. Ala al-Din would spend a great deal of time dressed in rags and acting as a shepherd with Hasan, and whilst his father was roving around the mountains, Rukn al-Din would emerge from the harem to conspire with the leaders of Alamut. These conversations seem to have centred on ensuring that Ala al-Din did not change his policy of continued appeasement of the Mongols. The old man had begun to speak more and more of unleashing the *fidai'in* on Qaraqorum. There was also equally a concern that Ala al-Din might send Assassins against his own son. At this time too, the Ismaili state was suffering from the grand master's increased removal from worldy business, as well as suffering what appears to have been a crime wave, with highway robbery becoming a daily event.

Things came to a head in 1255, when Rukn al-Din stated at one of these meetings that, 'my life is not safe with my father', and that he planned to flee to Syria. Juvaini states that he then went on to offer a form of ultimatum to the leaders of Alamut, in which he stated that because 'of my father's evil behaviour the Mongol army intends to attack this kingdom and my father is concerned about nothing. I shall secede from him and send messengers to the Emperor of the Face of the Earth and to the servants of his court and accept submission and allegiance.'* Rukn al-Din was unable to carry out any such plan because he then fell seriously ill, but his sickness eventually turned out to be serendipitous. He had been ill for about a month and none of the leaders of Alamut could decide how to proceed. It seemed impossible to depose Ala al-Din, especially now that his heir was gravely sick, and none of them could bring themselves to contemplate regicide. In the end, the affair was settled by Hasan, who appears to have been unable to endure any more beatings from his elderly lover.

One evening towards the end of the year, in one of his shepherd's huts, Ala al-Din and Hasan started a drinking session with with some slaves and fellow shepherds. The grand master fell into a drunken stupor and the next morning his decapitated body, complete with the head neatly placed beside it, were found outside the hut. A tribunal was set up and all the grand master's drinking companions were questioned. Eventually the blame worked its way round to Hasan, chiefly through the admission of

---

* Juvaini, p. 708.

Hasan's wife, who had also been Ala al-Din's mistress, that her husband had beheaded the imam.

Rukn al-Din had Hasan quietly done away with. He sent him out to tend his father's now sherperdless sheep and sent a *fidai* after him armed with the large double-headed axe that the Assassins always carried when on guard duty. The *fidai* struck Hasan from behind, and took his head off cleanly in one quiet stroke. His son and two daughters were also put to death, and so the whole affair was neatly closed. Only the accusations of Rukn al-Din's mother and sisters, that he had actually murdered his father, disturbed the peace. It was but an small episode of blood-letting, restricted only to a small mountain state, and was as nothing compared to the carnage that was to come, so very soon, to the whole of Persia.

6

THE WHITE DONKEY
AND THE WAR CHARGER

SINAN AND SALADIN

Warfare is deception. If you find a tithe collector, kill him. Go in the name
of God and in God and in the religion of the Prophet of God! Do not kill the
very old, the infant, the child, or the woman. Bring all the booty, holding
back no part of it. Maintain order and do good, for God loves those who
do good. Accept advice to treat prisoners well. Looting is no more lawful
than carrion. He who loots is not one of us. He has forbidden looting and
mutilation. He has forbidden the killing of women and children. He who
flees is not one of us. The bite of an ant is more painful to the martyr than
the thrust of a weapon, which is more desirable to him than sweet, cold
water on a hot summer day.

*Attributed to the Prophet Muhammad in the writings of Al-Muttaqi**

T
HE FALL OF EDESSA to Zangi in 1144 sparked panic in the petty
Muslim states of Syria, as well as Europe. The European response
would come in the form of the Second Crusade. Meanwhile,
the Damascenes reached out to the Crusaders to seal a mutual defence
policy against the new threat from the Jazira, whilst remaining officially
non-aligned. The Assassins of Syria fell back on their well-tried tactic of
withdrawal to their castles in the mountains of Jabal Bahra and Jabal al-
Summaq to await events.

By the time the Crusade reached the Holy Land in 1148, Zangi had
already been dead for two years and his possessions had been shared out
equally between his two sons, as Turkish tradition required. Nur al-Din
inherited Aleppo, whilst his brother, Sayf al-Din Ghazi, was bequeathed
Mosul. The generally friendly relationship that endured between the two

---

went very much against the grain of the normal deadly sibling rivalry of Turkish princes. The division did, however, weaken Nur al-Din's ambitions in Syria because he could not draw, as his father had, on the military and economic reserves of Mosul. He still had the core of his father's Mamluks and the *askaris* of his emirs, as well as the Turcoman irregulars, but it was obvious that he needed more men if he was ever to be able to bring Damascus under his dominion. He therefore employed the Kurdish clan of the Ayyubids, and with these forces he was able to crush a Crusader attempt to retake Edessa in 1147.

Nur al-Din had secured his physical possessions in readiness for the challenge of the coming Crusade. However, he knew he also needed to rekindle the union of the Sunni-Syrian population's religious and civilian leaders with the Turkish men of the sword that had taken place during the reign of Zangi. He therefore abolished the Shiite prayer formula, previously used to call the faithful to prayer in Aleppo, and began a furious propaganda assault on the populace of Damascus, identifying himself as the champion of *jihad* and the only hope for Muslim Syria against the coming infidel assault.

He almost did not need to bother with the war of words. The Second Crusade did more to push Damascus into Nur al-Din's arms than any number of epistles could ever have managed. The whole venture had started to unravel, with a heavy defeat of the German knights by Turcoman forces as they crossed Anatolia. The few knights that continued their journey into Syria soon found that their efforts would be wasted by leaders who had no experience of the complex politics of the region. The problem was that King Fulk had died in 1143, and his son Baldwin III was very much under the control of his mother. His weakness on the throne meant that he could not secure control over the new Crusaders. Moreover, the counsel of the Palestinian knights was ignored by the knights of Europe, who decided to attack Damascus – the one Muslim city in Syria on which they could rely for alliance and even assistance. The resulting Crusader siege of the city, and its break-up before the advance of Nur al-Din's forces, effectively finished the Second Crusade and also killed the hope that Muslim Syria would never unify against the *Franj*. By their own blundering, the Crusaders had effectively forced the Damascenes to abandon their policy of non-alignment.

The Assassins looked down from their castles' ramparts in horror. Their own policy of hindering any extension of Turkish rule in Syria had been completely ruined by the Crusaders' actions. Nur al-Din's removal of the

Shiite rite in Aleppo also gave them full warning that the Sunni drive on Jerusalem and beyond to the Mediterranean, hailed by Nur al-Din as the aim of his *jihad,* also had them very much in its sights. The presence of Nizari troops, led by a Kurd named Ali ibn Wafa, in the forces that Prince Raymond of Antioch brought to his campaign against Aleppo in 1149, is therefore not surprising. Unfortunately for the Assassins, both Wafa and Raymond were killed at the Battle of Inab in 1149. Nur al-Din rewarded the takers of the heads of the Crusader prince and the Assassin leader with handsome gifts.

Damascus came over to Nur al-Din bloodlessly in 1154, and things looked grim for Franks and Assassins alike. Then in August 1157, as rumours circulated in Damascus that Nur al-Din was readying himself to take Jerusalem, nature disturbed all the plans of men, as an immense earthquake devastated all of Syria. Nur al-Din had to concentrate all his energies on just repairing the fabric of his cities.

In October of the same year he was taken seriously ill. Ibn al-Qalanasi tells us how serious this was for Muslim Syria:

> The armies of the Muslims dispersed, the provinces were thrown into confusion, and the Franks were emboldened. They proceeded to the town of Shaizar, entered it by assault, and slew citizens, took prisoners, and plundered. Then there assembled from various parts a great host of the men of the Ismailis amongst others, and these defeated the Franks, slew a number of them, and drove them out of Shaizar.*

So why were the Ismaili Assassins now defending one of Nur al-Din's possessions against the *Franj*? Put simply, in their attempts to solidify borders against the now-united Muslim state of Syria, the Franks were coming into conflict with the Assassins' ambitions for independence from all powers. In 1152, because of just such a boundary conflict, Count Raymond II of Tripoli fell to the *fidai'in*'s daggers at the gates of his own city. Ralph of Merle and another knight, who were with the Count, tried to save him and also perished. King Baldwin III of Jerusalem, who was also in Tripoli at the time, ordered a majestic funeral for Raymond and let loose a frenzy of retaliation on local Muslims. A large number were massacred by Tripoli's Christians and the king then sent the Templar Knights into the Jabal Bahra to raid croplands and Ismaili villages. This destruction eventually forced the Nizaris to parley, and start paying the Templar Order an annual tribute of some two thousand gold pieces.

---

* Gibb, *The Damascus Chronicles,* 1932, p. 341.

All this is highly ironic, given that much has been written on the great similarity between the Assassins and the knights of the Templar, Hospitaller and Teutonic Orders. Many writers have suggested that the Templars' organisation, in particular, replicated both the Assassins' hierarchy and their 'uniform'. White gowns were certainly used by both orders, with the Templars substituting a red cross for the Assassins' red dagger emblazoned on their breasts. It has even been suggested that the military orders were formed as a direct response to the religious brotherhood of the *fidai'in* that Crusaders had encountered in Syria.

Such a hypothesis seems extremely unlikely, however, given that medieval Europeans remained almost completely ignorant of Shiism and its structure – let alone that of the secretive Ismailis – and its differences to Sunnism. Even William of Tyre, one of the best informed of the Crusader chroniclers, summed up his knowledge of the distinction between the two creeds in 1180, by declaring that, according to the Shiites, God had intended to give the message of Islam to Ali, the only true Prophet, but the angel Gabriel had mistakenly handed the message to Muhammad.*

The reasons for the formation of the military orders undoubtedly lie elsewhere. There is an almost universal tendency among writers from all eras, including our own, to label the Assassins as religious fanatics. In the long view of history, this seems a rather odd position to take. The chroniclers recording the deeds of the pilgrim soldiers of Europe were, in fact, recording an action largely built on religious fanaticism. The creation and success of the First Crusade and later of the military orders, was both built on, and then developed further, a union between the Church and the men of the sword. Later, this would lead to the bloody extinguishing of the Albigensians in the Crusades against Christians in southern France, as well as the Teutonic Knights drive to the East in the thirteenth century.

This union required the production of religious fervour within European society, particularly among the knights, upon who the papacy relied during the conflict between the popes and the Holy Roman Emperors over investitures in the eleventh century. During this conflict, knights were invested by the pope as *Milites San Petri*, or 'soldiers of Saint Peter'. The union was achieved partly through the blessing of battle banners and weapons, just as the *fidai'in*'s daggers were consecrated by their grand master. The *Milites San Petri* were initially a small movement, but one can see the seeds of the later 'pilgrim in arms' of the First Crusade and military orders in this organisation. Tales, such as the expulsion

---

* F. Daftary, *The Assassin Legends: Myths of the Ismailis*, London, 1994, p. 24.

of the emperor's antipope's forces from Rome by the crusading Prince Hugh of Vermandois, who fought under the banner of Saint Peter, were highly influential, in the same way that Alamut's *fidai'in* roll of honour was, in creating a lore of sacrifice. The battle cry *Deus lo volt!* or 'God wills it!', and Holy Banners such as the *Vexillum San Petri* (Banner of Saint Peter) and the *Vexillum Cruces* (Banner of the Cross) were central to the identity of a Crusader and Templar. The Assassin guards' axes and their consecrated daggers worked in the same manner.

The link between faith and war therefore developed rapidly in the late eleventh century in Europe. The process of 'Christianising' the bloody business of war was chiefly undertaken through the granting of indulgences that ensured a safe passage to Heaven without the soldier's soul having to traverse Purgatory or risk Hell as his destination. Church-sanctioned murder – killing for the faith – guaranteed a direct passage to Heaven, just as the Assassin masters promised Paradise to the *fidai'in*.

The Templars were also, in theory, only answerable to the pope, not to kings. From the Council of Clermont and Urban's call for the liberation of the Holy Land onwards, there was a willingness among much of the nobility of Europe to see the pope, rather than the emperor, as the leader of 'the army of the faithful'. Such attachment to a spiritual leader, even when undertaking the bloody business of earthly war, connects the men of the knightly orders once again with the *fidai'in*, but attachment to faith leaders was not unique to the Ismailis in Islam. There was a long history of *ghazis* – these fighters for the faith would leave safe homelands to fight on the borders of the *Dar al-Islam* against the Turks or Byzantines, and live together as communities in *ribats*, fortified Muslim monasteries. In eleventh- and twelfth-century Syria there were also *futuwwa*, or brotherhoods, such as the Nubuwiyya, whose central principle was the eradication of Shiism from the region. These brotherhoods were associations of young men, with distinct ranks and rites to mark the attainment of manhood. Most were followings of holy men and had cult practices; they were deeply mistrusted by orthodoxy, just as the Templars would be at the close of their history.

The discipline that the Templars showed within their strict hierarchy was directly related to the religious nature of their brotherhood. This reflected the ecclesiastical discipline based on celibacy and rejection of worldly honours and desires that had been instilled by Urban II into the church, and by the Cluniac philosophy of Gregory the Great. The monkish lifestyles of the grand masters would have recommended itself to the clerics of Cluny and the monks might even have understood the dual nature of existence that Ismaili theology described. The dualism of Ismaili teaching, that described the presence of the heavenly in everyday things, has a strong parallel in the ideal Crusader – he fought to free the Holy Land but also retained a higher ideal of the 'other' Jerusalem, the celestial city that existed above the ordinary gore and dross of this earth.

Whilst parallels between the Templars and the *fidai'in* are not hard to uncover, the only real link between the Templars and the Assassins was that the weapon of assassination was ineffective against the Templars. Even the murder of their grand master would only lead to a small and short-lived level of disorganization. He could be immediately and easily replaced by a fellow knight. The Assassins would face the same problem in the thirteenth century, when they found the one-generation nobility of the Mamluk sultanate similarly impossible to intimidate.

With the payment of tribute to the Templars, and Nur al-Din's recovery, the Assassins in Syria were undoubtedly in trouble. However, they were then saved by the appearance of a man who, according to the chroniclers, arrived at Masyaf castle on a white donkey, in 1162. The writers chose to have Rashid al-Din Sinan arrive on a white donkey because, of course, this historically had been the colour of resistance for all Shiites, being the opposite to the Abbasids' black. Sinan was to become the very epitome of resistance, both to the Sunni *jihad*, and to the Crusaders, who gave him another title; 'Old Man of the Mountain'. He was to make the Syrian mission very much his own, and whilst there was certainly lip service paid by this redoubtable man to Alamut, there can be no doubting that under Sinan, the Syrian Assassins' operation became very much a personality cult. A traveller through the region between 1160 and 1173, Rabbi Benjamin of Tudela, tells us that:

> Under Mount Lebanon . . . reside the people called Assassins, who do not believe in the tenets of Mohammedanism, but in those of one whom they consider like unto the Prophet . . . They fulfil whatever he commands them, whether it be a matter of life or death. He goes by the name of Sheikh al-Hashishin, or their Old Man, by whose commands all the acts of these mountaineers are regulated. The Assassins are faithful to one another by the command of their Old Man, and make themselves the dread of everyone, because their devotion leads them gladly to risk their lives, and to kill even kings when commanded. They are at war with the Christians, called Franks, and with the Count of Tripoli . . .*

---

* Komroff, p. 269.

Sinan came to Masyaf as a representative of the Persian grand master, Hasan II. He is recorded as having been a handsome individual with astonishingly dark, almost hypnotic, eyes. More important than his physical make up, however, was his learning, eloquence and innate intelligence; he claimed to be the son of a noble Shiite of Basra. He was probably born around 1130, and among the other trades assigned to him by the writers of the time, he was listed as an alchemist. After a family quarrel he left home penniless and travelled to Alamut. Sinan continues the tale of his early life as recorded by Kamil al-Din, the chronicler of Aleppo:

> I made my way until I reached Alamut and entered it. Its ruler was Kiya Muhammad, and he had two sons called Hasan and Husain. He put me in school with them, and gave me exactly the same treatment as he gave them, in those things that are needful for the support, education, and clothing of children. I remained there until Kiya Muhammad died, and was succeeded by his son Hasan. He ordered me to go to Syria. I set forth as I had set forth from Basra, and only rarely did I approach any town . . . I entered Mosul and halted at the mosque of the carpenters and stayed the night there, and then I went on, not entering any town, until I reached Raqqa. I had a letter to one of our companions there. I delivered it to him; he gave me provisions and hired me a mount as far as Aleppo. There I met another companion and delivered him another letter and he too hired me a mount and sent me on to Kahf. My orders were to stay in this fortress, and I stayed there until Sayh Abu Muhammad, the head of the Mission, died on the mountain.*

It is possible that Sinan was in Syria as early as 1157 and was lamed by a rock fall, during the terrible earthquakes of that year. However, his activities until his arrival at Masyaf, in 1162, are unknown. In 1169, Sinan is said to have come to the chief *dai* of Syria, Abu Muhammad, and apprised him of the fact that he was about to die. He then showed Abu Muhammad a letter from Alamut. The letter was from seven years earlier and appointed Sinan to replace Abu Muhammad as chief *dai* in Syria. Abu Muhammad soon died, just as Sinan had predicted, but Hwaga Ali Ibn Masud succeeded him without Alamut's approval. He was, however, killed shortly after, as he left his bath, by men sent by Abu Muhammad's nephew. Orders then came from Alamut, that those involved in the conspiracy against Masud should be arrested and put to death. A further

---

* B. Lewis, 'Kamal al-Din's Biography of Rashid al-Din Sinan', *Arabica. Revue D'Etudes Arabes. Extrait*, Tome XIII, Fascicule 3, 1966, pp. 231–2.

message came with the order ratifying the position of Sinan as grand master in Syria.

There was a backlash against Alamut's imposition of a master by some members of the Syrian mission, which was already showing a degree of independence from its Persian parent. Plots were formed against Sinan, but he had already developed an internal network of informers inside Masyaf and the putsch planned against him was discovered easily enough. His handled and gathered information so skilfully that upon discovering that they had been exposed, many of the plotters assumed Sinan to have supernatural powers. Some even submitted to him without waiting for evidence of their guilt to be produced. Sinan also appears to have worked hard to create an illusion of preternatural powers.

His Ismaili biographer, Abu Firas, rehashed tales of Hasan-i-Sabbah's deeds and applied them to Sinan, but Sinan also seems to have adopted a persona that invited tales to be created about him. He lived his public life as a pious ascetic dedicated to prayer and good works. He also made sure he was seen fervently conversing with invisible beings and claimed to know the secrets of the afterlife. He even prevented his *fidai'in* guards from killing a large snake one day, because he said it was the soul of an Assassin who had died recently. Another tale, genuinely believed at the time, was that one day, after he spoke gently to a horse it dropped dead. Sinan claimed that, through Allah's intercession, he had released the horse, a princess in a previous life, from a harsh master. Sinan's telepathic powers were also recounted as being so powerful that he could read thoughts and unopened letters.

It seems, however, that not all his contemporaries were convinced of his unnatural abilities. Complex tales of fraud were recorded, including one of a *fidai*'s apparently decapitated head on a gold tray chatting with the grand master whilst really being quite fully attached to a body hidden below the floor. Kamal al-Din's verdict was that whilst Sinan was undoubtedly 'an outstanding man', he was also little more than a juggler, 'with power to incite and mislead hearts', who used 'the vile and the foolish for his evil purposes'.*

Sinan showed his loyalty to the Persian mission by recognising the Resurrection that Hasan II had proclaimed from Alamut. There were, however, too many excesses carried out in Syria in celebration at the end of the law. Assassins were recorded, not surprisingly by Sunni writers, as defiling their mothers, sisters, and daughters during the *Qiyama*. Even

---

* Lewis, 'Biography of Rashid al-Din Sinan', pp. 231–7.

if these accusations are exaggerated there does appear to have been an acute breakdown in the Ismaili order resulting from the Resurrection. In 1176 Sinan had to carry out a campaign of virtual extermination against factions in the Jabal al-Summaq that were ignoring all calls for a return to discipline. The Resurrection and its aftermath made Sinan favour a fuller break from Persian control, and in the 1170s there were any number of attempts on his life by Assassins sent from Alamut, but every one failed and every Assassin sent was either killed or switched to Sinan's patronage.

Sinan's position at the head of the Syrian mission was now secure. His external policy was complex but retained his personal stamp, which is undoubtedly why he became the archetypal Assassin for the Crusader historians, and the stuff of legend in Europe. Indeed, his recognition as a man of great importance in the Levant was not limited to Christian writers. The Muslim traveller, Ibn Jubayr, recorded during his journey through Syria in 1185 that

> a sect has diverged from Islam, and which claims that the divinity resides in a human being. A demon with a human face, called Sinan, has appeared among them. They acknowledge him as their god whom they worship, and on whose behalf they are ready to sacrifice their lives. So completely have they become accustomed to obeying his orders, that if he orders someone to throw himself from the top over the precipice he does so at once.*

Between the two powers of the region, the Crusaders and Nur al-Din, the main contest was over Egypt. The Crusaders had realised that there could be no attempt to reclaim their losses against Zangi and Nur al-Din without the resources of Egypt, and Egypt looked ready to fall. Indeed, the Assassins' murder of Caliph al-Amir had, as we saw earlier, brought the Fatimid Dynasty virtually to its knees, and ended Egypt's ability to act as a regional power. In the 1150s and 1160s, the throne and the office of the *wazir* had been fought over by numerous candidates, and so weak was the kingdom that it began to pay tribute to the Franks. In 1163, an ousted *wazir*, Shawar, fled to Nur al-Din's court to seek aid against his successor. Amalric, the King of Jerusalem, invaded Egypt and would have taken Cairo, if he had not been halted by the city's defenders cutting dykes to release the Nile floods.

Nur al-Din's resources were stretched at this time, but he sent the Ayyubid, Shirkuh, with only a small force, to attempt to take Cairo.

---

* R. Broadhurst, *The Travels of Ibn Jubayr*, London, 1952, p. 264.

Shirkuh and his nephew, Saladin, were surprisingly successful and put Shawar back in office. However, Shawar then double-crossed Shirkuh and Saladin and called Amalric to his aid. Amalric advanced towards Cairo again, but Nur al-Din recommenced operations in Palestine and this was enough to force Amalric to conclude an armistice, based on the withdrawal of both the Crusaders' and Shirkuh's forces from Egypt. It was only a temporary ceasefire, however, and Shirkuh returned to Egypt in 1167. Shawar again appealed to Jerusalem and Amalric came in force, but was defeated by Shirkuh at al-Babayn, in March. The Franks also besieged Alexandria and its new governor, Saladin, managing to force a stalemate that saw both armies evacuate Egypt once again. Amalric was left in a slightly better position, in that the tribute paid to him by the Fatimids was increased, and he had troops and a military attaché garrisoned in Cairo itself.

In 1168 Amalric attempted to bring Egypt under full control and invaded once more. He took Bilbays on the Cairo road and it looked as if the capital would fall. Shawar opened protracted negotiations with the king, but also sent to Nur al-Din once again for aid. Shirkuh set out in December 1168 from Syria and the arrival of his forces in Egypt was enough to force the withdrawal of the Frankish army, which was suffering from disease. Shirkuh took the position of *wazir* and executed Shawar. Shirkuh's death soon after left Saladin at the helm of the Egyptian state, but in a tricky position. He was *wazir* to a Shiite-Ismaili caliph and had only a small body of Syrian troopers to counter the still large, if virtually unmanageable, forces of the Fatimid army. Fortuantely Saladin was a mature thirty year old, and was already a seasoned warrior and politician. Despite all his later great achievements, what he managed to do in Cairo, in these early years, may have been Saladin's finest deeds in terms of simple political acumen. He started by seizing lands and properties from senior Fatimid emirs, whilst still maintaining his loyalty to the Fatimid caliph. He then used the funds and property he garnered from this to both buy the services of Turkish Mamluks, and to supply his own men with *iqtas* in Egypt. By these actions, he both increased his own forces and tied the troops to his personal fortunes.

In 1169, he was able to meet and suppress a revolt among the Black troops of the Fatimid army, and by 1171 he simply had to wait for the sickly Fatimid caliph al-Adid to die in order to bring Egypt fully under his own control. Nur al-Din meanwhile, was placing increasing pressure on his lieutenant to finish the Fatimid line and impose Sunnism, and adherence to the Abbasid caliph, on Egypt. It has been suggested that Saladin could not bring himself to kill the young al-Adid, but it is obvious that he was also attempting to ensure that Egypt remained very much under his own control as a satellite to, rather than a province of, Nur al-Din's sultanate. Then, without warning, in September 1171, a citizen of Mosul, who was visiting Cairo, entered a mosque, climbed the pulpit ahead of the Ismaili preacher, and said the *khutba* in the name of the Abbasid caliph. There was no protest from the congregation, or riots, or insurrections over the following days. The Fatimid-Ismaili cause seemed to have died quietly, as did its last caliph, in his sleep, only a few days later.

Saladin then began to play a clever game: he assisted Nur al-Din in the sultan's campaigns against the Franks in Jordan, in 1171 and 1173, but during both campaigns he withdrew early from the conflict, citing concern over Cairo's politics – effectively allowing the Franks to escape serious defeats. Doubtless the ruler of Egypt realised that the Crusaders were effectively both distracting Nur al-Din from a march on Egypt and dividing Muslim Syria from Saladin's state. He also realised how dangerous this game was, and in February 1174, he sent his brother to Yemen to secure a bolt-hole for the Ayyubid family, should the whole empire-building project in Egypt come to nothing. Incidentally, this action pushed the Ismaili community, who had controlled Yemen since the tenth century, out of the country – they departed for India, where today they are known as the Bohoras.

The Ayyubid safe-haven plan certainly seems wise as the very next month a grand conspiracy against Saladin was discovered. It involved the now-disbanded Black troops of the former caliphal guard, Armenian Mamluks and diehard Fatimid Ismailis. The plotters had also opened negotiations with the Franks and, if a letter from Saladin to the caliph is to be believed, with Sinan, who, Saladin suggested, was colluding with the Franks over the future of Egypt at this time. In the end, a Christian agent in Saladin's secret service brought all the details of the plot to him and, acting quickly, he was able to round up all the ring leaders and have them crucified.

The Yemen bolt-hole plan might have been needed again later in the same year, when Nur al-Din sent an inspector to Egypt to check whether Saladin had been remitting tribute proportional to Egypt's revenue to Damascus. The inspector submitted a far-from-glowing report about the sultan's man in Cairo. The report was damning enough for Nur al-Din to begin mustering his forces in May 1174 for an expedition to Egypt, when fortunately for Saladin, he died on the fifteenth of the month after a fit of apoplexy brought on by a rather over-vigorous polo match.

The Assassins' daggers had been sheathed all this time. The *Qiyama* and the anarchy it caused were doubtless factors in this, but the focus of the main powers in Syria on Egypt had also meant there was a period of peace for Sinan to work on the infrastructure of his little kingdom. He established an efficient carrier pigeon service between the castles and improved the fortifications at all of the key strongholds. In 1173, in a decidedly strange episode, Sinan also seems to have opened negotiations with King Amalric on a possible conversion of the Assassins to Christianity. It could be that, by undertaking such negotiations, Sinan simply hoped that the king would force the Templars to revoke the annual tribute they had been paid by the Assassins since 1152. The talks may also, however, have been linked to possible assistance from the Assassins in the Egyptian plot.

The Templars, however, scuppered all these negotiations by ambushing and massacring Sinan's envoys, as they returned from an audience with the king. The Assassins continued quietly paying the Knights for peace, but their contact with Amalric gave William of Tyre an opportunity to study the sect reasonably thoroughly. The picture he has left us is one of a small but powerful state with a healthy population size and a very effective if intellectually lacking foreign policy:

> In the province of Tyre in Phoenicia and in the diocese of Tortosa there lives a tribe of people who possess ten fortresses with the villages attached to them. Their number, as we have often heard, is about sixty thousand or possibly more. It is the custom of this people to choose their ruler, not by hereditary right, but by the prerogative of merit. This chief, when elected, they call the Old Man, disdaining a more dignified title. Their subjection and obedience to him is such that they regard nothing as too harsh or difficult and eagerly undertake even the most dangerous tasks at his command. For instance, if there happens to be a prince who has incurred the hatred or distrust of this people, the chief places a dagger in the hand of one of or several of his follower; those thus designated hasten away at once, regardless of the consequences of the deed or the probability of personal escape. Zealously they labour for as long as may be necessary, until at last the favourable chance comes which enables them to carry out the mandate of the chief. Neither Christians nor Saracens know where this name, the Assassins, is derived from.*

---

* Quoted in Daftary, p 71. From the *Historia Rerum in Patribus Transmarinis Gestarum*.

With Nur al-Din's death, however, there was a new opportunity for expansion in Muslim lands, as the state created by the 'Saint King' was rapidly breaking up. Senior officers of Nur al-Din's government fought each other as they sought to control Nur al-Din's heir, al-Salih Ismail, who was only eleven at the time of his father's death.

Saladin also saw an opportunity to bring the former dominions of Nur al-Din into his possession and this remained his main aim in the years between 1174 and 1186. By his desire to re-unify and rule all of Syria he made himself number one on Sinan's most-wanted list. In addition, there was the fact that when the lands of the Assassins were raided by ten thousand Nubuwiyya, in one of their anti-Shiite operations, Saladin took advantage of the destruction of al-Bab and Buzaa and the Nubuwiyya's killing of as many as thirteen thousand Ismaili supporters in the two centres, to raid Sarmin and Jabal al-Summaq on his way up to Aleppo.

In October 1174, Saladin was virtually invited by the emirs of Damascus to take possession of the city. Al-Salih Ismail was taken by his *atabeg*, Gumushtigin, to Aleppo. The *atabeg* then contacted Sinan and it seems very likely that the Assassins were paid to make an attempt on Saladin's life. A group of *fidai'in* were dispatched to Saladin's camp, but they were challenged by an emir as they attempted to enter his tent. They stabbed the emir and one Assassin got into the tent, only to have his head slashed off by a guard's sabre. The other *fidai'in* then forced their way into the tent, but were met by a rapidly increasing number of Saladin's entourage, who killed them to a man.

In April 1175, Saladin crushed the combined forces of Mosul and Aleppo at the Battle of the Horns of Hama, near the River Orontes, and then concluded a truce, leaving him in undisputed possession of Damascus and a large part of northern Syria, including Homs, Hama and Baalbak. He fought the Mosul–Aleppo allies again, a year later at Tall al-Sultan and again routed them. Then in May 1176, as he was preparing to once again besiege Aleppo, while he was resting alone in the tent of one of his emirs, a *fidai* rushed in and struck at him with his dagger. Saladin was saved by the mail coif covering his head and neck. The Assassin slashed at his throat, but Saladin, obviously a powerful man, struck his attacker's wrist and deflected the blow. An emir rushed in and grabbed at the dagger and the Assassin was overpowered and killed. Then another attacker hurtled into the tent and attacked Saladin. By this time though the tent was full of emirs and the Assassin was literally hacked to pieces.

It was only after the event that it became clear that both of the *fidai'in* were members of Saladin's close personal bodyguard.

It was almost certainly in revenge for this last assault that Saladin set out to besiege Masyaf, after closing the siege of Aleppo in August 1176 through negotiation with al-Salih Ismaili's minders. As he approached Masyaf, however, and was riding under a walnut tree, a *fidai* dropped from the tree to murder him. Fortunately for Saladin, the Assassin's timing was out and he landed on the horse's rump, fell backwards to the ground, and was trampled and hacked to death by Saladin's bodyguard who were riding close behind. Saladin was not dissuaded from pressing the siege of Masyaf by the free-falling *fidai*, and he and his men settled in to starve the impressive fortress's garrison out.

Sinan's response was certainly worthy of any modern psychological operations unit. Whilst there is controversy over the reasons for Saladin's eventual raising of the siege, it seems highly likely that the tactics employed by Sinan against the new strongman of Syria played a major part in the withdrawal of Saladin's forces from Masyaf. First, there were letters between the two and one of Sinan's replies was recorded by Kamal al-Din:

> O you who threaten me with strokes of the sword, May my power never rise again if you overthrow it! The dove rises up to threaten the hawk. The hyenas of the desert are roused against the lions! He tries to stop the mouth of the viper with his finger, let the pain his finger feels suffice him. We have read the gist and details of your letter, and taken note of its threats against us with words and deeds, and by God it is astonishing to find a fly buzzing in an elephant's ear and a gnat biting statues. Others before you have said these things and we destroyed them and none could help them . . . If indeed your orders have gone forth to cut off my head and tear my castles from the solid mountains, these are false hopes and vain fantasies, for essentials are not destroyed by accidentals, as souls are not dissolved by diseases. We are oppressed and not oppressors, deprived and not deprivers.
>
> The common proverb says: 'Do you threaten a duck with the river?' Prepare means for disaster and don a garment against catastrophe; for I will defeat you from within your own ranks and take vengeance against you at your own place, and you will be as one who encompasses his own destruction . . .*

The duck and its water that Sinan referred to was the *fidai* and his love of death, and if such notions did not put fear in Saladin's heart,

---

* Lewis, 'Biography of Rashid al-Din Sinan', pp. 234–5.

then he must, after reading the phrase 'from within your own ranks', at least have looked warily through the register of his own *askari*. The fact was that Saladin had increased his standing bodyguard's size, with the purchase of Turkish Mamluks, and the permanent employment of Turcoman irregulars. Among the Turkish tribes continuing to enter Syria there were many who had been affected by extremist Shiite propaganda in the East.

Saladin, at this point, had a tall wooden tower built, in which he would sleep at night and he was never seen without mail during the day. Even these precautions, however, did not make him feel completely safe, so when he received an ambassador from Masyaf in his tent, he took the extra precaution of ringing the emissary of the Assassins with his most trusted bodyguards. The envoy was searched for weapons, and only then allowed to approach Saladin. When he refused to deliver his message in the presence of so many outsiders, Saladin acquiesced, but retained two Mamluks who he had raised from boyhood in his own household. Still, the emissary insisted on a one-to-one meeting. Kamal al-Din tells us that the resulting exchange went like this:

> Saladin said. 'These two do not leave me. If you wish deliver your message do so, and if not go'.
>
> He said. 'Why do you not send away these two as you sent away the others?'
>
> Saladin replied. 'I regard these two as my own sons, and they and I are as one'.
>
> Then the messenger turned to the two Mamluks and said. 'If I ordered you, in the name of my master, to kill this sultan would you do so?'
>
> They answered yes and drew their swords, saying. 'Command us as you wish'.
>
> Sultan Saladin [God have mercy on him] was astounded, and the messenger left, taking them with him. And thereupon Saladin [God have mercy on him] inclined to make peace with him and enter into friendly relations with him. And God knows best.*

There were certainly other reasons for Saladin's rapprochement with the Assassins. The Franks' invasion of the Biqa Valley and advance towards Baalbak called the sultan away from the siege of Masyaf. Many of Saladin's troops were also weary and wanted to return home to enjoy their booty. Ibn al-Athir also tells us that Sinan threatened to murder

---

* Lewis, 'Biography of Rashid al-Din Sinan', 1966, pp. 236–7.

'all the people of Saladin' if Saladin's kinsmen did not encourage him to withdraw.*

From the world of myth we have been given one final reason for Saladin's change of heart. The story goes that one night Saladin awoke in his tower and witnessed Sinan shining like a glow-worm and gliding above the ground and out of the door of the tower. Looking down to his bedside the sultan then saw a dagger pinning a leaf of paper to the floor. The page apparently carried the lines 'We acquaint you that we hold you, and that we reserve you till your reckoning be paid.' The creator of this story, Abu Firas, Sinan's Ismaili biographer, at least had the decency to state that he had only heard of this episode of levitation, as he was absent from Masyaf at the time.

Through the mediation of the emir of Hama a *modus vivendi* was reached between Saladin and Sinan. The secretive nature of the agreement allowed Saladin to complain to the caliph that the Zangid leaders of Aleppo were trying to derail his holy mission of ejecting the Franks from Syria. He claimed that the Aleppans had sent Assassins to attack him while he was in fact employing these same blades against Zangi and Nur al-Din's household. The former *wazir* of Nur al-Din was murdered on 31 August 1177 in Aleppo. The Assassins, when captured, stated under torture that they had been sent by Gumushtigin, who was still using the boy-sultan al-Salih Ismaili as a puppet on the throne. It is likely that the Assassins were told by Sinan that Gumushtigin was their 'employer' but Saladin was in fact the paymaster. Looked at in its simplest terms, there was nothing for Gumushtigin to gain from the murder whilst Saladin could only profit from increased confusion and mutual distrust within the house of Zangi.

Sinan carried out his own personal feud with the Zangids too. In 1180, Assassins infiltrated Aleppo and set fire to the great bazaar in reprisal for the seizure of some of their villages. Such targeting of economic assets of enemies was exceptional and the fact that every *fidai* returned from the mission was highly novel too.

Saladin continued his conquest of Muslim Levant by acquiring Aleppo in 1183, and imposing his suzerainty on Mosul in 1186. The Crusaders faced, once again, a unified Syria, but now the sultan had the additional resources of Egypt fully under his control. The King of Jerusalem, Guy, should at this point have taken a leaf from the Assassins' book of political survival by retiring to his fortified places to await events. Muslim history

---

* B. Lewis, 'Saladin and the Assassins', *Bulletin of the School of Oriental and African Studies*, Vol. 15, No 2, 1953, pp. 239–45.

had shown again and again that even polities as apparently strong as Saladin's was now, would soon enough break down. Indeed, the king's predecessors, despite their constant manpower shortages, and through their judicious use of their field army and superb understanding of castle strategy, had been reasonably successful in the Levant, until Guy recklessly sacrificed the flower of Jerusalem's chivalry on the Horns of Hattin on 4 July 1187.

It has been suggested that Assassins fought with Saladin against the army of the Franks at the battle, and given their continued payment of tribute to the Templars, it is possible that Sinan might have sent a force to aid the sultan. If he did, however, he might soon enough have regretted it since the Assassins homeland was essentially in the hinterland between the Muslims and Christians. Saladin's great victory very nearly put an end to the existence of any such no-man's land. The sultan quickly took Acre and Jerusalem and it seemed likely, for a time, that the Latin state was going to be pushed into the Mediterranean. Soon only Tyre, saved by the skilled and brave defence of Conrad of Montferrat, as well as Tripoli and Antioch, remained in Christian hands.

Whilst the pope hurriedly preached a Crusade and the Norman King of Sicily sent a fleet to supply the beleaguered cities, it was 1190 before the first Crusader army under the German Emperor Barbarossa marched eastward. The emperor drowned in Anatolia, whilst fording a river, but his son Frederick of Swabia was at least able to bring a thousand men down to Acre, where he joined King Guy, who had obviously crossed his fingers whilst swearing to Saladin that he would never again bear arms against the sultan after his capture at Hattin.

Guy was now engaged in besieging the city, whilst being surrounded himself by Saladin. Between April and June 1191, the King of France, Philip Augustus, and the King of England, Richard Couer de Lion, arrived at the siege. The squeeze was now really placed on Saladin's Acre garrison and they capitulated in July. Richard then marched south to relieve the coastal ports, after beheading the three thousand men of the garrison, and then defeated Saladin at the Battle of Arsuf. He went on to take Jaffa and twice struck towards Jerusalem, at one point coming within only a few miles of the city.

Despite Saladin's success in capturing Jerusalem, it seems at this point that there was a very real chance that he would lose everything. The sultan's health was failing and so was his revenue. Things were looking grim and negotiations were started with Richard through Saladin's brother. The princes of the Jazira began to desert, and despite continued calls for assistance to Iraq, no new help came. Al-Fadil wrote, 'tongues are generous with advice but hands are miserly with help,'* and Saladin spoke to his troops of the situation: 'Only our army is facing the army of infidelity. There is none among the Muslims who will come to our succour and there is none in the lands of Islam who will help us.'

Perhaps the sultan exaggerated a little, however, since there was one group of Muslims who would strike against the Crusaders, and whose hands carried daggers that in the past had proved to be more effective than any amount of talk. They struck on 28 April 1192, right at the centre of the Latin government, with the murder of the Marquis Conrad of Montferrat, hero of the defence of Tyre, and the man awaiting coronation as the new king of the Crusader kingdom:

> One day the marquis was returning from an entertainment given by the bishop of Beauvais, at which he had been a guest. He was in a very cheerful and pleasant humour and had just reached the customs house when two young men, without cloaks, approached him. These Assassins suddenly rushed upon him with poniards, which had been concealed in their hands. Stabbing him to the heart, they turned and fled away at full speed. The marquis instantly fell from his horse and rolled dying on the ground; one of the murderers was immediately slain, but the second took shelter in a church. In spite of this sanctuary, he was captured and condemned to be dragged through the city until his life should be extinct. Before he expired, he was closely questioned to discover at whose instigation, and for what reason, they had done the deed: he confessed that they had been sent a long time before, and had done it by command of their superior, whom they were bound to obey. This turned out to be true; for these young men had been some time in the service of the marquis, waiting for a favourable opportunity to complete the deed. The Old Man of Masyaf had sent them over to assassinate the marquis within a certain space of time; for every one the Old Man judged deserving of death, he caused to be assassinated in the same manner.
>
> The Old Man of Masyaf, according to hereditary custom, brings up a large number of noble boys in his palace, causing them to be taught every kind of learning and accomplishment, and to be instructed in various languages so that they can converse without the aid of an interpreter in any country of the known world. Cruelty of the greatest degree is also inculcated with profound secrecy; and the pupils are carefully and anxiously trained to follow it up. When they reach the age of puberty, the senior calls them

* M. Cameron Lyons and D. Jackson, *Saladin: The Politics of the Holy War*, Cambridge, 1982, p. 320.

to him and enjoins on them, for the remission of their sins, to slay some great man, whom he mentions by name; and for this purpose he gives to each of them a poniard of terrible length and sharpness. From their devoted obedience, they never hesitate to set out as they are commanded; nor do they pause until they have reached the prince, or tyrant, who has been pointed out to them; and they remain in his service until they find a favourable opportunity for accomplishing their purpose, believing that by so doing they shall gain the favour of heaven.*

Other versions of the killing say that the Assassins offered the marquis a letter for his attention before slaying him and that they were able to approach him easily, because they had been living for over six months in the Crusaders' camp, disguised as Christian monks. This seems unlikely given that the Assassins were certainly not trained in foreign languages. However, such fabrications, and the fact that the daring murder had taken place in the heart of the Crusaders' new capital in daylight, would soon enough carry the Assassins' fame in poems and tales to all the courts of Western Europe. Other chroniclers wrote that the marquis was only going to dine with the bishop because he was fed up with waiting for his wife, who was taking too long in the bath. While it might seem de rigueur for the medieval monks who were the recorders of events to blame a woman for the marquis's death, the fact remains that Conrad's murder has left us with an intriguing medieval whodunit because, whilst Sinan's men were undoubtedly responsible for the killing, a number of other respectable individuals, including his wife, were likely accessories to the fact.

The 'tidiest' explanation for the marquis's murder is that given by Ibn al-Athir, an admittedly hostile historian of Saladin's time, who claimed that the sultan commissioned Sinan to have both Conrad and Richard killed, but that Richard's murder had proved impossible. Certainly, given the apparent near exhaustion of Saladin's resistance to Richard and the fact that Conrad had been the saviour of the Latin Kingdom by his resistance at Tyre, such a plan would have been appealing, and as we have seen, a *modus vivendi* had already been reached between the sultan and Sinan. Ibn al-Athir also claims to know the amount the Assassins were paid for the planned double murder. Ismaili sources state, unconvincingly, given the history of the sect in the cities of Syria, that Sinan was promised houses

---

* *The Third Crusade: An Eyewitness Account of the Campaigns of Richard Couer De Lion in Cyprus and the Holy Land*, ed. K. Fenwick, London, 1958, p. 51. The author of the chronicle is anonymous but the original work is known as the 'Carmen Ambrosii' and Ambroise, a Norman troubadour, went with Richard to the Third Crusade.

of propaganda in Aleppo and Damascus by the sultan. A later Syrian source, as well as other Crusader writers, also identify that Sinan had his own reasons for assassinating Conrad. The marquis had offended Sinan by seizing a ship laden with a rich cargo belonging to the Assassins, and could only have increased the grand master's fury by then drowning its crew.

This is the simplest explanation of the killing, but Acre was a complex place in the late twelfth century. Suspicion also fell on Henry of Champagne, who had been a rival of Conrad for the throne of Jerusalem. He had certainly had extensive contact with the Assassins, and had even enjoyed Sinan's hospitality, during which, the writer who continued William of Tyre's history claimed, he witnessed two *fidai'in* showing their dedication to their master, by leaping from one of Masyaf's battlements to their deaths. The same story had, of course, been applied to Hasan-i-Sabbah a century before, and such a display was, according to Kamal al-Din, also laid on by Sinan for the benefit of Muslim emissaries. Historians never let a good story go to waste, but the fact remains that Henry married Conrad's widow within the week of the killing and was acclaimed King of Jerusalem in May 1192.

Even this explanation, of one man killing another for the throne and his wife, common though it is in history and Shakespearean in its telling, does not, however, reveal fully the fault lines that ran through Outremer, just as they had through the Muslim empires and states that the Assassins' daggers had previously brought down. Henry was just one man, but there were larger forces at play in the city. The orientalised Latins of Outremer, such as the Templars and Hospitallers, had a vested interest in keeping Conrad from the throne. They favoured Guy re-ascending the throne. He had already proved himself to be a weak king who was easily led by the military orders, whilst Conrad came from a powerful Crusading 'dynasty'. Conrad's brother was also a Palestinian baron and his nephew, Boniface, would later be a leading participant in the Fourth Crusade.

There was also the competition between the Italian maritime republics over the trade of the Levant, which continued right through to the Crusader kingdom's final extinction in 1291. The Genoese had favoured Conrad's claim to the throne, whilst their rivals, the Pisans, favoured Guy. An anonymous and contemporary chronicle of the Third Crusade tells us how at Acre, just before Conrad's murder:

> The Pisans were favourers of King Guy, whilst the Genoese were on the side of the marquis chiefly on account of the oath of fidelity by which

he was bound to the King of France. Hence arose discords which ended in bloodshed and mutual attacks, and the whole city was in a state of confusion. As they had been approaching the city the French had heard a great uproar, and the noise of the people exhorting each other to fight; upon which they, and the duke of Burgundy, in full armour, hastened to give succour to the Genoese. For all that the Pisans, when they saw them coming, went forth boldly to meet them. Falling upon the duke of Burgundy they surrounded him, and having pierced his horse with a lance, threw him to the ground; then they retreated to the city and closed and bolted the gates as a precaution against any unforeseen accidents which might happen. For they had heard that the Genoese had sent to the marquis to ask him to come as quickly as possible and seize the city of Acre, which they promised to deliver over to him. The Pisans, therefore, took every precaution against this faction, for their safety and for that of the city.

The marquis, without a moment's delay, came to Acre with a large number of armed men, in the hope of seizing the city unawares. On their arrival, the Pisans attacked him with mangonels and, confiding in their own valour and the justice of their cause, they fought bravely and sent a message to King Richard [he was at Caesarea] to inform him of the state of affairs, bidding him come with all speed . . .*

So now we have Richard and Philip, King of France, involved in the succession dispute. Suspicion for instigating the murder of the marquis later therefore fell on Richard, as Conrad had taken service under Philip, whilst Guy was a vassal of Richard:

In the confusion which now prevailed amongst the people, it was whispered by certain of the French who sought to veil their own wickedness by such a falsehood, and infused it into the minds of all the people that King Richard had vilely brought about the death of the marquis, and that he had hired these men from the Assassins for that purpose. Nor were they content with defaming the character of King Richard in those quarters, but also sent a warning to the King of France to be on his guard against the satellites of the Old Man of Masyaf . . .†

Indeed, in a further French version of the killing of Conrad, one *fidai* fled to the same church that the marquis's attendants had carried Conrad to, in order to dress his wounds. The *fidai*, seeing that his intended victim was not yet dead, emerged from his refuge and plunged his poniard into Conrad's body once more. The writer goes on to say how, when tortured with slow fire and flaying, the Assassin claimed that he had acted on

---

* Fenwick, p. 52.
† Fenwick, p. 54.

behalf of Richard Couer de Lion. English versions of the murder however, have the marquis dying in the arms of his wife, who presumably had, by now, finished her bath. In these versions of the story the marquis enjoined his wife to resign his possession, the city of Tyre, to no one save King Richard and, as noted above, within a week she had wed Richard's nephew, Henry.

The English writers also invented two letters supposedly written by Sinan: one sent to Leopold of Austria, who captured and held Richard for ransom as the king was travelling home across Europe; the second to the other princes of Europe, clearing Richard's name. They also wrote of how the king was reconciled with the marquis just before Conrad's murder, because the Crusader army had entreated him to do so, as well as asking to give them Conrad as their king before Richard's departure for England.

Richard's admirers worked hard to exonerate the king, but the fact remains that Philip had already left Acre for France to try to grab Flanders from its now-dead count. Along with Prince John of England's conspiring with the French king, this placed Richard's domain of Normandy in jeopardy, and required his rapid return to Europe. He could not secure the accession of his candidate, Guy, for the throne before his departure, so it seems extremely likely that he arranged for the Assassins to remove a tricky political problem for him with their daggers. This accusation was made by Muslim writers, as well as many of the Christian chroniclers.

This does not remove the likelihood that Saladin may have had a hand in the killing too. The death of Conrad certainly would have made Richard's departure from the Holy Land more likely and Saladin would have known that the king's leaving would effectively bring the Crusade to a close. It is possible then that Saladin, or rather his brother Sayf al-Din, known to the West as Saphadin, might have expedited the king's return to Europe by removing a prickly political problem for him. Certainly Saphadin and Richard grew close during their protracted negotiations. On Palm Sunday, Richard, amid much splendour in Acre's cathedral, girded Saphadin's son with the belt of knighthood. Perhaps this honour was bestowed on Saphadin's family for allowing Richard to profit from the working relationship that Saladin, and thereby Sayf al-Din, had with the Assassins. Back in France, Philip spread rumours that he was to be killed by a group of Assassins who had come from the Middle East at the instigation of Richard.

Richard took care of his other business in the Levant in a more orthodox fashion. The contest with Saladin had reached a stalemate and in August 1192 an accord was signed which left the coastal cities as far south as Jaffa to the Christians and gave access to Jerusalem for pilgrims. In March 1193, Saladin died in Damascus and later the same year Sinan took his knowledge of Conrad's murder with him to the grave.

Sinan had died after a rule of thirty years. He had been as a king, perhaps even a demigod, among his followers, and it is notable that with his passing, full control of the Syrian mission quickly reverted back to Alamut. His successor was a Persian named Nasr, but with the passing of Sinan and the adoption of Alamut's policy of alliance with the Sunni caliphate of Baghdad in 1211, the glory years in Syria were most definitely over. From the death of Sinan until their eventual extinction, the Assassins in Syria had none of the religious fervour and discipline that had held the mission together through the trials of the twelfth century. At many points in the thirteenth century they were to be little more than knives for hire.

7

DESTRUCTION IN THE HOMELAND

THE MONGOL CONQUEST OF PERSIA

That the joys of mortal men be not enduring, nor worldly happiness long lasting without lamentations, in this same year a detestable nation of Satan, to wit, the countless army of the Tartars, broke loose from its mountain-environed home, and piercing the solid rocks [of the Caucasus], poured forth like devils from Tartarus, so that they are rightly called Tartari or Tartarians. Swarming like locusts over the face of the earth, they have brought terrible devastation to the eastern parts [of Europe], laying it waste with fire and carnage. After having passed through the land of the Saracens, they have razed cities, cut down forests, killed townspeople and peasants. If, perchance, they have spared any suppliants, they have forced them, reduced to the lowest condition of slavery, to fight in the foremost ranks against their own neighbours. Those who have feigned to fight or have hidden in the hope of escaping have been followed up by the Tartars and butchered . . . For they are inhuman and beastly, rather monsters than men, thirsting for and drinking blood, tearing and devouring the flesh of dogs and men, dressed in ox-hides, armed with plates of iron. Short and stout, thickset, strong, invincible, indefatigable, their backs unprotected to prevent retreat, their breasts covered with armour, drinking with delight the pure blood of their flocks, with big, strong horses, which eat branches and even trees . . . They are without human laws, know no comforts, and are more ferocious than lions or bears . . . They have one-edged swords and daggers, are wonderful archers, spare neither age, nor sex, nor condition . . .

From Matthew Paris's Chronica Majora *for the year 1240*

IN 1251 BATU, THE Mongol Khan of the Golden Horde of Russia, and the sons of the House of Tolui formed an alliance and placed Mongke, Tolui's eldest son, on the throne of the Great Khans. Batu was paid off by being allowed virtual independence in his own lands, and the branches of the family emanating from Ogedei and Chaghatai were effectively disinherited from any chance of obtaining the throne of Chinggis Khan.

Mongke then partied with his supporters for a week, consuming two-thousand wagon loads of wine, three hundred horses and oxen and three thousand sheep, before neatly parcelling out the empire to his three brothers. Qubilai was assigned the conquest of the Song Empire in southern China, while Ariq Boke was given Mongolia. Hulegu was to be dispatched to the west. His mission would be to bring Persia fully under control. His more specific instructions were to ensure that the Abbasid caliph accepted Mongol suzerainty and to destroy, utterly, the Assassins.

A quick recap of the Assassins' relations with the Mongols in the first half of the thirteenth century shows how the Assassins had, like the caliph, at first found the Mongols to be a convenient counterweight to the Khwarazm shah. Their favourable impression of the new raiders from the East could only have been increased by the Mongols' sparing of the Assassin centre of Quhistan during their reduction of Khurasan. With the extinction of Khwarazm in 1231, however, relations deteriorated. As we have seen, in the 1240s Assassin ambassadors spent long periods in Qaraqorum, but were not received because of the political confusion of the Mongol state during this period. The Assassins were only one of the many panicked polities of Asia and Europe vying for the Great Khan's attentions. Lastly, of course, there was the simple reason that the Mongol chiefs feared an Assassin's blade too much to engage too closely with their emissaries. The Assassins' reputation, for once, worked against them and they were also let down by an uncharacteristic indiscipline in their ranks.

Despite the rapprochement that had taken place between the caliph, the Sunnis of western Persia and the Assassins, it seems that the war between the Sunni *ulama* and the *fidai'in* was still rumbling on in the east – even as close to Alamut as Qazvin. Juvaini wrote of there being a 'frontier' of Sunnism against the heretic Ismailis in the 1240s and 1250s. This was despite a redoubling of efforts to live in peace with his Sunni neighbours, especially the Gilanis, by Rukn al-Din. The Mongols became aware of this continued conflict through the *qadi* of Qazvin; he headed a delegation of several Sunni governors put into their positions by the Mongols before their withdrawal from Khurasan. The deputation complained to the Khan that they had to wear armour all day and night just in order to feel safe from the daggers of the Assassins.

Baiju, the Mongol commander in the Middle East, backed this up with a report to Mongke to the effect that the caliph and the Ismailis were the biggest obstacles to Mongol government in the region. Baiju's ire against the Ismailis was also stoked by the Assassins' murder of Chaghatai Qorchi, one of the senior Mongols who had been involved in the destruction of the Khwarazmians in the 1230s.* The Mongols may not have cared too much about the governors and religious judges, but they did care about their own kind and they liked orderly government, because order meant the free flow of revenue. The Assassins' disturbance of that and their unexplained murder of Chaghatai Qorchi were reasons enough for the Khan to countenance their destruction. But there was worse to follow. In his final years, Ala al-Din had been showing less and less desire for continued deference to Gog and Magog† and one last mission under the old man's rule had set out for Qaraqorum before his death and the accession of Rukn al-Din. The journal of Friar William of Rubruck briefly records a panic at the Mongol court:

> Following the court, we arrived here on the Sunday before Ascension. The next day we were called by Bulgai, first secretary of state and a great judge, as well as the monk and his whole family and all the ambassadors and the strangers who frequented the monk. We were separately brought into the presence of Bulgai and they asked us where we came from, and why, and what we wanted. And they proceeded to question us minutely, because it was reported to Mongke Khan that [four hundred] Assassins had arrived under various disguises to kill him . . . ‡

A later western traveller, Friar Odoric, who wrote of his journey to the East between 1318 and 1330, tells us how this one mission was part of a broader campaign against the Mongols:

> When the Tartars had subdued a great part of the world, they came to the Old Man, and took from him the custody of his Paradise, who being incensed by this, sent abroad many desperate and resolute persons and

---

* T. May, 'A Mongol–Ismaili Alliance? Thoughts on the Mongols and Assassins', *Journal of the Royal Asiatic Society*, Vol. 14, No. 3, 2004, pp. 231–9.

† Gog and Magog, or *Yajuj* and *Majuj*, in the Quran are the nations under the dominion of Satan. In the medieval Islamic mind the numerous barbarians of North Eastern Asia were the personification of *Yajuj* and *Majuj*. The expectation of the vast size of this army is expressed in Sura 21, v. 96: 'Until, when Gog and Magog are let loose, and they hasten out of every mound.'

‡ Whilst the quotation here is taken from Komroff, p 167, I have a made a small adjustment to the text. The number of Assassins sent to kill Mongke has been settled at four hundred and not forty as many versions of the friar's journal have it. See, *The Mission of Friar William of Rubruck: His Journey to the Court of the Great Khan Mongke, 1253–1255*, trans. P. Jackson and D. Morgan, Hakluyt Society, Aldershot, 1990, p.222.

caused many of the Tartar nobles to be slain. The Tartars, seeing this, went and besieged the city where the Old Man was, took him, and put him to a most cruel and miserable death.*

Ultimately, the mission failed, simply because the Mongol security arrangements, as discussed earlier, were so tight that not even the *fidai'in* could slip through. The attempt was an obvious *casus belli*, but the fact that the Assassins still maintained independent statelets that were not fully submitted to Mongol rule, was a simple affront to the Khan's vision of world conquest and was in fact reason enough. Indeed, there is evidence that the Mongols had planned the destruction of the Ismailis several years before Mongke ascended the throne. As noted above, the death of the Khwarazm shah Jalal al-Din in 1231, and the reduction of the Saljuqs in Anatolia in 1243, really meant that the Ismailis were the only power left in the old Saljuq lands who were capable of resistance. Certainly at Guyuk's coronation in 1246, the envoy of the Ismailis was driven from Qaraqorum and insulted by the Mongols. Guyuk then sent a Mongol force into the vicinity of Alamut to assault the Ismaili castles. The danger, however, passed with Guyuk's death in 1248, because as we have seen there was then a long interregnum and dispute over the throne that only ended with Mongke's ascension in 1251.

Mongke was very clear in his plans for the Assassins. They had outlived their usefulness to the Mongols in Persia. In fact, their value had expired once they had used their skills of masquerade and espionage to discover the whereabouts of the Khwarazm shah Jalal al-Din and then to convey this information to the Mongols, back in 1231. Ibn al-Athir tells us how:

> An official of the Ismaili Heretics was sent to the Tatars. He made known to them the weakness of Jalal al-Din, with his defeat. He urged [the Mongols] to proceed to him, and follow up on [Jalal al-Din's] weakness. And [the Ismaili official] guaranteed to them victory over [Jalal al-Din] truly if they proceed to him.†

The Mongols then chased Jalal al-Din to his death in Kurdistan – with his passing, the last effective counterweight to the Mongols' ambitions in Persia disappeared. Giving up the shah's whereabouts to the Mongols

---

* Komroff, p 247.
† Ibn al-Athır, al-Kamil fi al-Tarıkh, cited by May. I am extremely grateful to Dr Timothy May for pointing out to me the mechanics of the flowering and subsequent decay of the Ismaili–Mongol alliance.

may very well have secured the Ismailis the right not to supply troops to the Mongols and not to send tribute, but by doing so they also effectively sealed their own fate.

Hulegu's expeditionary forces began their invasion in 1253, and at this point all the leaders of the Islamic lands were sent letters requiring their submission. Hulegu, however, did not begin marching with his main force until later the same year. He spent the summer of 1254 in Turkistan and then moved across Khurasan. He did not reach Assassin territory until 1256. By this time Rukn al-Din had been grand master for just under a year and he certainly had not had time to bring the Assassins' organisation fully under his control or to grasp fully the state of affairs in Persia. This might explain the series of errors he made in dealing with Hulegu.

Whilst it is difficult to be exact about the size of the army that Rukn al-Din was going to have to face, we can be sure it was vast. The number of *tumen* commanders mentioned in the sources is generally about seventeen – this gives a figure of one hundred and seventy thousand men if each *tumen* was at full strength. This was, however, commonly not the case and there may have been as few as one hundred and twenty thousand Mongols accompanying Hulegu. His ranks would, however, have been swollen by Turkish freebanders and fifteenth-century sources give us a figure of about three hundred thousand men marching west to overwhelm Persia.

Hulegu's expeditionary forces had faired badly against the small forces available to the Assassins and had been beaten off from Quhistan by a counter-attack. At Girdkuh, his forces failed to make any headway against the castle's impressive walls and in the absence of any siege engines, they withdrew quickly. The preparations made for the main invasion were obviously influenced by these previous failures:

And he sent to Khitai to fetch mangonel experts and naphtha-throwers; and they brought from Khitai one thousand households of Khitai mangonel men, who with a stone missile would convert the eye of a needle into a passage for a camel, having fastened the poles of the mangonels with sinews and glue that when they aimed from the nadir to the zenith the missile did not return.*

An impressive logistics system was also put in place. Ahead of the army's move across Mongol, controlled territory pastureland was

---

* Juvaini, p. 608.

reserved, bridges were repaired and roads were cleared. Provisioning for the men included wineskins and flour, and Muslim emirs, who either governed Mongol-annexed territory or who were en route in lands still to be conquered, were equally expected to provide provisions for the army's passing. Hulegu was preparing for a long campaign and it was obvious that he was not going to leave Persia empty-handed.

The Mongol prince moved slowly, however, and enjoyed tiger hunts and countless revels, as well as the spectacle of his troops flattening the city of Firdaus and driving its entire population out into the countryside, before killing every person over the age of ten. These activities were, of course, diversions from his mission against the Assassins, but they also served a purpose in that they brought more and more of the local Turkish lords of eastern Persia to the Mongol standard, either through the attractions of the Mongol prince's evident wealth and power, or through fear of his army's obvious brutality. Hulegu's displays of splendour and of carnage therefore eliminated the need for battle and gathered troops to him for the reduction of the Assassins' strongholds. Juvaini tells us that, 'Orders were then given for the fastening of banners and standards [to lances] and the massing of troops for the purpose of making holy war and uprooting the castles of the Heresy. And all the forces in that region, whether Turks or Taziks, put themselves in readiness.'*

Rukn al-Din's will to fight, as we will see, collapsed quickly upon the approach of the Mongols. It could have been the sight of a multitude of banners and a vast siege train that caused this disintegration of spirit, or perhaps it was the fact that Mongol troopers were so inured to hardship that no siege seemed likely to end with their withdrawal through hunger. William of Rubruck wrote of them,

> they feed fifty or one-hundred men with the flesh of a single sheep, for they cut it up in little bits with salt and water, making no other sauce, then with the point of a knife or a fork made specially for this purpose . . . they offer to each of those standing around one or two mouthfuls.†

Even if sheep were in short supply, there were alternatives:

> Their food consists of everything that can be eaten, for they eat dogs, wolves, foxes, and horses and when driven by necessity, they feed on human flesh. For instance, when they were fighting against a city of the Khitai, where

---

* Juivani, p. 610.
† J. Smith, 'Mongol Campaign Rations: Milk, Marmots and Blood?', *Journal of Turkish Studies*, Vol. VIII, 1984, p. 223.

the emperor was residing, they besieged it for so long that they themselves completely ran out of supplies and, since they had nothing at all to eat, they thereupon took one out of every ten men for food. They eat the filth that comes away from mares when they bring forth foals. Nay, I have even seen them eating lice. They would say, 'Why should I not eat them since they eat the flesh of my son and drink his blood?'*

Either way, at the very word of Hulegu's arrival at Quhistan, the grand master of the Assassins opted for negotiation with his adversary, rather than an attempt on his life. He sent to one of Hulegu's lieutenants a message full of reproach for his father's hardening of attitude towards the World Emperor, and stated that he was looking for *il* with the Mongols. The Mongol word *il* is decidedly double-edged: it means peace but it also means absolute submission – the only way in which one could be at peace with the world conquerors. It is possible that this was exactly what Rukn al-Din planned for his little kingdom. However, despite being told to report in person to Hulegu, Rukn al-Din, in fact, only sent his brother, Shahanshah, to the Mongol prince's court. It is possible, therefore, that he was just playing for time in the hope that something would come up or that by procrastination he could at least arrange more favourable terms for his realm.

Hulegu seems to have foreseen any such tarrying and decided to speed along Rukn al-Din's decision about total submission by an invasion of Alamut's environs in June 1256. This was met by stiff resistance from the mountains around the castle, from both the Assassins and local Daylamite mountain villagers, and the Mongols withdrew after burning Alamut's croplands. Hulegu then tried a different tack. He sent to Rukn al-Din telling him that he did not hold him accountable for his father's crimes and would treat him as a vassal ruler, provided that he destroyed all his strongholds and submitted to him in person. The grand master continued to play for time; doubtless he thought that his show of resistance in June had strengthened his hand with the prince. He ordered the dismantling of some of the minor fortresses around Alamut and Mongol emissaries were sent by Hulegu to monitor this, but the main castles of Alamut and Lamasar only suffered cosmetic demolitions of their defences.

Rukn al-Din requested a year's grace to complete the work before appearing before Hulegu to do homage. He also ordered his lieutenants in Quhistan and east of Rayy to submit to the Mongols fully. However, either through *sub rosa* instructions from the grand master, or because

---

* John of Plano Carpini in Smith, p. 224.

Rukn al-Din did not have enough authority over the Assassins outside of the Alamut region, this was not fully carried out, and the castle of Girdkuh refused to surrender. Perhaps Rukn al-Din was still playing for time, knowing that winter snows would make any full-scale assault on Alamut impossible, as the valleys below the castle would become impassable. He would have been disappointed in this, however, by the curiously mild winter that settled on Persia that year. Hulegu also used this time to send detachments to the north and west of the Alamut region, to begin an encirclement of the Assassins' main castles.

Hulegu then ordered Rukn al-Din to come in person to court within five days, or to send his son. The grand master sent a seven year-old, but Hulegu was not convinced of the child's parentage – Juvaini tells us it was the child of a Kurdish woman and the bastard of Ala al-Din – and perhaps thinking to grab another hostage, he suggested that Shahanshah should be replaced by another of the grand master's brothers. At this point, Hulegu and his main force were only three days from Alamut and Shahdiz. The great castle south of Isfahan had fallen after only two days to Hulegu's lieutenant, Kit Buqa. Juvaini tells us that the arrival of Hulegu's forward troops with his banners had sent Rukn al-Din and all his advisers into a panic and that the grand master had, by September, made up his mind to surrender, only being deflected from this plan by the unwise counsel of women and other 'short-sighted people'.

Negotiations continued into October, and were hurried along in November by the launching of an all-out assault by Hulegu, despite the doubts of some of his generals over their ability to supply the army high in the mountains with winter coming on. It seems that Hulegu overcame the reservations of his recalcitrant lieutenants by conducting the campaign personally:

> The Monarch himself, blessed in action and in counsel, moved forward with an army in full array, of such great numbers that Gog and Magog themselves would have been destroyed by the waves of its battalions . . . And the centre he adorned with men of experience who consider the day of battle the wedding-night, and connect the blades of flashing swords with the cheeks of white-skinned women, and deem the pricks of lances to be the kisses of beautiful maidens.*

Juvaini's hyperbole aside, the Mongols made reasonable progress towards Alamut through the pass of Hazar-Cham and two castles on

---

* Juvaini, p. 625.

the lower slopes of the mountain range, Aluh-Nishin and Mansuriyya, were encircled and cut off. In fact, Hulegu only had to campaign among the peaks of the Elburz for a fortnight. The reported size of his army was enough to sway the Assassins' leadership towards surrender and in the meantime, the noose was also tightening around Rukn al-Din's men. The Mongol forces that Hulegu had sent around the Caspian Sea coast during the earlier negotiations, now also closed in and the castles of the Alamut region were completely surrounded.

Rukn al-Din himself was cut off from Alamut and besieged in the castle of Maymundiz by Hulegu in person. Juvaini described the siege. 'And now the inmates of the castle saw how a people as numerous as ants had, snake-like formed seven coils around it,'* and how the fruit trees of Alamut and Maymundiz were cut down to form the mangonels that the Mongols' Chinese siege engineers were preparing to bring the castles' walls down with. There was a response from the Assassins' own mangonels but the Mongols severely limited the use of the siege engines mounted on the castle ramparts by an almost unending rain of arrows. From wooden towers the Chinese engineers used ballistas to send quarrels, oversized crossbow bolts, flying into the battlements of the castles. Often these bolts were headed by naphtha and many of the castle's defenders were incinerated during artillery exchanges.

This barrage had the desired effect, and by now the Assassin leadership was split into factions over the simple question of whether to capitulate totally to the Mongols or not. Rukn al-Din totally failed as a general at this point and gave no decisive leadership. He was swayed in the end towards total submission to the Mongols and a hope for mercy. The Sunnis inside Maymundiz, many of whom had fled to Ismaili lands during the initial Mongol invasions, were influential in his choice and the chronicles record how decisive the astrological calculations of the Sunni philosopher al-Tusi were in this. He informed Rukn al-Din how portentous the stars were for such a move, but now the grand master sent an apologetic note to Hulegu saying that, whilst he wished to surrender, many men in the castle would kill him if he was seen to leave.

Hulegu returned to the offensive and gave orders that:

Every one, whoever he was, should advance and join battle with his opponents. And from the whole circumference of the castle, a distance of a *parasang* or more, the battle cry was blended with its echo; and from the

---

* Juvaini, p. 630.

rolling of the boulders hurled from above a trembling fell upon the limbs and members of the mountains. As for the mangonels that had been erected it was as though their poles were made of pine trees a hundred years old and as for their fruit, their fruit is as it were the heads of Satan; and with the first stone that sprang up from them the enemy's mangonel was broken and many were crushed under it. And great fear of the quarrels from the crossbows overcame them so that they were utterly distraught and everyone in the corner of a stone made a shield out of a veil whilst some who were standing on a tower crept in their fright like lizards into crannies in the rocks. Some were left wounded and some lifeless and all that day they struggled but feebly and bestirred themselves like mere women . . .*

It was enough to break the resolve of those who were holding the grand master back from capitulation. On 19 November 1256 the imam, along with his family and treasure, descended to Hulegu's camp under the protection of a *yarligh*, or edict, from Hulegu, drawn up by Juvaini, guaranteeing their safe conduct. Juvaini later recorded how the master's wealth was not as grand as it had been reported, but it was certainly gratifying for the Sunni writer to see Rukn al-Din kissing the threshold of Hulegu's audience tent.

Rukn al-Din was, in fact, then well received by the Mongol prince and this was not surprising as Hulegu obviously felt he had in his hands the key to every one of the Assassins' castles. This was certainly true of almost all the strongholds – following the appearance of the grand master and his calls to abandon and demolish a castle, his orders were generally carried out. Only Lamasar, Girdkuh and Alamut ignored his calls to surrender, although at Maymundiz there was a brief flaring up of resistance from a faction of *fidai'in*, who, following the grand master's safe passage to Hulegu's camp, started once again to work their mangonel. They were silenced forever, after four days of heavy Mongol bombardment.

It has been suggested that the commanders and *fidai'in* of these castles may have believed that Rukn al-Din was acting in *taqiyya*.† Such an idea is difficult to countenance, however, given that the grand master had given away almost every asset that would have been required for a return to the fray with the Mongols, in such a very brief period. Given this fact, there is no evidence that Rukn al-Din was dissimulating his beliefs in order to carry on fighting for Ismailism. He had shown himself to have neither the courage, discipline nor even the guile for such a venture. Perhaps

---

* Juvaini, p. 633. A *parasang* is a Persian measurement of about three miles. 'Their fruit is as it were the heads of Satan', is from the Quran: Sura 37, v. 3.
† Lewis, *The Assassins*, p. 94.

it is apt therefore, that two of the great fortresses that refused his calls for surrender were those of the first and greatest of the Assassin leaders, Hasan-i-Sabbah. Hasan had been a man very much the opposite of Rukn al-Din, who now progressed in his career as Hulegu's lackey to marriage with a Mongol girl and an unusual passion for a certain sport:

> And in the cauldron of his fancy he cooked a mania for stallion Bactrian camels and was always discussing them with anyone who had any knowledge about them. One day, accordingly, the king gave him a hundred head of female camels. He refused them saying, 'How can I wait for them to breed?' And he asked for thirty stallions because of his mania for watching camels fighting.*

Alamut surrendered in December 1256, and it was obvious that all the fire had gone out of the Assassin cause. The Mongols entered and began the onerous task of attempting to level the walls of the castle. Juvaini entered Alamut before this was undertaken and reported how the Assassins had made galleries and deep tanks for supplies in the cavities of the rock upon which Alamut stood. The tanks were filled with wine and vinegar and one intrepid Mongol had to be saved from a tank of honey into which he had waded, but then found it to be deep enough to try to swim in and easily deep enough to drown in. Juvaini also records how some of the foodstuffs dated from the time of Hasan-i-Sabbah, and that their freshness was taken by the Assassins as evidence of the first grand master's sanctity.

Juvaini also examined the library, burned its undesirable heretical books, and preserved whatever he felt was of value for his writing of the history of Hulegu's campaign and that of the Ismailis, including an autobiography of Hasan-i-Sabbah. He also took scientific and astronomical instruments, all of which ended up in the Mongols' soon-to-be-built observatory in Maragha. Tusi, the astrologer who had convinced Rukn al-Din of the stars' approval of his surrender, would later find work there under the Ilkhans. The Mongols then attempted to destroy Alamut, though it took them some time to work out how to level walls as their stones were bound together with lead. They finally settled on fire.

Lamasar held out for another year but then quietly submitted. Rukn al-Din sent letters to Syria ordering the *dais* there to submit to the Mongols, now that Hulegu's army had moved on to the conquest of that

---

* Juvaini. p 722.

state too, but his orders were generally ignored by the Syrian Assassins. The Syrian mission had a little more time ahead of it yet.

Rukn al-Din had very little time left. His usefulness to Hulegu was now exhausted. At his own request he was dispatched to the Great Khan Mongke, the very man whose attempted killing by the Assassins had brought such ruin to Persia and to Rukn al-Din. He went via Girdkuh, where he failed to negotiate the surrender of the castle, and eventually reached Qaraqorum. After the grand master's departure, a mass slaughter of the Ismailis began. Many of them had already been concentrated by the Mongols in camps around the city of Jamalabad near to Qazvin. Juvaini tells us that so many men, women and children were slaughtered in the concentration camps that afterwards, 'sent to Jamalabad' became common parlance in Persia for meaning someone had been killed.

Mongke Khan's original orders had called for none of the Ismailis to be spared and this was carried out with aplomb. Even babes in their cradles were not allowed to live. Rukn al-Din's family were reserved for slaughter by a Mongol named Bulaghan, whose father had been killed by the last desperate attacks of the *fidai'in* at Maymundiz, who, ironically, were acting against Rukn al-Din's orders for surrender. Juvaini claims that the Assassins and their supporters were destroyed wherever they were and over one hundred thousand people were probably slaughtered in this holocaust. However, many of the *rafiqs*, the low-level ordinary adherents of the Assassin cause, managed to flee across Persia to a new homeland in Sind and some higher-ranking members of the organisation even remained in Persia after the Khan's genocide.

Mongke Khan was disinterested in the grand master and refused him an audience until he had brought Girdkuh and Lamasar to surrender. Indeed, the great Khan seems to have been peeved at Hulegu because of the pointlessness of Rukn al-Din's journey. The grand master was immediately sent off on a return journey, but he never made it back to Persia. He was led off the road by his escort and there kicked to death and finished off with the sword. His body was never found and the only epitaph to the last Assassin grand master and his Persian followers was hardly an encomium:

> Let those who shall come after this age and era know the extent of the mischief they wrought and the confusion they cast into the hearts of men. Such as were on terms of agreement with them, whether kings of former times or contemporary rulers, went in fear and trembling and [such as were] hostile to them were day and night in the straits of prison for dread of

their scoundrelly minions. It was a cup that had been filled to overflowing; it seemed as if a wind had died. This is a warning for those who reflect, and may God do likewise to all tyrants.*

Hulegu moved on to the next part of his operation. He arrived just north-east of Baghdad in 1258. Mongol forces that had been stationed just to the east of Anatolia since the 1240s moved down the Tigris. According to Marco Polo, as Hulegu's forces approached the gates of the city, the Mongol prince

trusted rather to stratagem than to force for its reduction, and in order to deceive the enemy with regard to the number of his troops, which consisted of a hundred thousand horse besides foot soldiers, he posted one division of his army on the one side, and another division on the other side of the approach to the city in such a manner as to be concealed by a wood, and placing himself at the head of the third, advanced boldly to within a short distance of the gate.†

It seems that the caliph's army was lured out by the prospect of defeating this apparently small force, led by Hulegu. The Mongols then used their usual feigned retreat to draw the caliph's men about thirty miles away from Baghdad and to lure them into marshy land that inhibited both their manoeuvres and then their attempts to escape encirclement by the other Mongol divisions. They were massacred almost to a man.

The Muslim writer, Abu'l-Faraj, certainly suggests quite strongly that Caliph al-Mustasim was not the brightest Abbasid to have sat on the throne of Baghdad:

He was devoted to entertainment and pleasure, passionately addicted to playing with birds, and dominated by women. He was a man of poor judgment, irresolute, and neglectful of what is needful for the conduct of government. When he was told what he ought to do in the matter of the Tatars, either to propitiate them, enter into their obedience and take steps to gain their goodwill, or else to muster his armies and encounter them on the borders of Khurasan before they could prevail and conquer Iraq, he used to say, 'Baghdad is enough for me, and they will not begrudge it me if I renounce all the other countries to them. Nor will they attack me when I am in it, for it is my house and my residence.'‡

---

* Juvaini, p. 725.
† *The Travels of Marco Polo*, p. 44.
‡ Lewis, *Islam from the Prophet Muhammad to the Capture of Constantinople*, Vol. II, p. 23.

And of course he was wrong. The Mongols would begrudge him his city and indeed his life and they made preparations to take both from him. The caliph attempted a defence of his city but it was a hopeless attempt at resistance:

> Baghdad was defended, and mangonels were set up, with other instruments of defence, which, however, cannot avert any part of God's decree. As the Prophet said, 'Caution does not avail against fate', and as God said, 'When God's term comes it cannot be deferred' . . . The arrival of Hulegu Khan at Baghdad with all his troops, numbering nearly two-hundred thousand fighting men, occurred on Muharram of this year [January 19, 1258] . . . he came to Baghdad with his numerous infidel, profligate, tyrannical, brutal armies of men, who believed neither in God nor in the Last Day, and invested Baghdad on the western and eastern sides. The armies of Baghdad were very few and utterly wretched, not reaching ten thousand horsemen. They and the rest of the army had all been deprived of their *iqtas* so that many of them were begging in the markets and by the gates of the mosques.*

Even at this calamitous moment, when it seemed that the age of Islam was at an end, the old Shiite–Sunni conflict was very much in evidence. It was said in the streets of Baghdad that the poor condition of the army was due to the scheming of the Shiite *wazir*, Ibn al-Alqami. The rumour-mongers said that the *wazir* had seen Shiites turned out of their homes the previous year in rioting and street fighting between Sunnis and Shiites, and had decided to betray Baghdad to the Mongols. He had therefore deliberately denuded the army of supplies and money. The fact that he was the first of the ministers to go out to parley with the Mongols after the defeat of the caliph's army was taken as further evidence of his collusion with the heathens.

The *wazir* tried to negotiate on the basis of half the land tax of Iraq for Hulegu and half for the caliph, but Hulegu insisted on the caliph coming out of Baghdad to parley with him directly:

> The caliph had to go with 700 riders, including the *qadis*, the jurists, the Sufis, the chief emirs, and the notables. When they came near the camp of Sultan Hulegu Khan, all but seventeen of them were removed from the sight of the caliph; they were taken off their horses and robbed and killed to the very last man. The caliph and the others were saved. The caliph was then brought before Hulegu, who asked him many things. It is said that

---

* Abu'l-Faraj in Lewis, *Islam from the Prophet Muhammad to the Capture of Constantinople*, Vol. II, p. 24.

the caliph's speech was confused because of his terror at the disdain and arrogance which he experienced.*

The caliph returned to Baghdad with the *wazir* and also Nasir-al-Din Tusi, who we last met giving appalling astrological advice to Rukn al-Din. He was now in the service of Hulegu and had accompanied him to Baghdad, where he was now about to give more of his, perhaps not entirely unbiased, advice to the caliph. Great quantities of gold and jewels and other treasures were offered to Hulegu for peace, but this display of Baghdad's wealth only made the Mongols keener to get into the city and begin looting.

The second interview between the caliph and Hulegu was cut short by the Mongol prince calling his guards to take the caliph into custody, then the Mongols

came down upon the city and killed all they could, men, women and children, the old, the middle-aged, and the young. Many of the people went into wells, latrines, and sewers and hid there for many days without emerging. Most of the people gathered in the caravanserais and locked themselves in. The Tatars opened the gates by either breaking or burning them. When they entered, the people in them fled upstairs and the Tatars killed them on the roofs until blood poured from the gutters into the street; 'We belong to God and to God we return'. The same happened in the mosques and cathedral mosques and dervish convents.†

After witnessing the destruction of his city the caliph was then murdered. Marco Polo describes his end as having a certain poetic justice:

The caliph himself was made prisoner, and the city surrendered to the conqueror. Upon entering it, Hulegu discovered, to his great astonishment a tower filled with gold. He called the caliph before him, and after reproaching him with his avarice, that prevented him from employing treasures in the formation of an army for the defence of his capital against the powerful invasion with which it had long been threatened, gave orders for his being shut up in this same tower, without sustenance and there, in the midst of his wealth, he soon finished a miserable existence.‡

---

* Abu'l-Faraj in Lewis, *Islam from the Prophet Muhammad to the Capture of Constantinople*, Vol. II, p. 24.

† Abu'l-Faraj in Lewis, *Islam from the Prophet Muhammad to the Capture of Constantinople*, Vol. II, p. 24.

‡ *The Travels of Marco Polo*, p. 44.

In fact, the unfortunate caliph was wrapped in a carpet and kicked to death. The Mongols never spilt blood in the execution of princes. And so, the Ismailis' ideological enemy of five centuries was extinguished, but there was no victory in this for them, as by now they too had gone the same way as the sons of Abbas.

Hulegu then withdrew from the city, as the stench of death was said to be too overpowering to stay within the circular walls. Then the vast Mongol army decamped to the pastureland of Azerbaijan, where it remained for over a year, before embarking on a campaign in Syria against Saladin's descendants, the Ayyubids.

Just as Sunni Islam did not end with the extinction of the caliphate, the history of the Assassins in Persia also did not end with the death of their last grand master. Girdkuh held out until 1270, and legend has it that the garrison only surrendered because their clothes had rotted away to scraps. In 1275, Assassins under the command of one of Rukn al-Din's sons, called Abu Dawlut, recaptured Alamut, which the Mongols had been unable to destroy, even with fire. The new garrison was finally crushed by the Mongols the next year. Other minor forts in Quhistan fought on in the same way.

From these facts, and from Juvaini's description of Alamut's readiness for siege, it seems impossible that the Mongols could have made particularly easy work of reducing Alamut and Lamasar and the other Assassin castles without Rukn al-Din's compliance. So the question remains, why did the Assassins give in to Hulegu's men when a unified resistance might well have, at the very least, enabled the Assassins to obtain better terms?

The answer certainly lies partly with the Mongols. They were the irresistible force of the medieval age and their seemingly unstoppable run of success would not be broken until their defeat by the Mamluk sultanate at the Battle of Ain Jalut in Syria, in 1260. Resistance against such a superpower might just have seemed impracticable and futile to the Assassins. The Mongols also used terror in a way that no other invader of Persia had before.

Previous to the Mongols' irruption into the Middle East, the true end of military activity was the capture of fortified places, deposing of the previous dynasty and exploitation of the state's resources. Von Clausewitz's perhaps now somewhat hackneyed declaration that, 'war is a mere continuation of policy by other means', is in fact true when applied to the polities that had fought over Persia, previous to the Mongols' total war. The Mongol war aim was different simply because they were antagonistic against anything of the pre-existing state and were focused on its total destruction. William of Rubruck, who knew them first hand, said of them: 'When they make peace with any one, it is only to destroy them.'*

Even the Khwarazmians had been Muslims and this had perhaps restrained them from even worse atrocities against their co-religionists than those that are recorded as having been committed by Ala al-Din Muhammad and the other shahs. Juvaini, the panegyrist of Hulegu, occasionally forgets himself and refers to the Mongols as 'Tartar devils' and 'strangers to religion'. The Mongols' savagery has been recorded by both Islamic and European chroniclers, and the spread of this terror was far ranging, as the Mongols were more numerous than any other previous invader. Ibn al-Athir, a contemporary of the Mongol invasions, wrote in the opening passage of one of his books that:

> I have been avoiding mentioning this event for many years because I consider it too horrible. I have been advancing with one foot and retreating with the other. Who could easily write the obituary of Islam and the Muslims? For whom could it be easy to mention it? Would that my mother had not given birth to me. Would that I had died before it happened and had been a thing forgotten. However, a group of friends urged me to record it since I knew it first-hand. Then I saw that to refrain from it would profit nothing. Therefore we say this deed encompassed mention of the greatest event, the most awful catastrophe that has befallen time. It engulfed all beings, particularly the Muslims. Anyone would be right in saying that the world, from the time God created humans until now, has not been stricken by the like. Histories contain nothing that even approaches it. In fact nothing comparable is reported in past chronicles. It may well be that the world from now until its end will not experience the like of it again, apart perhaps from Gog and Magog.†

There were no empty threats from the Khans; they had both the manpower and the will to decimate populations. They were the real terrorists of the Middle Ages, in that they used terror on a vast scale to achieve their goal – the acquisition of territory and wealth. It was no wonder that Juvaini, their apologist, had to cast them in the role of God's judgment on His sinful people, but he too, then goes on to write of the

---

* Komroff, p. 171.
† S. Virani, 'The Eagle Returns: Evidence of Continued Ismaili Activity at Alamut and in the South Caspian Region Following the Mongol Conquests', *Journal of the American Oriental Society*, Vol. 123, No. 2, 2003, pp. 351–70.

hopeless desolation to which the conquerors had reduced Khurasan, his homeland. Then there was the fact that the Mongols applied siege warfare in a manner unseen in the Middle East prior to their arrival. They had learnt much from their Chinese campaigns against the great-walled cities of the Jin state and brought expert Khitai and Chinese engineers with them to batter at the walls of the Assassin castles.

This said, and even if we accept that the Mongol army was capable of feeding itself off lice and carrion, there was still the question of fodder, a problem that every cavalry army from Alexander's to Napoleon's faced. Juvaini's rendition of Hulegu's campaign against the Assassins tells us how the Mongol army had to move from relatively fertile areas after only a month or so, because the pasture had been denuded. Later, the Mongols would face a logistical nightmare in Syria whilst trying to maintain an army in the field against their doughty opponents, the Mamluks.

The fact remains therefore that the Assassins, despite all the problems of facing down the Mongol war machine, should still have been able to hang on longer, simply because the time the Mongol army could spend in one location besieging castles was limited by their horses' needs.

In the final count, the Assassins of Rukn al-Din did not resist as their predecessors would have, and whilst some of the reasons for Rukn al-Din's easy surrender to Hulegu doubtless lie with the frightening military ability of the Mongols, along with the grand master's own weakness of character, this cannot be the whole answer. The neighbours of the Assassins, the Gilanis, maintained their independence from the Mongols until the early part of the fourteenth century. Even when a Mongol army was sent into the jungles south of the Caspian Sea, in an attempt to bring them to heel, it was slaughtered. A subsequent punitive campaign could not make effective contact with an enemy who just kept melting away into the forest. Eventually the Gilanis obtained quite favourable terms from the Mongols for their surrender, and of course the Ilkhanate, the Mongol state of Persia, collapsed in 1336, freeing the Gilanis from their yoke.

What was more important for the Assassins was that they had lost the will to fight on. Under earlier grand masters, they would have maintained themselves in their castles and the *fidai'in* would have brought about the sort of crises within the Mongol state that the killing of Nizam al-Mulk and of other political luminaries had caused in previous regimes. The Mongols were also, of course, heathens and any action against them by the *fidai'in* might even have allowed the Assassins to appear as the saviours of all of Islam. They could not save Islam from the Mongol rage – that job would fall to the Mamluks of Egypt. One of the reasons for this was that, under the grand master Jalal al-Din, they had come in from beyond the pale and become good Muslims following the edicts of the Sunni caliph.

In short, the radical fire of the Assassins had been put out by a desire among the later grand masters to join the society of nations and to be seen as kings rather than as revolutionaries. They had sold out for earthly power, whilst what had made the early *fidai'in* so feared was their rejection of this world and their apocalyptic desire to attain the next. The last Assassins had forgotten what Hasan-i-Sabbah had known so completely – the *sirat-i-qiyamat*, the bridge from this world into Paradise, is more slender than a hair and sharper than a sword. Absolute discipline and total belief are needed in order to cross it.

8

MAMLUKS, MONGOLS AND CRUSADING KINGS

THE END OF THE SYRIAN MISSION

When we were children we went to the Master for a time,
For a time we were beguiled with our own mastery;
Hear the end of the matter, what befell us:
We came like water and we went like wind.

*Omar Khayyam**

THE DEATH OF SALADIN broke up Sunni Muslim unity in Syria and Egypt, just as the Assassins' daggers had in the past. The patrimonial share-out of the sultan's possessions, once again, put brother against brother and uncles against nephews. Syria was parcelled out among Saladin's relatives. Egypt, at least, remained intact as a state, but independent of Syria. It could have been a wonderful time to be an Ismaili Assassin, but there were troubles ahead. As discussed briefly at the end of chapter six, in 1211 the Syrian Assassins had adopted the policy of the Persian grand master Hasan III, that of alliance with the Abbasid caliph. The fast of Ramadan was enforced by the compliant new chief *dai* and there would be no leaders worthy of the title of grand master in Syria after Sinan's passing.

---

* The Persian poet Omar Khayyam was linked in legend as being one of three schoolfellows in Nishapur, along with Nizam al-Mulk and Hasan-i-Sabbah. The three allegedly made a vow that the first of them to achieve success in life would help the other two in their careers. Nizam al-Mulk achieved this, but after offering Khayyam a regular stipend he double-crossed Hasan who vowed to take revenge. The tale is impossible, by simple virtue of the dates of birth of the protagonists but Khayyam was mentioned in the Ismaili text *The Seven Chapters of the Father of Our Lord* and he was certainly a radical by reputation, as well as being a brilliant mathematician. In 1074 he reformed the Persian calendar for Malikshah. See G. Sarton, 'The Tomb of Omar Khayyam', *Isis*, Vol. 29, No 1, 1938, pp. 15–19.

Alamut's control over the Syrian mission was now very much in evidence, a Syrian Assassin inscription records how:

> In that year 608 [1211] an ambassador of Hasan, the grand master of Alamut came, to announce that they were liberated from *Batinism*, that they had built mosques and prayer houses and re-established worship and prayer meetings and the fast of Ramadan. The public and the caliph felt great joy at this. The princess daughter of Hasan undertook the pilgrimage and received a warm welcome from the caliph.*

Saladin's truce with Sinan and the above accord between the Assassins and the caliphate seems to have been enough to maintain fairly friendly relations between the Ayyubids and the Syrian Nizaris. The Ayyubid princes found themselves in a similar situation to that which the Turkish princes of Syria had found themselves in 1099 – petty princes controlling only one city or province and surrounded by suspicious neighbours. Stirring up a hornet's nest by attacking Assassin possessions would have been unwise. Likewise the Assassins turned away from the killing of Muslims and towards the murder of Crusaders in this period. This was not undertaken for ideological reasons, but simply because the Crusader princes of the Levant were now placing more and more pressure on the Assassin territories.

In 1213 Raymond, the son of Prince Bohemond IV of Antioch, was killed in the main church of Tortosa during prayers, and the response of his father is not all that surprising. He sent an expedition to the nearest Assassin castle of al-Khawabi and began a fierce assault on it, then settled in for a siege. The Assassin leaders called for assistance from the Ayyubid prince of Aleppo. When this was not sufficient to push the Franks from their position surrounding the castle, a further appeal was made to Damascus. The Franks were finally turned away from the fortress in 1215.

There was nothing of *jihad* in all this – the Ayyubids competed with the Franks for trade routes and croplands in Syria, but there was no ideology evident in the warfare of early thirteenth-century Syria, and this extended to the Assassins and the military orders. The Knights Hospitallers managed, through raiding of Ismaili villages and destruction of their agriculture, to force the Syrian Assassins to pay them tribute, as they did already to the Templars. In 1230, presumably as an attempt to pay

---

* M. Van Berchem, 'Epigraphie des Assassins de Syria', *Journal Asiatique*. Serie IX, Mai-Juin 1897, pp. 453–501. Translated from the French by M. McCrystall.

them in kind and to vent their spleens against Bohemond, the Assassins sent a military force along with the Hospitallers of Crak des Chevaliers, who were raiding Bohemond's lands as part of a long-running feud that the order had been pursuing against the lord of Antioch. Bohemond's relationships with his fellow Crusaders were fairly appalling generally, and he was excommunicated in 1208 by the Patriarch of Jerusalem. His feud with the Hospitallers also suggests that the Assassins might have had some encouragement from the Knights for their killing of Raymond.

Considering the degree of contact the Assassins had with the Hospitallers in this period, it should be noted, once again, that the weapon of assassination was ineffective against the military orders. Murdering the grand master of the Hospitallers would just lead to one of the knights replacing him from the hierarchy below. The Templar and Hospitaller Orders of knighthood were institutions built on hierarchy and non-familial loyalty. Medieval Muslim polities generally had neither of these qualities. They were centralised, autocratic states based on personalities and transient ties. As the Lord De Joinville described it:

> At that time he [the chief dai] used to pay tribute to the Temple and the Hospital; for they feared the Assassins not at all, seeing that the Old Man of the Mountain had nothing to gain by having the master of the Temple or Hospital put to death; for he knew very well, that if he had one of them killed, he was immediately replaced by another just as good; and for that reason he did not want to waste his Assassins in a quarter where he had nothing to gain by it.*

The eventual nemesis of the Assassins in Syria, the Mamluk Dynasty, was the Muslim equivalent of these non-aristocratic military brotherhoods. It was made up of slave soldiers without parentage whose ties to each other were based on a barracks culture and a military code.

In order to make their payments to the Knights Hospitallers and Templars, the Assassins, in a very businesslike manner, turned to offering asylum for a price to political dissidents from the petty states of Syria, as well as simple extortion. Minor Muslim and Christian lords were shaken down for protection money, and in 1228 they even tried it on, to good effect, with an emperor. Frederick II came on Crusade and sent gifts totalling some eighty-thousand dinars to Majd al-Din, the chief dai, to guarantee his safe conduct, whilst he visited the holy sites of Palestine. The Crusade itself was curiously bloodless, with the qadi of Jerusalem

---

* Wedgwood, pp. 234–5.

being so friendly towards Frederick that the muezzins were told to hold their evening call to prayers for fear of disturbing the emperor's sleep. Frederick also managed to negotiate with al-Kamil, the most powerful of the Ayyubid princes and de facto sultan, for Jerusalem to return bloodlessly to Christian control. His success and efforts in the Holy Land were not viewed warmly, however, by the pope back in Rome, who still seemed to be of the opinion that the only good Muslim was a dead Muslim. Besides, Frederick had been excommunicated prior to his departure on Crusade and was therefore ineligible to wear the Cross.

Majd al-Din failed to send the Holy Roman Emperor's treasure on to Alamut, because he claimed the roads had become too dangerous. There was at least a scrap of validity in this assertion – ever since the complete destruction of the Khwarazm shah's empire by the Mongols in the 1220s, unemployed bands of Khwarazmian soldiers had been turning up in Syria and making trouble for just about everyone. They then exceeded even their own normally high standards of brutishness in 1244, while they were supposed to be working for the new Ayyubid sultan of Egypt, al-Salih, in Syria. They entered the open city of Jerusalem, slayed at least two thousand of its Christian residents, destroyed the tombs of the Latin Kings of Jerusalem and only then moved on to join their employer's army in Egypt. Their act of desecration was enough to bring the largest army that Outremer had put in the field since Hattin, to Egypt's frontier. The Crusaders pulled troops from every part of the kingdom and allied with the Ayyubids of Syria, who had also suffered at the hands of al-Salih's Khwarazmian mercenaries. Al-Salih's Mamluk army and his Khwarazmians met the allies in battle at Harbiyya.*

The allied forces outnumbered their enemy, but the Egyptian Mamluks stopped the Crusader charge dead, and the Khwarazmians, from a position out to the right of the Mamluks, swung down upon the Syrian Ayyubids and smashed into their flank. There was panic among most of the Syrian Muslims, who fled and left only the men of Homs and the Crusaders on the battlefield. The Khwarazmian drive pushed the Crusaders and their few remaining allies into the arms of the Mamluks, who proceeded to massacre them with bow, mace and axe. At least five thousand Crusaders were killed and eight hundred taken prisoner. It was a defeat on the scale of Hattin, and it triggered renewed calls for Crusade in Europe.

---

* The battle is known in the European sources as La Forbie.

The new Crusade came in the summer of 1249, under the pious King of France, Louis IX. Louis aimed to wrest Egypt from Islam – the logic for this being that Egypt was in fact the key to the Holy Land, as without Egypt's economic and agrarian resources, Syria's interior lands were extremely difficult to defend and maintain, especially as the Crusaders still retained the Syrian coastline. The same kind of amphibious attack as Louis contemplated had been tried in 1218, and had very nearly succeeded. It was only when the Crusader advance from al-Mansura had been halted by Nile floods that the Egyptians had been able to encircle them and then cut them off totally, by bringing down river dams to flood the area to their rear.

Louis's endeavour, however, failed, after al-Salih's Mamluks defeated his army at al-Mansura, just north of Cairo, cut it off from its supply route up the river Nile, and let disease and starvation force the king to surrender himself and his forces. As an aside to all this, al-Salih died during the Crusade and his Mamluks then rebelled against his heir. A junior emir named Baybars killed the Ayyubid prince as he tried to escape across the Nile and the Mamluk Dynasty was born on the river's muddy banks.

Louis was eventually ransomed and sailed for Acre, where he spent some four years strengthening the city's defences and carrying on a long-distance negotiation with the Mongols, who had by now conquered Anatolia, and obviously had designs on the whole of the Middle East. The king was also an enticing target for extortion by the Assassins. There were already tales circulating in Europe that Assassins had been sent to Europe to kill King Louis when he was a child but these were just a by-product of the slanders against Richard Couer de Lion, that claimed he had brought *fidai'in* back from the Levant with him to kill kings for him. Now, however, Louis faced emissaries of the Assassins in his own quarters:

> Whilst the king was dwelling in Acre, there came to him messengers from the Old Man of the Mountain. When the king returned from mass, he made them come before him. The king made them be seated in the following order. In front was an emir, well dressed and well equipped; and behind this emir was a youth well equipped, grasping three knives in his hand; so that if the emir had been rejected, he might have offered these three knives to the king, in token of defiance. Behind him who held the three knives, there was another that carried a sheet wound around his arm, which he

too would have presented to the king for a shroud to wrap him in, had he refused the request of the Old Man of the Mountain.*

The emir then asked the king if he knew of his master and Louis replied calmly that he had heard of him. He obviously did not appear impressed enough for the emissary:

> Then since you have heard of my lord, I marvel greatly, that out of your possessions you have not sent him such gifts as would have secured him for your friend; even as the Emperor of Germany, the King of Hungary, the sultan of Egypt, and the rest do every year; because they know for certain, that they can only live as long as it shall please my lord. And if you do not choose to do this, then let him receive quittance of the tribute that he owes to the Hospital and the Temple, and he will consider your score cancelled.†

The king had obviously acquired a very acute understanding of the mechanics of Palestinian politics, because he asked the emissary to attend on him later the same day. The Assassin entourage did so but when their chief entered the king's salon:

> He found the king seated thus: the master of the Hospital on one side, and the master of the Temple on the other. Then the king bade him repeat what he had said to him in the morning; and he replied that he had no mind to repeat it, save before those who had been with the king in the morning.
>
> Then the two masters said to him: 'We command you to speak it'. And he said, that, since they commanded him, he would repeat it to them. Then the two masters caused him to be told in Arabic, that he was to come and speak with them the next day at the Hospital; which he did. Then the two masters said to him that his lord was a very bold man, to dare to send such harsh language to the king.‡

The counter-threat from the two masters was very obvious and there were no attempts on the king's life while he was at Acre. The only gift the Assassins ever received from him was reciprocated by the chief *dai*, and tribute continued to be paid to the Templars and Hospitallers. As if all this was not bad enough, in 1256 word came of the destruction of the Assassins in Persia. Despite the 'interregnum' of Sinan, there had always been an umbilical connection to Persia for the Syrians. There is even evidence of Assassin activity as far north as Azerbaijan, and as discussed

---

* Wedgwood. pp. 233–4.
† Wedgwood, p. 234.
‡ Wedgwood, pp. 234–8.

earlier, through a corridor between north-west Persia and Northern Syria that passed through Mosul. The killings in the Azerbaijan region seem to have been an elemental part of the attempt to keep communications open between Alamut and its colony. There were certainly a number of unresolved murders of princes of Azerbaijan and Mosul, but whether the Ismailis operated through allies or directly in this region, we shall probably never know. There are no known Assassin fortresses between Persia and Syria and very little in the chronicles beyond an ambiguous reference in the writings of Benjamin of Tudela, and a vague mention by Marco Polo who wrote 'He [the grand master] had also constituted two deputies or representatives of himself, of whom one had residence in Damascus, and the other in Kurdistan; and these two pursued the plan he had established for training their young dependants.'* This connection was strong right up until the moment the Mongols extinguished Alamut. And whilst the Syrians refused Rukn al-Din's calls for them to surrender, there must have been an awful feeling of isolation descending on the Assassin castles of Syria in the last years of the 1250s.

The Mongol invasion of Syria began in January 1260 with Aleppo's bloody fall. Damascus then capitulated rapidly, and probably wisely, upon the approach of Hulegu's army. The Mongols then proceeded to disestablish Islam as the official religion of the area. The Christians of Damascus drank openly during Ramadan, and it is to be wondered whether the Syrian Assassins, so long committed to the idea of the destruction of the Baghdad caliphate, but now wedded to the corpse of its caliphate, might possibly have thought of celebration too. This, however, seems unlikely. With the Mongol conquest of Damascus, the Assassins' castles were now flanked on two sides, and to their rear Bohemond VI, of Antioch and Tripoli, made submission to Hulegu. Four of the Assassin castles in the Jabal al-Summaq were besieged by the Mongols and they surrendered. Only Egypt, a few isolated cities and castles in Syria and the Arabian Peninsula were now left to Islam in its historic heartland. Hulegu sent envoys to Kutuz, the Mamluk sultan in Cairo, demanding his surrender, but once Kutuz had had the envoys cut in half and placed their heads on the gates of the city, he started to mobilise his troops for battle in Syria. It was to be a battle that would essentially decide the fate of the Islamic world.

News reached Syria that Mongke Khan had died, of natural causes, while on campaign in China with his brother Qubilai – this sowed the seeds of

---

* *The Travels of Marco Polo.* p 77.

a great Mongol civil war. This was just what Ala al-Din Muhammad had tried to effect by his abortive dispatch of four hundred *fidai'in* to Mongke Khan's court in 1253. Certainly, there had been previous divisions and conflict within the House of Chinggis Khan over the succession. Upon the death of Mongke, however, the rifts between the Mongol princes became so great and irreparable that the death knell of the Mongol Empire was struck in 1259. Hulegu was distracted from his coming conflict with the Mamluks by the death of his brother and its sequelae, far to his east. His brothers Qubilai and Ariq Boke were both prepared to undertake war on each other for the succession. Hulegu never really seems to have counted himself as a candidate, but he did have concerns about the outcome of the contest. Ariq Boke was backed by most of the Chinggisid family in Mongolia and, most importantly for Hulegu, by the Golden Horde's Khan Berke. Qubilai, meanwhile, held the support of most of the generals of the Mongol army, and, what was more, he held China – the Mongols' most prized possession.

What would really have concerned Hulegu was that Berke's forces lay directly to his north in the Caucasus region. As was discussed earlier, Batu Khan had been made virtually independent ruler of this area by the agreement that brought Mongke to the throne in 1251, and there were unresolved issues over rights of conquest in Persia between Hulegu and Berke, Batu's successor. Moreover, Hulegu had now conquered Anatolia, which had originally been part of the sphere of influence of the Golden Horde and Berke had also converted to Islam, whilst Hulegu had been persecuting that same religion since his arrival in the Middle East. Hulegu was then caught between wanting to support his brother Qubilai for the throne, but having very real concerns over upsetting his powerful neighbour, who had already sent to Hulegu, claiming ownership of the pasturelands and silver trade routes of Azerbaijan, which formed the border of their territories.

Hulegu, therefore, never really committed himself to the support of either candidate for the throne, although he was viewed by members of the Ariq Boke faction as very much pro-Qubilai. The evolving Mongol conflict then had immediate consequences for the Muslims of Syria when Hulegu went to Maragha to be in a good position to meet any invasion of the Golden Horde. For the Mamluks, he was far enough away to give them at least a chance against the remainder of his force, which he had left behind to mop up Syria under Kit Buqa, one of his most experienced and trusted lieutenants.

The Mamluks met the Mongol army at Ain Jalut, the Spring of Goliath, at the foot of Mount Gilboa on 3 September 1260 and in a bloody battle, that lasted from dawn till midday, completely defeated them. Kit Buqa was killed, and as a result of the battle, the Mongols had to evacuate Damascus, Hama and Aleppo. Syria was saved, but Kutuz, the sultan who had won the battle, did not survive to see the real fruits of his victor – he was killed by the emir Baybars, now twice a regicide, who took the throne.

The Mongols suffered a further defeat at the hands of a mixed Mamluk–Ayyubid army at Homs in December 1260, and by now Syria was firmly welded to Egypt, under the firm control of Baybars. The Assassins must, of course, have been overjoyed at the Mongols' defeat, but it soon became very obvious that Baybars was not content with pushing just one group of infidels from Syria. He now embarked on the same kind of Sunni *jihad* that had led Zangi, Nur al-Din and Saladin on their journeys of conquest. The Franks were the obvious target for Baybars' new Holy War, but it again became very obvious that any such project required the suppression of all heresy within the state, and that there be no other loyalties, other than to the new Sunni sultan. To drive this point home, Baybars had also found himself a puppet caliph – a refugee from the Abbasid family had been placed on a new caliphal throne of Cairo, and the Mamluks would maintain the caliphate as a tool of their legitimacy, until their eventual conquest by the Ottomans in 1517.

Baybars's war against the Crusaders was also fought to preclude any Mongol–Crusader alliance that would require him to fight a war on two fronts, and he began it with aplomb. Mamluk raids on Antioch brought it close to collapse in 1261, and in 1262 its port was looted. 1263 saw the fall of Nazareth and the encirclement of Acre. Caesarea fell in 1265, as did Haifa, along with practically all the inland Crusader castles. In 1271, the White Castle of the Templars and Crak des Chevaliers, as well as the castles of Gibelcar and Beaufort, fell to the Mamluks' siege engines. Christian Armenia was also devastated in 1266.

During all this, Baybars found time to send his lieutenants, between 1265 and 1273, to effectively put the Assassins out of business. Baybars had revolutionised siege warfare in Syria, just as the Mongols had in Persia. Gone were the long desultory encirclements of cities that attempted to starve out garrisons. The Mamluks became experts at delivering rapid destruction to bastions and strongholds. The cavalry would appear suddenly at the walls of a fortification and begin the attack with a hail of arrows and Greek Fire, thrown from hand slings. Then the light artillery of *arradas* and wheel-crossbows would be added, while the heavy artillery of counterweighted mangonels were being constructed; these would then be added to the assault. The whole thing gave defenders the impression of an ever-increasing spiral of violence.

At the same time the defenders also had to worry about the ground dropping out from under their feet, as the Mamluks were also adept at both sapping and filling in moats under cover of moveable shelters or *dabbaba*, which were similar to the Romans' testudo. Added to this was the simple fact that the Mamluks were the most highly disciplined troops of the medieval world, fired with *jihad*. They were quite prepared to storm castles and cities without waiting for the artillery to do its work, as they did at Caesarea, when they made ladders from their horses' tack to scale the city's walls. The Assassins would also have been distracted by the constant and morale-sapping beating of huge paired drums, carried on the backs of up to three hundred camels, that attended Mamluk siege warfare. Several castles fell, and the Assassins soon enough made it clear that they were willing to take suzerainty under the sultan.

In 1266 Baybars also, however, made his conclusion of a truce with the Knights Hospitallers, who were also desperate for some respite from the Mamluk war machine, dependant on them forgoing the payment of tribute from the Assassins. In this way he effectively offered the Assassins protection, and made it clear to them that they were his subjects. His solution to the Assassin problem was therefore a twofold one: he brought them to heel, but did not plan their total extinction. By this policy he both received the tribute that the Assassins formerly paid to the Holy orders, and gained the benefit and convenience of deploying Assassins for his political killings as required, and the sultan had plenty of work for them.

Just how tame the Assassins were is difficult to assess. Certainly as early as 1260 Baybars granted *iqtas* to some of his emirs based on the revenue drawn from Assassin lands, and in 1265 he garnered taxes from the money that the Assassins continued to extort from Crusader princes and minor Muslim emirs. All this was accepted without a murmur from the cowed chief *dai*, Najm al-Din. In 1270, Baybars dismissed the chief *dai* from his post and, at this point, seems to have literally taken over from Alamut as the Assassins' parent. However, his new appointee, Sarim al-Din, double-crossed him and, through trickery, managed to eject the Mamluk garrison from Masyaf castle and reoccupy it, before raising the banner of rebellion against the sultan. The revolt was short-lived and soon enough Baybars had reappointed Najm al-Din as chief *dai*, with his son Shams al-Din as his heir, dependant on an increased payment of tribute. He then had Sarim al-Din imprisoned in Cairo, tortured a little and then poisoned.

All this time, Baybars was also preparing to meet the threat of a new Crusade by Louis IX, that had been in preparation since 1267. Louis's reputation had been enough to bring even the kings of Aragon and England into the project and he had also been corresponding with Hulegu, and then with Abagha, the new Khan of Persia following Hulegu's death in 1265. Baybars therefore had to prevent the Crusade from finding any friendly disembarkation point. He responded to calls for a truce from Acre with an agreement allowing a temporary cessation of operations against the city, and then completely demolished Ascalon, rendering it useless as a port for the Crusade. Despite the truce, he still arranged for the Assassins to eliminate the leading baron of Acre, Philip of Montfort, in 1270, to ensure that the local Franks would be leaderless if King Louis's forces should arrive. In the event, the Crusade was a disaster, and following its diversion to Tunisia, on the rather odd assumption that the sultan there was a likely convert to Christianity, King Louis and many of his men died of dysentery whilst fighting on the North African coast.

Perhaps in revenge for the murder of Philip, and for his loss of Antioch to Baybars in 1268, Bohemond VI of Tripoli employed two *fidai'in* to assassinate the sultan, but the men were discovered and arrested by Baybars in March 1271. Shams al-Din was also arrested and charged with complicity in the crime. Such collusion was, however, unlikely as by this point the movement seems to have lost virtually all cohesion. Indeed, the *fidai'in* had come from a castle no longer under the full control of the *dai*. The charge was convenient, however, for Baybars, and though Shams al-Din was released after his father had pleaded his innocence, both men were made to reside, not in their castles, but in Cairo where they could be watched. Baybars also sent messages to Bohemond in April, threatening him with a fate identical to that which the count had planned for the sultan.

The freedom of action that Baybars enjoyed in this period was entirely due to the ongoing dissent among the Mongol princes. By 1264, Qubilai had decisively defeated Ariq Boke, but there was still a vast amount of dissatisfaction within Mongolia proper towards the new Great Khan. This discontent was lead by Qaidu, from the line of Ogedei, who managed to maintain a great deal of control over the Central Asian lands and obtain de facto leadership of the Chaghatai Horde, in what is today roughly Uzbekistan. The Chaghatai branch of the family had lost out in the first round of succession disputes, after the death of Chinggis Khan, and retained a vehement hatred for the house of Tolui, from which Mongke Khan, Qubilai Khan and Hulegu sprang. From 1264 onwards, Hulegu had had to endure raids and conflict on his north-eastern border, as Qaidu used the Chaghatai Horde to strike at Qubilai through Hulegu.

In the spring of 1266, the Golden Horde invaded Persia and the fighting continued into the summer. Abagha Khan was distracted, once again, from Syrian affairs by an extensive invasion of Khurasan by the Chaghatai Mongols in 1270, who he defeated at the Battle of Herat in July of the same year. In 1271, as a reprisal, he sent a large division of his forces into the Chaghatai Horde's lands to sack and burn Bukhara. The *Pax Mongolica* was slowly but surely falling apart.

Baybars next employed his Assassins against his Mongol enemies. Juvaini, on whose writing most of our understanding of Hulegu's campaign against the Assassins of Persia is based, was the object of an unsuccessful attack by *fidai'in* in Baghdad in 1271. Certainly his polemics against the Assassins would have been reason enough for them to wish his end, but in his position as governor of Baghdad, he was also an important part of the Mongol administration, and Baybars's cold war against the Persian Khans was built on such acts. Espionage, the poisoning of water sources and the 'turning' and double-crossing of Mongol officials were second nature to Baybars.

Given Baybars's skills for intrigue, then, it is more than a little surprising that he was caught napping by Shams al-Din in June 1271. The junior chief *dai* requested permission to leave Cairo and to return to the castles in the Syrian mountains to deal with some minor points of administration. He was allowed to do so, but once there he began to organise a revolt against the sultan. Baybars got to hear of the uprising early on in its planning and the Mamluks' siege engines were quickly employed again against Shams al-Din's bolt-hole. Shams al-Din was given surprisingly good treatment by the sultan – even after Baybars discovered further plots to assassinate several of his emirs, he did no more than return Shams al-Din to house arrest in Cairo. Perhaps Baybars enjoyed the fear his domesticated Assassin inspired in others and he was already planning new operations for the *dai*'s followers.

Prince Edward, the future King of England, had arrived in the Holy Land in June 1271. His Crusader army had reached Tunisia only after Louis's death and, not wanting to return empty-handed to Europe without having fulfilled his Crusading vows, he had sailed to Cyprus and then on to Acre. Baybars was concerned that Edward might be preparing to use his, admittedly small, Crusading army, in conjunction with the Latin army and navy of Cyprus, in a concerted attack on Muslim Syria with the Mongols. His fears seemed well founded: Edward struck into the Plain of Sharon near Mount Carmel, and Abagha sent a Mongol force of ten thousand troopers from Anatolia to Syria, at the prince's behest.

The Mamluk garrison of Aleppo fled under Baybars's orders as he wanted to try to draw the Mongols further into Syria, closer to his main force at Damascus. As the Mongols advanced towards Maarat al-Numan, Baybars started to move north with his heavy cavalry, but the Mongols denied him battle by quickly evacuating Syria. The Mongol incursion had been too brief for Edward to be able to achieve anything, but it did bring Baybars to the negotiating table. He decided to grant a truce to Acre in order to reduce the risk of future Mongol–Crusader operations against him. The peace was signed on 22 May 1272 and negotiated to last ten years, ten months, ten days and ten hours, the standard timeframe for *hudna* – the truce that can interrupt *jihad*, if there is an advantage to be gained by the Muslims from a cessation of hostilities against the infidel.

As a further guarantee of peace from Edward in the future, Baybars sent a *fidai* to assassinate him. The Mamluk governor of Ramla sent to Edward, intimating that he was prepared to betray the sultan. He then sent him a messenger with gifts for both himself and his wife. The messenger was admitted several times to Edward's presence as the negotiations progressed – on his fifth visit, on 18 June, the *fidai* took his chance. After being searched for weapons he was permitted to see the prince. Edward, suffering in the Syrian heat, was wearing only a light tunic and was resting on a couch. He took the emir's letter from the messenger who, as he bent towards the prince to answer a question, drew a thin dagger from the inside of his belt and struck a blow at his intended victim. Edward caught the blow on his arm, and, knocking the Assassin to the ground, jerked the dagger from his grasp and stabbed him with his own blade. The prince's servants came running and battered the *fidai*'s brains out with a foot stool.

Edward seemed to have survived the attack relatively unscathed. Unfortunately, the dagger was poisoned and over the next few days

Edward became seriously ill. There is a story of Eleanor, Edward's young wife, trying to suck the poison from her husband's wound, but not surprisingly, this seems to have been a romantic Italian invention of later years. The master of the Temple gave him what was felt to be the antidote, but his condition continued to deteriorate and the wound on his wrist began to suppurate. The prince only began to recover once all the dead flesh from around the original stab mark was excised by a surgeon. Fifteen days later he was seen on his horse in the streets of Acre. As soon as he was well enough he departed for England. It is to be wondered what effect this brush with the Assassins had on Edward. Certainly as King of England he gained a reputation as being both calculating and distant.

The story leads credence to the idea that by this stage the Assassins were little more than hit men. A poisoned blade would never have been contemplated by the devotees of the past. They were now the compliant tools of the Mamluk sultan, who by 1273 had occupied all their castles. Even after the death of Baybars in 1277,* they continued in the service of the Mamluk sultans. The fourteenth-century traveller Ibn Battuta wrote of their servile existence:

> When the sultan wishes to send one of them to kill an enemy, he pays them the price of his blood. If the murderer escapes after performing his task, the money is his; if he is caught his children get it. They use poisoned knives to strike down their appointed victims. Sometimes their plots fail and they themselves are killed.†

In 1400, the Mamluk sultan, Faraj, dispatched Assassins to kill the new invader from the East, Tamerlane, as he besieged Damascus, but they were caught and returned without either ears or noses to their employer. Tamerlane brought terror to Syria and Persia on a scale unimaginable, even under the Mongols. Compared to Tamerlane's slaughter of men, women, children and the still to be born, the killings of the Assassins – a sect of supposedly bloodthirsty demons – pale into insignificance.

---

* For a full account of the remarkable career of Baybars, from being sold as a child slave to becoming one of the greatest leaders of the medieval world, see, Waterson, chapters five and six.
† H. Gibb, *The Travels of Ibn Battuta*, Cambridge, 1958, Vol. I, p. 106.

9

BOTH FORGOTTEN AND REMEMBERED

THE MEANING AND THE MYTH OF THE ASSASSINS

Io stava come frate che confessa
Lo perfido assassin . . .

I stood there like the friar who takes
Confession from the treacherous assassin . . .*

I N 1291, ACRE FELL to the Mamluks and the Crusaders were pushed out of the Levant. In 1322, the Mongols of Persia, exhausted from both their attempts to wrest Syria from the Mamluks, and from wars with their kinsmen, signed a peace treaty with the slave soldier dynasty. The Ilkhanate, the Mongol state of Persia, collapsed in 1336. Thus, two of the Assassins' most inveterate enemies both died out shortly after the *fidai'in*'s own disintegration into hired killers. There could be no comfort in this however for the refugees of the Assassin states: victory over both had been achieved by a state that was, however nominally, under the spiritual guidance of a Sunni caliph.

Whilst the Abbasids of Cairo were certainly little more than puppets to the Mamluk sultans, the sultans themselves were a direct product of the fusing together of Sunni *jihad* with military men. The Mamluk sultanate was in its essence an orthodox Sunni state, run by Turks. The seeds of this state had been sown by the reaction of Sunni jurists in Aleppo and Damascus, back in the first decades of the twelfth century. The call for *jihad*, that the *qadis* of Syria made, was a direct reaction, not only to the Crusaders' presence in the Holy Land, but also to the unholiness of the *fidai* and the disgust and fear that their killings brought to Sunnis. In many

---

* Dante Alighieri, *La Divina Commedia: Inferno*, Canto XIX, Verses 48–9. c.1308. English translation by M. McCrystall.

ways then, the Assassins were not only responsible in large part for the success of the First Crusade, with their killing of Nizam al-Mulk, which shattered the unity of the Saljuq Empire. They were also responsible for the counter-Crusade that brought Zangi, Nur al-Din and Saladin to the fray with the Crusaders, and ultimately led to the Mamluk war machine that finished Outremer's existence.

The Franks had been a potent military force whose courage, religious fervour, unity and sense of purpose were key elements in their successful exploitation of the situation in the Middle East in the late eleventh and early twelfth centuries. They rapidly established a strong state, with much of its security indebted to impressive fortifications. The parallels between the early pilgrim soldiers of the *expeditio* and the early Assassins are obvious, and both states fell only when they lost their unifying sense of mission and their enemies united.

Equally the Assassins were, along with the Abbasid caliph's refusal to undertake Mongol suzerainty, the direct cause of Hulegu's destruction of Persia, but they might also just have been Persia's only hope of avoiding the Mongol rage. It is easily arguable that the Mongols were coming to pillage and conquer in Persia anyway, whatever the *fidai'in* and the caliph did. Expansionism was a basic tenet of the Mongol world view, as their continued attempts to bring Japan and Syria into their empire make obvious. Furthermore, when Mongke did die, there was a falling apart of the Mongol Empire that would see even China revert to native rule, under the Ming, by 1368. Just one *fidai* breaking through the Mongol guards around the Khan might have caused just the same result before Persia was ruined and the Assassins would have been the saviours of their nation. Perhaps Chinggis Khan had foreseen all this when:

> One day he called his sons together and taking an arrow from his quiver he broke it in half. Then he took two arrows and broke them also. And he continued to add to the bundle until there were so many arrows that even athletes were unable to break them. Then turning to his sons he said: 'So it is with you also. A frail arrow, when it is multiplied and supported by its fellows, not even mighty warriors are able to break it but in impotence withdraw their hands there from. As long, therefore, as you brothers support one another and render stout assistance to one another, though your enemies be of great strength and might, yet shall they not gain victory over you.*

---

* Juvaini, p. 41. The story is also found in the *Secret History of the Mongols* (see suggested further reading).

In the end, of course, the *fidai'in* failed to cause the bundle to break apart early enough to save Persia, and in an ironic twist, the Mongols, before their extinction in Persia, converted to Islam – though not the Shiite form the Assassins had killed and died for. Like the Saljuqs before them, they took up the Sunni creed and it seemed that a wave of orthodoxy had flowed smoothly over all the Islamic lands. Indeed, Persia would remain Sunni until the birth of another personality cult on a par with that of Hasan-i-Sabbah, when the enigmatic Shah Ismail gathered devoted Turcoman tribesmen around him in the sixteenth century. Even then, however, it would be the Twelver Shiite tradition that would triumph in Persia.

The Assassins place in history then is a largely forgotten one, but they have certainly obtained a place in myth. In 1332, King Philip VI of France was advised, during his planning of a Crusade to retake the Holy Land, by a German priest called Brocardus:

> I name the Assassins, who are to be cursed and fled. They sell themselves, are thirsty for human blood, kill the innocent for a price, and care nothing for either life or salvation. Like the devil, they transfigure themselves into angels of light, by imitating the gestures, garments, languages, customs and acts of various nations and peoples; thus, hidden in sheep's clothing, they suffer death as soon as they are recognised. Since indeed I have not seen them, but know this of them only by repute or by true writings, I cannot reveal more, nor give fuller information. I cannot show how to recognise them by their customs or any other signs, for in these things they are unknown to me as to others also; nor can I show how to apprehend them by their name, for so execrable is their profession, and so abominated by all, that they conceal their own names as much as they can. I therefore know only one single remedy for the safeguarding and protection of the king, that in all the royal household, for whatever service, however small or brief or mean, none should be admitted, save those whose country, place, lineage, condition and person are certainly, fully and clearly known.*

Brocardus tells us that he only knew of the Assassins' ways from 'true writings' and that must have been how Dante had come to hear of them too. Indeed, there were many 'true writings' circulating in Europe at this time, feeding an audience hungry for tales of the mystical East. We have already met Marco Polo's description of the Old Man of the Mountain's gardens of Paradise. His description was no more ridiculous than Dante's Assassin confessing to a friar, and at least showed a little less invention

---

* From Brocardus's *Directorium ad Passagium Faciendum*, in Lewis, *The Assassins*, p. 2.

than the anonymous author of a chronicle of the Third Crusade. This writer tells us that the 'Vetus de Montanis', Sinan the Old Man of Masyaf, brought up a large number of noble boys in his palace who were then taught every kind of learning and accomplishment and instructed in various languages before being called before the grand master at pubescence. At this audience the boys would then be told that for the remission of their sins they would have to slay some great man. The writer then tells us that the youth was then given a poniard of terrible length and sharpness and would, in order to complete his mission, remain in a prince's service until he found an opportunity for killing him. The anonymous writer's tale was certainly designed to inspire fear in his audience.

Friar Odoric's tale however was created, like Marco Polo's, to dazzle his untravelled audience:

> I arrived at a certain country called Melistorte, which is a very pleasant and fertile place. And in this country there was a certain aged man called the Old Man of the Mountain, who round about two mountains had built a wall to enclose them. Within this wall there were the fairest and most crystal fountains in the whole world: and about the fountains there were most beautiful virgins in great number, and goodly horses also, and in a word, everything that could be devised for bodily pleasure and delight, and therefore the inhabitants of the country call the same place by the name of Paradise. The Old Man, when he saw any proper and valiant young man, would admit him into his Paradise. Moreover, by certain conduits he makes wine and milk to flow abundantly. This Old Man when he has a mind to revenge himself or to slay any king or baron, commands him that is governor of the said Paradise, to bring there one of the youths, permitting him a while to take his pleasure therein, and then to give him a certain drug of sufficient force to cast him into such a slumber as should make him quite void of all sense, and so being in a profound sleep to convey him out of his Paradise, who being awaked, and seeing himself thrust out of the Paradise would become so sorrowful that he could not in the world devise what to do, or whither to turn. Then would he go to the Old Man, beseeching him that he might be admitted again into his Paradise, who says to him: 'You cannot unless you will slay such or such a man for my sake, and if you will give the attempt only, whether you kill him or no, I will place you again in Paradise, that there you may remain always'. Then would the youth without fail put the same in execution, endeavouring to murder all those against whom the Old Man had conceived any hatred. And therefore all the kings of the East stood in awe of the Old Man, and gave him great tribute. *

---

* Komroff, p. 247.

Listing the luxuries of the lands of the East was a staple for medieval European writers and this is not entirely surprising. Compared to the merchandise available in the West, the imported products of Islam were fine beyond all measure, and this is reflected in the number of Persian words that made their way into European languages along with these goods of desire – jasmine, crimson, taffeta, musk, candy, saffron and the ultimate extravagance, pyjamas.

Marco Polo's description, however, gave only 'the most beautiful women and girls' to the *fidai'in*, but Odoric trumped that with the much more erotic and romantic idea of virgins. Romance was central to the tales. In the western medieval mind, that is where the Assassins belonged – in a world of romance and eroticism, fringed with dark acts and violence. By the fourteenth century, they were both perfect material for, and an inspiration to, the poets.

The troubadour Aimeric de Peguilhan wrote to his lady, 'You have me more fully in your power than the Old Man his Assassins, who go to kill his mortal enemies, even if they were beyond France.' Blind obedience in love was obviously seen as a virtue, part and parcel of chivalry – that knightly ideal that had done so much to create the myths of the Crusade, and of Saladin and Richard. Love was to be obeyed without regard for consequences, 'just as the Assassins serve their master unfailingly, so I have served Love with unswerving loyalty,' as the troubadour Bernart de Bondeilhs would have it. An anonymous troubadour even went as far as to say to his lady, 'I am your Assassin who hopes to win Paradise through doing your commands.' While Aimeric de Peguilhan, who seems to have fallen in love with his theme as much as with his lady, likened his heart to an Assassin, since it kills him for his Lady's sake, Giraut de Bornelh, hopefully as a compliment, describes his desire for his lady thus: 'My Lady's love is an Assassin, which kills me.'*

All of this was, of course, very far from the truth, and Ismailis, although their communities survived the passing of the Mongol Ilkhanate of Persia, continued an extremely unromantic struggle against enemies such as the Zaydites, who, like the Ismailis, were leftovers from the old days of Shiite radicalism. In 1378 Zaydites, under their leader, Ali Kiya, fought the Ismailis of the Caspian region and beheaded their chief in battle. Refugees from the battle settled in Qazvin, until they were pushed

---

* The poems, both in the original French and with selected English translations, can be found in F. Chambers, 'The Troubadours and the Assassins', *Modern Language Notes*, Vol. 64, No 4, April 1949, pp. 245–51.

from there and suffered a further massacre at the hands of Tamerlane's troops. And yet the sect remained quite visible in Persia, right up until the sixteenth century.

A son of Rukn al-Din had survived the Mongol onslaught and went on to sire the line of imams now titled the Aga Khans, as the Ismailis scattered over eastern Persia, Afghanistan, Central Asia and southern Pakistan. In these places, they survived as a peaceful underground sect with the old days of the *fidai'in* behind them. Similarly in Syria, small communities survived the destruction of the Mamluks and were still to be found in the late Ottoman Empire, dotted along the coastal mountains of Syria.

In the nineteenth century, the Aga Khan led a revolt against the Shah of Persia, but the rising was unsuccessful. After a brief stay in Afghanistan, he decamped to India. He finally settled in Bombay, where oddly enough it was a British law court that decreed him to be the true head of the Ismaili sect, to whom all the various sects of the faith should pay dues. He had been taken to court by a group of Ismailis, who claimed that he had no right to interfere in their religious business. The Aga Khan, in response, showed the court evidence of his descent from the imams of Alamut. In December 1866 an organisation that had previously settled such disputes with rather more pointed arguments, listened quietly to the verdict of a British judge. The judgement was that the Indian Ismailis were entirely subject to the spiritual authority of the Ismaili imams, the latest of whom was the Aga Khan. The judge had inspected the Aga Khan's genealogy and found him to be descended from the Lords of Alamut, and by virtue of that, from the Fatimid caliphs of Egypt, and so, ultimately, from the Prophet Muhammad.

The nineteenth-century British judge certainly showed more interest in Islamic history than did the Assassins' medieval contemporaries and this accounts for much of the mythologising of the Assassins. Western knowledge of Islam in the medieval period was scant, despite the Crusades and the daily contact that had existed between Europeans and Muslims in both Spain and Sicily. The Quran was translated into Latin by Robert of Ketton in 1143, as were the philosophical treatises of al-Kindi and al-Farabi. Ibn Sina, or Avicenna as he was known in the West, an early sympathiser with Ismailism, was also translated by Gerard of Cremona.

Generally, however, westerners were not interested in gathering accurate information about the Muslims' religion or civilization. Of course there were exceptions, such as De Joinville, who at least noted that there was a schism between Sunnis and Shiites, although he assumed that Sunnis were followers of Muhammad, and that Shiites followed only Ali. He also believed that the law of Ali was that when a man died in executing his lord's commands his soul passed into a 'happier body'. He suggested that this was why the Assassins were happy to lay down their lives when their lord commanded it. This was a reasonable assumption given the report of a certain Brother Ives who visited Sinan and then reported back to De Joinville:

> Brother Ives found a book at the head of the Old Man's bed, in which were written several sayings of Our Lord to Saint Peter, when he walked on earth. And Brother Ives said to him, 'Ha! For God's sake, Sir, read this book often for these are passing good sayings'.
>
> The Old Man told him that he often did so. 'For I hold my lord St. Peter very dear for in the beginning of the world, the soul of Abel, when he was slain, passed, into the body of Noah and when Noah died, it returned in the body of Abraham and from the body of Abraham when he died, it passed into the body of Saint Peter, when God came upon earth.'*

However, it seems even Brother Ives had an eye for the sensational, and like the troubadours and adventurers who gave their audiences gardens of Paradise, hashish-addicted devotees and murderers lurking in every throne chamber, ready to strike down kings, Brother Ives gave his readers the grand master in all his majesty riding forth like Death, the final Horseman of the Apocalypse, across a landscape of fear:

> When the Old Man went riding, a crier went before him, carrying an axe with a long handle all covered with silver, and stuck full of knives, who kept crying out. 'Make way before him who bears the death of kings in his hands!'†

---

* Wedgwood, pp. 238–9.
† Wedgwood, p. 239.

SUGGESTED FURTHER READING

THE REFERENCED WORKS ARE the obvious starting point for any reader interested in further reading about the Assassins, the Mongols, the Saljuqs, the Fatimids and the other clans and individuals who have graced us with their presence in this slim volume. For those readers who wish to pursue their studies a little further the following works are suggested. Most are readily obtainable, but because of the relative immaturity of English language studies into both the Assassins, and particularly into the Fatimids, some could be considered 'specialist'.

Amitai-Preiss, R. and Morgan, D. (eds), *The Mongol Empire and its Legacy*, Leiden, 2000.

Biran, M., *The Empire of the Qara Khitai in Eurasian History: Between China and the Islamic World*, Cambridge, 2005.

Bosworth, C., 'The Political and Dynastic History of the Iranian World 1000–1217', in Boyle, J. (ed.), *The Cambridge History of Iran, Volume Five: The Saljuq and Mongol Periods*, Cambridge, 1968.

Boyle, J., *The Mongol World Empire 1206–1370*, London, 1977.

Cahen, C., 'The Mongols and the Near East', in Setton, K. (ed.), *A History of the Crusades, Volume Two*, Madison, 1969, pp. 715–32.

Cahen, C., 'The Turkish Invasion: The Selchukids', in Setton, K. (ed.), *A History of the Crusades, Volume One*, Madison, 1969.

Chambers, J., *The Devil's Horsemen: The Mongol Invasion of Europe*, London, 1979.

Cleaves, F. (trans.), *The Secret History of the Mongols*, Cambridge, MA, 1982.

Daftary, F., 'A Short History of the Ismailis: Traditions of a Muslim Community', *Islamic Surveys Series*, Edinburgh, 1998.

Daftary, F. (ed.), *Medieval Ismaili History and Thought*, Cambridge, 1996.

Daftary, F., *The Isma'ilis: Their History and Doctrines*, Cambridge, 1990.

Daftary, F., 'Ismailis in Medieval Muslim Societies', *Ismaili Heritage Series, Number Twelve*, London, 2005.

Dauvillier, J., 'Guilliame de Roubrouck et les Communautes Chaldeenes d'Asie', in *Histoire et Institutions des Eglises Orientales au Moyen Age*, London, 1983.

De Rachewiltz, I., *Papal Envoys to the Great Khans*, London, 1971.

Edbury, P. and Rowe, J., *William of Tyre, Historian of the Latin East*, Cambridge, 1988.

El-Azhari, T., *The Seljuqs of Syria during the Crusades: 1070–1154*, trans. Winkelhane, Berlin, 1997.

Fink, H. (ed.), *Fulcher of Chartres: A History of the Expedition to Jerusalem 1095–1127*, Tennessee, 1969.

Firro, K., *A History of the Druzes*, Leiden, 1992.

Gabrieli, F., *Arab Historians of the Crusades*, trans. Costello, E., London, 1969.

Hammer-Purgstal, J. von, *The History of the Assassins Derived from Oriental Sources*, trans. Wood, O., London, 1835.

Humphreys, R., *From Saladin to the Mongols: The Ayyubids of Damascus 1192–1260*, Albany, 1977.

Jackson, P., *The Mongols and the West, 1221–1410*, Harlow and New York, 2005.

Morgan, D., 'The Mongols in Syria 1260–1300', in Edbury, P. (ed.), *Crusade and Settlement*, Cardiff, 1985.

Morgan, D., 'The Great Yasa of Chingiz Khan and Mongol Law in the Ilkhanate', *Bulletin of the School of Oriental and African Studies*, London, 1986, pp. 163–76.

Peters, P., *Jihad in Medieval and Modern Islam*, Leiden, 1997.

Pipes, D., *Slave Soldiers and Islam: The Genesis of a Military System*, Yale, 1981.

Rashid al-Din, *The Successors of Chinggis Khan*, trans. Boyle, J., New York and London, 1971.

Saunders, J., *The History of the Mongol Conquests*, London, 1971.

Spuler, B., *History of the Mongols*, London, 1972.

INDEX